THIRUKKURAL

Pearls of Inspiration

THIRUKKURAL

Pearls of Inspiration

Translated by
M. Rajaram

RUPA

Published by
Rupa Publications India Pvt. Ltd 2009
7/16, Ansari Road, Daryaganj
New Delhi 110002

Sales centres:
Allahabad Bengaluru Chennai
Hyderabad Jaipur Kathmandu
Kolkata Mumbai

Translation copyright © M. Rajaram 2009
Foreword copyright © APJM Nazema Maraikayar 2015
Edition copyright © Rupa Publications India Pvt. Ltd 2009

While every effort has been made to verify the authenticity of the information
contained in this book, the publisher and the author are in no way liable for
the use of the information contained in this book

ISBN: 978-81-291-1467-9

Twenty-first impression 2018

25 24 23 22 21

The moral right of the author has been asserted.

Printed at Yash Printographics, Noida

Dedicated

to

World Peace

CONTENTS

INTRODUCTION

Thirukkural as a book that deals with *the art of living* is gaining increasing acceptance. It transcends national boundaries, historical, social limitations and language barriers. It makes great sense and relevance even today and for all times. Among the ethical works in Indian languages, **Thirukkural** stands supreme.

Thirukkural was written 2000 years ago. It was more truly presented in a language that was in vogue at that time. *Thiruvalluvar,* who brought out **'Thirukkural'**, the **book for all ages,** was an eminent and exceptional scholar endowed with divine quality.

He was not only a sage with a humane heart but also a psychologist with a deep insight into the complexities of human nature and a philosopher with an urge to reform. As *Subramania Bharathi,* the Indian national poet, has rightly observed, **"Tamil Nadu gave unto the world Valluvar and thereby won great renown."** *Shri Sane Guruji* goes on to say, **"Great thinkers belong to the world. More truly, Thiruvalluvar belongs not only to Tamil Nadu but also to the whole world." Thiruvalluvar** has been compared with *Socrates, Plato, Aristotle, Confucius, Rousseau* and the like.

Thiruvalluvar has not dwelt upon any abstract thought or dogma. He is intensely conscious of the practical world. The noble as well as the ignoble, the haves as well as the have-nots, the honest as well as the dishonest dwell side by side. He is solely concerned with the present world. To him, how one lives at present is a matter of supreme importance. He does not consider ascetic life better than family life. He gives the ploughmen the highest place in the society because they provide food for all.

Thirukkural is recognized as a classic in the literature of the entire world and it is a part of world literature. It is not only a work of great aesthetic and literary value but also a guide to the art of living with nuggets of valuable wisdom sprinkled everywhere. It consists of 133 chapters of 10 couplets each, totalling in all 1330 couplets. They have been systematically arranged in three parts - **Virtue, Wealth** and **Love.** All of them deal with various aspects of human activities like devotion to God, ascetic life, family life, charity, kingship, military spirit, friendship, love, etc.

Thirukkural covers subjects like ethics, statecraft, citizenship, etc in myriad forms. The profound thoughts of the great saint-poet, **Thiruvalluvar,** are encapsulated in the shortest Tamil metre called 'Kural' which means anything short. **Thiru** means **sacred, beautiful,** etc. Each couplet conveys maximum sense in minimum words. It is **appealing to the mind, sweet to the ear and delicious to the tongue.** We can say, **"Age cannot wither it nor custom stale its infinite variety."**

It is not easy for all to comprehend the real meaning of the **Kural** at the first reading itself. *G.U.Pope,* who translated this work into English metric verse a century ago, explains poetically the beauty of **Thirukkural** thus: **Their construction resembles that of a design in a mosaic. The materials fitted together are sometimes mere bits of coloured glasses, but sometimes also very precious stones and pure gold.**

Thirukkural was among the earliest of the Tamil classics translated by the Christian missionaries. *Rev.Fr.Beschi* (1700-1742) translated it into Latin. There are also versions of

Thirukkural in French by *Monsieur Ariel* and in German by *Dr.Graul*. The great attraction of **Thirukkural** for the missionaries and others has been its ethical content.

The dynamics of **Thirukkural** has been richly complimented by various scholars. *Dr.Albert Schweitzer* says, **"There hardly exists in the literature of the world a collection of maxims in which we find so much of lofty wisdom."** *Mahatma Gandhi* calls it **'a textbook of indispensable authority on moral life'** and goes on to say, **"The maxims of Valluvar have touched my soul. There is none who has given such a treasure of wisdom like him."** He has also said that he came to know about **Thirukkural** from *Leo Tolstoy*, who had said that the concept of non-violence was taken by him from a German version of the Kural. And so he expressed his desire to learn Tamil so as to study **Thirukkural** in original. As *Sri Aurobindo* states, **"Thirukkural is gnomic poetry, the greatest in planned conception and force of execution ever written in this kind."** *Rajaji* says, **"It is the gospel of love and a code of soul-luminous life. The whole of human aspiration is epitomized in this immortal book, a book for all ages."**

According to *K.M. Munshi*, **"Thirukkural is a treatise par excellence on the art of living."** It cuts across castes, creeds, climes, ages, etc and has a freshness which makes one feel as if it is meant for the present time. *Dr. Zakir Hussain*, late President of India, says, **"Thirukkural is a treasure house of worldly knowledge, ethical guidance and spritual wisdom."** *Monsieur Ariel* calls it **'a masterpiece of Tamil literature,** one of the highest and purest expressions of human thought.'

E.J. Robinson finds that it contains all things and there is nothing which it does not contain. Rev. Emmons E.White opines, "Thirukkural is a synthesis of the best moral teachings of the world." As Rev.J.Lazarus declares, "No Tamil work can ever approach the purity of the Kural. It is a standing repute to modern Tamil."

There are several translations already made available by eminent scholars like F.W. Ellis, Rev.G.U. Pope, Rev.W.H.Drew, Dr.John Lazarus, Yogi Suddhananda Bharathi, Rajaji, K.M.Balasubramaniam, P.S.Sundaram, J.Narayanasamy and others. Then, what is the need for one more English translation of this Tamil classic?

Although there are numerous translations of Thirukkural, the fact remains that no translation could render full justice to the original. As the ancient Tamil poet, Avvaiyar, observes, "Thiruvalluvar pierced an atom and injected seven seas into it and compressed it into what we have today as Kural." Dr. Graul rightly states that no translation can fully convey the charming effect of Thirukkural.

Because of its universality, social philosophy and non-denominational nature, it finds its echoes in the teachings of every religion.

The present translation is an attempt to bring out the Tamil text of Thirukkural into English in a complete form.

Dr M. Rajaram

Dr. APJ Abdul Kalam
Former President of India

December 29, 2008

सत्यमेव जयते

FOREWORD

I congratulate Dr.M.RAJARAM, IAS for the efforts he has made in translating the original work of poet saint Thiruvalluvar, the famous Thirukkural. It is considered to provide the code of conduct for the humanity of the planet earth for all time, which makes the past meet the present and creates the future.

Dr. Rajaram's translation of Thirukkural on the three parts i.e. **Virtue, Wealth and Love** - makes a garland of knowledge guiding the people on the right path always and every time. There have been a number of translations of Thirukkural by many authors. The present translation is unique in its simplicity, elegance and maintenance of poetic rhythm on the lines of original Thirukkural. Dr. Rajaram has made special efforts to see that the spirit of Thiruvalluvar is not compromised through his translation.

I would like to cite a few examples of translated couplets to demonstrate the rhythmic feature of translation.

Smile, charity, pleasant words and civility
These four are marks of true nobility.
Dig deeper the sand-well, more water flows,
Read deeper, more wisdom grows.

The translated couplets virtually provide the intended meaning conveyed by Thiruvalluvar. This document will certainly be useful to Non-Tamil speaking people to understand the richness of Tamil culture and its civilizational heritage. Also it will be a friend to the Tamil community who are not fortunate to educate the new generation in Tamil living in various parts of the world.

I am sure the book will be read by a number of people, understood and become a part of their guide in their day to day living leading to the promotion of an enlightened citizen who in turn will make the realization of peaceful, happy and harmonious planet earth.

I congratulate Dr.Rajaram for making this notable contribution for propagating the richness of Thirukkural to world citizens.

APJ Abdul Kalam

PUBLISHER'S NOTE

Thirukkural is the greatest ancient Tamil classic. It embodies the entire gamut of Indian ethics. It ensures individual, social and cultural harmony. It is a treasure not only for the Tamils but also for the entire humanity. It has a universal appeal and acceptability. To publish a book of such great values is a great privilege for us. The reason for bringing out the Tamil work and its meaning in simple, lucid English is to make the renowned Indian classic better known to the people of the entire world.

We sincerely acknowledge *Dr. A P J Abdul Kalam, Former President of India,* for his foreword and *Dr M. Rajaram, IAS* for his commendable efforts in translating **Thirukkural** into English.

PUBLISHER

ACKNOWLEDGEMENT

I owe my understanding of **Thirukkural** to my revered teachers and beloved friends who inspired me to make an endeavour of an English translation of this greatest Tamil classic. I deem it a rare privilege and great fortune to have the blessings of *Dr. A P J Abdul Kalam, Former President of India*, in the form of a foreword. This rendering would not have been possible without the intellectual support of my good friends, Prof S.Jayabaskaran Charles, Mr.P.Jeyaraj, Mr.D.J.Bethelraj, Mr.A.Rajamanickam, Mr.P.M. Dharmalingam of the Ideal Resort, Mr.M.Chakravarthi of Savera Hotel, Mr. D.Varadarajan, Mr.C.S.Kalyanasundaram, Mr P.Saravanan, Mr.L.J.I.Jayaraj and Mr.S.Ravichandran. I extend my profound thanks to the erudite scholars, Dr.G.Joseph Panneerselvam, Mr R.Chellaraman, Mr R.Balakrishnan, Mr D.Joseph Soundararaj, Mr J.Narayanaswamy, Mr V.Kootha Nainar, Thirukkural K.Kaliaperumal and Mr V.Rajagopal for their able guidance in this work.

My profound thanks are due to *Mr S.Balusamy,* whom I cherish with fatherly regards for his moral support and blessings and *Rupa & Co*, *New Delhi* for their noble venture.

Dr M. Rajaram

அதிகாரங்கள்–CHAPTERS

I. அறத்துப்பால் –VIRTUE

III. இன்பத்துப்பால் - LOVE

I

அறத்துப்பால்

VIRTUE

பாயிரம் - Introduction
1. கடவுள் வாழ்த்து
GLORY OF GOD

1   அகர முதல எழுத்தெல்லாம் ஆதி
       பகவன் முதற்றே உலகு.

'A' is the beginning of all alphabets
God is the origin of the universe.

'A' is the first of all letters. Likewise, God is the
beginning of all the worlds.

2   கற்றதனா லாய பயனென்கொல் வாலறிவன்
       நற்றாள் தொழாஅர் எனின்.

Of what use is learning if it fails to lead
To the holy feet of all-knowing God?

Learning is of no use if the learner does not submit
himself to God.

3   மலர்மிசை ஏகினான் மாணடி சேர்ந்தார்
       நிலமிசை நீடுவாழ் வார்.

Who clasp the feet of God in flowery mind
Live long in this earthly abode.

Those who submit themselves to the sacred feet of
God live long in this world.

4   வேண்டுதல்வேண் டாமை இலான்அடி சேர்ந்தார்க்கு
       யாண்டும் இடும்பை இல.

No misery falls on those who hold
The feet of the unbiased God.

No sufferings come to those who hold the feet of God,
who is above likes and dislikes.

5   இருள்சேர் இருவினையும் சேரா இறைவன்
       பொருள்சேர் புகழ்புரிந்தார் மாட்டு.

Twin deeds of dark illusion, good and bad,
Won't be theirs who glorify God.

Those who praise the glory of God have no confusion
about right and wrong deeds.

6   பொறிவாயில் ஐந்தவித்தான் பொய்தீர் ஒழுக்க
     நெறிநின்றார் நீடுவாழ் வார்.
     They live long who follow virtuous ways
     Of God, who has curbed five senses.
     They who follow the virtuous ways of God, who has curbed
     the five senses, live long in happiness.

7   தனக்குஉவமை இல்லாதான் தாள்சேர்ந்தார்க்கு அல்லால்
     மனக்கவலை மாற்றல் அரிது.
     It is extremely hard for others to dispel distress
     Except to those at the feet of the Peerless.
     Only those who reach the feet of God, who has no equal,
     can be free from sorrows.

8   அறஆழி அந்தணன் தாள்சேர்ந்தார்க்கு அல்லால்
     பிறஆழி நீந்தல் அரிது.
     If men reach not the feet of the Oceanic Virtue
     It's hard to swim the sea of sin and woe.
     Those who do not seek the feet of God cannot overcome
     the evils and sufferings of life.

9   கோளில் பொறியில் குணமிலவே எண்குணத்தான்
     தாளை வணங்காத் தலை.
     Who bows not at the feet of eight-virtued God
     Has his head in vain like senses palsied.
     The head that does not worship the feet of God, who has
     eight virtues, is useless.

10   பிறவிப் பெருங்கடல் நீந்துவர் நீந்தார்
     இறைவன் அடிசேரா தார்.
     Vast sea of births can be crossed
     By those who clasp God's feet.
     Only those who surrender to the feet of God can overcome
     the sufferings of births.

2. வான் சிறப்பு
EXCELLENCE OF RAIN

11   வான்நின்று உலகம் வழங்கி வருதலால்
தான்அமிழ்தம் என்றுணரற் பாற்று.
**As the unfailing rain sustains the world
It is deemed a divine food.**
As the unfailing rain supports the world, it is consi-
dered a heavenly food.

12   துப்பார்க்குத் துப்பாய துப்பாக்கித் துப்பார்க்குத்
துப்பாய தூஉம் மழை.
**Rain produces food for all beings in the world
And rain itself serves as food indeed.**
Rain produces food for all living beings and the rain itself
forms part of their food.

13   விண்இன்று பொய்ப்பின் விரிநீர் வியனுலகத்து
உள்நின்று உடற்றும் பசி.
**The vast ocean-bound earth suffers
From famine if the sky fails.**
If it fails to rain, the world surrounded by the vast oceans
will be in hunger and distress.

14   ஏரின் உழாஅர் உழவர் புயலென்னும்
வாரி வளங்குன்றிக் கால்.
**Tillers won't plough and toil
If the rain is not genial.**
If there is no sufficient rain, the farmers will not
plough the land.

15   கெடுப்பதூஉம் கெட்டார்க்குச் சார்வாய்மற்று ஆங்கே
எடுப்பதூஉம் எல்லாம் மழை.
**It is rain that ruins and again it is rain
That lifts the ruined to gain.**
It is the rain that ruins people. It is also the rain that lifts
the ruined people.

16   விசும்பின் துளிவீழின் அல்லால்மற்று ஆங்கே
பசும்புல் தலைகாண்பு அரிது.
Not a blade of grass will be seen
If the sky showers no rain.
There will not be any vegetation on this earth if there is
no rain.

17   நெடுங்கடலும் தன்நீர்மை குன்றும் தடிந்துளழிலி
தான்நல்கா தாகி விடின்.
Even the boundless sea will shrink in nature
If the rainy clouds fail to shower.
Even the vast ocean on this earth will shrink in its
nature if there is no rain.

18   சிறப்பொடு பூசனை செல்லாது வானம்
வறக்குமேல் வானோர்க்கும் ஈண்டு.
If the sky dries up, rites and festivals
Won't be there even for gods.
When it fails to rain, there will be no festivals and rituals
even to gods.

19   தானம் தவம்இரண்டும் தங்கா வியன்உலகம்
வானம் வழங்காது எனின்.
Charity and penance will disappear
If the sky above fails to deliver.
There will be neither generosity nor penance in the
world, if it fails to rain.

20   நீர்இன்று அமையாது உலகுஎனின் யார்யார்க்கும்
வான்இன்று அமையாது ஒழுக்கு.
Without water life cannot sustain
Nor can virtue without rain.
Life cannot exist without water in this world. Similarly,
virtue cannot exist without rain.

3. நீத்தார் பெருமை
GREATNESS OF ASCETICS

21 ஒழுக்கத்து நீத்தார் பெருமை விழுப்பத்து
வேண்டும் பனுவல் துணிவு.
Scriptures praise the excellence of ascetics
Abiding by all in moral books.
Greatness of virtuous men who have renounced the world
is held in high esteem in moral books.

22 துறந்தார் பெருமை துணைக்கூறின் வையத்து
இறந்தாரை எண்ணிக்கொண் டற்று.
Measuring the greatness of ascetics
Is like counting the dead ones.
Greatness of ascetics is immeasurable. Measuring it is
as impossible as counting the dead.

23 இருமை வகைதெரிந்து ஈண்டுஅறம் பூண்டார்
பெருமை பிறங்கிற்று உலகு.
Who discern both and renounce the world alone
In this world brightly shine.
Those who analyse both good and bad and give up worldly
life alone are great.

24 உரன்என்னும் தோட்டியான் ஒரைந்தும் காப்பான்
வரன்என்னும் வைப்பிற்குஒர் வித்து.
Who by wisdom controls five senses
Is a seed of heavenly joys.
He who controls all his five senses by wisdom is a seed
of heavenly bliss.

25 ஐந்துஅவித்தான் ஆற்றல் அகல்விசும்பு ளார்கோமான்
இந்திரனே சாலும் கரி.
To a man who has curbed his five senses
***Indra* is a witness to his powers.**
Indra, the celestial king, is a witness to the might of a
man who has conquered his five senses.

26 செயற்கரிய செய்வார் பெரியர் சிறியர்
செயற்கரிய செய்கலா தார்.
The great ever perform rarer deeds
The mean can't do such deeds.
The great do extraordinary things but the petty-minded
can never do such things.

27 சுவைஒளி ஊறுஓசை நாற்றம்என்று ஐந்தின்
வகைதெரிவான் கட்டே உலகு.
The world belongs to those who quell
Taste, sight, touch, sound and smell.
Those who have complete control over their five senses
gain the whole world.

28 நிறைமொழி மாந்தர் பெருமை நிலத்து
மறைமொழி காட்டி விடும்.
The glory of the learned is amply revealed
In the scriptures of their land indeed.
Greatness of the learned men is shown in the
scriptures of the world.

29 குணமென்னும் குன்றுஏறி நின்றார் வெகுளி
கணமேயும் காத்தல் அரிது.
The ire of those on the mount of good
Tho' brief, can never be endured.
One cannot endure the anger of good men though it is
momentary.

30 அந்தணர் என்போர் அறவோர்மற் றெவ்வுயிர்க்கும்
செந்தண்மை பூண்டொழுக லான்.
The priests are the virtuous ones
Who show mercy to all beings.
The holy people are the virtuous who show compassion
to one and all.

4. அறன் வலியுறுத்தல்
INSISTENCE ON VIRTUE

31   சிறப்புஈனும் செல்வமும் ஈனும் அறத்தினூஉங்கு
      ஆக்கம் எவனோ உயிர்க்கு.
      Fame and wealth are bestowed by virtue
      What better gain can there be for you?
      Virtue gives fame and prosperity. There is no greater
      gain than this.

32   அறத்தினூஉங்கு ஆக்கமும் இல்லை அதனை
      மறத்தலின் ஊங்குஇல்லை கேடு.
      Nothing is greater than virtue to one's soul
      Forgetting the same is the worst evil.
      There is no greater gain than virtue. Forgetting the same
      brings ruin.

33   ஒல்லும் வகையான் அறவினை ஓவாதே
      செல்லும்வா யெல்லாம் செயல்.
      Always practise virtue in all possible ways
      And at all possible places.
      One should always perform righteous deeds in all
      possible ways and at all possible places.

34   மனத்துக்கண் மாசிலன் ஆதல் அனைத்துஅறன்
      ஆகுல நீர பிற.
      In spotless mind alone virtue is found
      Not in pomp and idle sound.
      Virtue is found only in the spotless mind but not in pomp
      and show.

35   அழுக்காறு அவாவெகுளி இன்னாச்சொல் நான்கும்
      இழுக்கா இயன்றது அறம்.
      Envy, greed, wrath and evil words —
      It's virtue to shun these ills.
      Avoiding the four evils such as envy, greed, anger and
      harsh words is a great virtue.

36   அன்றுஅறிவாம் என்னாது அறஞ்செய்க மற்றுஅது
      பொன்றும்கால் பொன்றாத் துணை.
      Always practise virtue; delay it not
      In death it's a prop that fails not.
      One should not postpone doing good which is an
      indestructible support at the hour of death.

37   அறத்தாறு இதுஎன வேண்டா சிவிகை
      பொறுத்தானோடு ஊர்ந்தான் இடை.
      The palanquin-bearers and the rider surely
      Show the fruits of their virtue openly.
      The men bearing the palanquin and the man in it are
      reaping rewards of their past deeds.

38   வீழ்நாள் படாஅமை நன்றுஆற்றின் அஃதொருவன்
      வாழ்நாள் வழியடைக்கும் கல்.
      The act of doing good deeds again and again
      Blocks rebirths like a stone.
      One's continuous good deeds serve as a stone blocking
      the chain of rebirths.

39   அறத்தான் வருவதே இன்பம்மற் றெல்லாம்
      புறத்த புகழும் இல.
      Real joy springs from virtue alone; all other joys
      Are painful and devoid of praise.
      Virtue alone gives real pleasure. Other pleasures are
      without fame.

40   செயற்பால தோரும் அறனே ஒருவற்கு
      உயற்பால தோரும் பழி.
      The only thing to do is virtuous deeds
      The thing to avoid is vicious deeds.
      One must do only acts of virtue and always avoid
      doing evil deeds.

இல்லறவியல் - Domestic Virtue
5. இல்வாழ்க்கை
DOMESTIC LIFE

41 இல்வாழ்வான் என்பான் இயல்புடைய மூவர்க்கும்
நல்லாற்றின் நின்ற துணை.
A man leading domestic life is he
Who supports the virtuous three.
A good family man is one who supports his parents, wife
and children.

42 துறந்தார்க்கும் துவ்வா தவர்க்கும் இறந்தார்க்கும்
இல்வாழ்வான் என்பான் துணை.
To the ascetics, the poor and the desolate
The family man is a support.
The family man is a support to the ascetics, the needy
and the deserted.

43 தென்புலத்தார் தெய்வம் விருந்தொக்கல் தான்என்றாங்கு
ஐம்புலத்தாறு ஓம்பல் தலை.
Ancestors, god, self, kindred and guests
Are a family man's chief interests.
Forefathers, god, himself, relatives and guests are the
prime concerns of a family man.

44 பழியஞ்சிப் பாத்தூண் உடைத்தாயின் வாழ்க்கை
வழியெஞ்சல் எஞ்ஞான்றும் இல்.
Progeny of those who shun evil and share
Their food ever prosper.
If the family men avoid evils and share food with others,
their descendants will ever prosper.

45 அன்பும் அறனும் உடைத்தாயின் இல்வாழ்க்கை
பண்பும் பயனும் அது.
If domestic life has love and virtue
There will be grace and gain true.
There will be grace and gift if family life is rooted in
love and virtue.

46 அறத்தாற்றின் இல்வாழ்க்கை ஆற்றின் புறத்தாற்றில்
போஒய்ப் பெறுவது எவன்?
What does he gain by resorting to ascetic life
When he leads a virtuous family life?
When a person leads a virtuous domestic life, he need
not aspire for ascetic life.

47 இயல்பினான் இல்வாழ்க்கை வாழ்பவன் என்பான்
முயல்வாருள் எல்லாம் தலை.
Who is virtuous in domestic life is the greatest
Of all who strive for a superior state.
One who leads a virtuous domestic life is the greatest
among all trying for a superior state.

48 ஆற்றின் ஒழுக்கி அறன்இழுக்கா இல்வாழ்க்கை
நோற்பாரின் நோன்மை உடைத்து.
Guiding others leading a virtuous domestic life
Is greater than the ascetic life.
Leading a virtuous family life and guiding others is
greater than the life of penance.

49 அறனெனப் பட்டதே இல்வாழ்க்கை அஃதும்
பிறன்பழிப்பது இல்லாயின் நன்று.
Domestic life is a virtue, especially
If it is pursued blamelessly.
Domestic life itself is a great virtue if it is really without
any blame.

50 வையத்துள் வாழ்வாங்கு வாழ்பவன் வான்உறையும்
தெய்வத்துள் வைக்கப் படும்.
Who leads an ideal life on this earth
Is a man of divine worth.
One who leads an ideal domestic life is considered
one among the gods in heaven.

6. வாழ்க்கைத் துணைநலம்
GOODNESS OF A WIFE

51   மனைத்தக்க மாண்புடையள் ஆகித்தற் கொண்டான்
       வளத்தக்காள் வாழ்க்கைத் துணை.

An ideal wife maintains dignity of home
And lives within her husband's income.

A good wife maintains the dignity of the family and
lives within the means of her husband.

52   மனைமாட்சி இல்லாள்கண் இல்லாயின் வாழ்க்கை
       எனைமாட்சித் தாயினும் இல்.

Barren is life when wife is not good
Other glories are only falsehood.

Domestic life, however dignified, will come to nothing
if wife is not good.

53   இல்லதென் இல்லவள் மாண்பானால் உள்ளதென்
       இல்லவள் மாணாக் கடை.

Nothing is really lacking when wife is worthy
What does one possess if she is unworthy?

A man lacks nothing if his wife is good. He has
nothing if she is not good.

54   பெண்ணின் பெருந்தக்க யாவுள கற்பென்னும்
       திண்மைஉண் டாகப் பெறின்.

There is nothing nobler than a wife
Who upholds chastity in life.

There is nothing of greater value to a man than a
woman of purity.

55   தெய்வம் தொழாஅள் கொழுநன் தொழுதெழுவாள்
       பெய்எனப் பெய்யும் மழை.

If a wife worships no other god but her husband
It will rain at her command.

Even if a wife does not worship god, but worships her
husband, it will rain at her command.

56 தற்காத்துத் தற்கொண்டான் பேணித் தகைசான்ற
சொற்காத்துச் சோர்விலாள் பெண்.
Who guards purity, tends her husband, upholds
Family fame and tires not is an ideal spouse.
One who guards chastity, nurses her husband,
preserves fame and remains tireless is an ideal wife.

57 சிறைகாக்கும் காப்புஎவன் செய்யும் மகளிர்
நிறைகாக்கும் காப்பே தலை.
Of what use is keeping women in confinement?
Guarding themselves by purity is paramount.
Nothing else can guard women's purity except their
own will.

58 பெற்றான் பெறின்பெறுவர் பெண்டிர் பெருஞ்சிறப்புப்
புத்தேளிர் வாழும் உலகு.
A woman who serves her husband well
Shall be honoured where gods dwell.
A woman who is devoted to her husband can gain
honour in the world of gods.

59 புகழ்புரிந்த இல்இலோர்க்கு இல்லை இகழ்வார்முன்
ஏறுபோல் பீடு நடை.
A man with a wife who preserves not honour
Has no lion's gait before his despiser.
A man without a good wife cannot walk majestically
like a lion before his slanderer.

60 மங்கலம் என்ப மனைமாட்சி மற்றுஅதன்
நன்கலம் நன்மக்கட் பேறு.
An excellent wife is indeed a domestic bliss
Good children are priceless ornaments.
A good wife is a blessing to the family and good
children are precious jewels.

7. மக்கட்பேறு
WORTHY CHILDREN

61   பெறுமவற்றுள் யாம்அறிவது இல்லை அறிவுஅறிந்த
மக்கட்பேறு அல்ல பிற.

Of all blessings we know nothing is greater
Than begetting children wiser.

There can be no better wealth than having good and
intelligent children.

62   எழுபிறப்பும் தீயவை தீண்டா பழிபிறங்காப்
பண்புடை மக்கள் பெறின்.

In all the seven births evil never touches one
With noble and blameless children.

In all the seven births, no evil will affect a person who
has virtuous children.

63   தம்பொருள் என்பதம் மக்கள் அவர்பொருள்
தம்தம் வினையான் வரும்.

Children are the real asset to the parents
And they are the fruits of their acts.

Children are parents' real wealth. The worth of good
children is the result of parents' own deeds.

64   அமிழ்தினும் ஆற்ற இனிதேதம் மக்கள்
சிறுகை அளாவிய கூழ்.

Food messed up by the hands of one's children
Is far sweeter than nectar divine.

Food messed up by the little hands of one's children
is sweeter than the divine nectar.

65   மக்கள்மெய் தீண்டல் உடற்கின்பம் மற்றுஅவர்
சொற்கேட்டல் இன்பம் செவிக்கு.

The touch of one's children thrills the body
To ears their words are sweet melody.

The touch of one's children and their sweet words
delight their parents.

66   குழல்இனிது யாழ்இனிது என்பதம் மக்கள்
மழலைச்சொல் கேளா தவர்.
Who have not heard their babies' babble
Say flute and lute are delightful.
Only those who have not heard the lisping of their
children say that flute and lute are enchanting.

67   தந்தை மகற்குஆற்றும் நன்றி அவையத்து
முந்தி யிருப்பச் செயல்.
Father's responsibility to his son lies
In placing him ahead of scholars.
The duty of a father to his son is to make him gain
the foremost place among the wise.

68   தம்மின்தம் மக்கள் அறிவுடைமை மாநிலத்து
மன்னுயிர்க்கு எல்லாம் இனிது.
Children wiser than parents give pleasures
To all the worldly beings.
Children wiser than their parents give delight to all
beings in the world.

69   ஈன்ற பொழுதின் பெரிதுஉவக்கும் தன்மகனைச்
சான்றோன் எனக்கேட்ட தாய்.
Mother rejoices indeed at her son's birth
But even more so on hearing his worth.
Mother rejoices at the birth of her son; but even more
so when he is praised as a noble man.

70   மகன்தந்தைக்கு ஆற்றும் உதவி இவன்தந்தை
என்நோற்றான் கொல்எனும் சொல்.
Son's duty to father is to make others wonder
What penance got such a son to the father?
The duty of a son is to conduct himself so well as to
bring honour to his father.

8. அன்புடைமை
POSSESSION OF LOVE

71   அன்பிற்கும் உண்டோ அடைக்குந்தாழ் ஆர்வலர்
புன்கண்நீர் பூசல் தரும்.
Is there any bolt to shut the doors of love?
Tears of the loved ones reveal the love.
True love can never be hidden. It is revealed through
the tears of the loved ones.

72   அன்பிலார் எல்லாம் தமக்குரியர் அன்புடையார்
என்பும் உரியர் பிறர்க்கு.
The loveless grab all for themselves
The loving give even their bones.
The loveless are selfish but the loving render their
service even risking their life.

73   அன்போடு இயைந்த வழக்கென்ப ஆருயிர்க்கு
என்போடு இயைந்த தொடர்பு.
The association of the soul and the body
Is the fruit of the life of love only.
The relationship between the body and the soul is the
result of benevolent life.

74   அன்புஈனும் ஆர்வம் உடைமை அதுஈனும்
நண்புஎன்னும் நாடாச் சிறப்பு.
Love begets the life of love for others
And amity of excellence it yields.
From love always springs affection and that gives
excellent friendship.

75   அன்புற்று அமர்ந்த வழக்கென்ப வையகத்து
இன்புற்றார் எய்தும் சிறப்பு.
Joy on earth and bliss in heaven above
Are the fruits of domestic life of love.
Joy on earth and bliss in heaven are certainly the
fruits of life of love.

76   அறத்திற்கே அன்புசார்பு என்ப அறியார்
மறத்திற்கும் அஃதே துணை.
'Love helps only virtue,' say the unwise
It also guards us from all evils.
The ignorant say that love helps virtue alone but it
also guards us against all evils.

77   என்பு இலதனை வெயில்போலக் காயுமே
அன்பு இலதனை அறம்.
As the sun burns the boneless worms
Virtue torments the loveless ones.
As the sun burns the boneless worms, virtue tortures
the loveless.

78   அன்பகத்து இல்லா உயிர்வாழ்க்கை வன்பாற்கண்
வற்றல் மரம்தளிர்த் தற்று.
Life bereft of love is like a tree sapless
Sprouting in utter barrenness.
To prosper in life without love is as impossible as a
dead tree sprouting in a barren desert.

79   புறத்துறுப்பு எல்லாம் எவன்செய்யும் யாக்கை
அகத்துறுப்பு அன்பி லவர்க்கு.
Of what avail is the body's every outward part
If there's no love within the heart?
The external organs of one's body are of no use if
one's heart is devoid of love.

80   அன்பின் வழியது உயிர்நிலை அஃதுஇலார்க்கு
என்புதோல் போர்த்த உடம்பு.
The soul of life is only the love within humans
Sans love man's body is but skin and bones.
Love is the substance and soul of life. Without it, a
man is a mere frame of bones covered with skin.

9. விருந்தோம்பல்
HOSPITALITY

81 இருந்துஓம்பி இல்வாழ்வது எல்லாம் விருந்துஓம்பி
வேளாண்மை செய்தல் பொருட்டு.
Keeping home and guarding riches
Is to help and entertain guests.
The purpose of leading a domestic life and protecting
wealth is to serve guests.

82 விருந்து புறத்ததாத் தான்உண்டல் சாவா
மருந்துஎனினும் வேண்டற்பாற் றன்று.
To keep out the guests is really bitter
Even while eating divine nectar.
It is undesirable to eat even divine nectar without
sharing it with the guests.

83 வருவிருந்து வைகலும் ஓம்புவான் வாழ்க்கை
பருவந்து பாழ்படுதல் இன்று.
One who daily entertains guests
Never suffers from wants.
The life of one who entertains guests every day will
never suffer from poverty.

84 அகன்அமர்ந்து செய்யாள் உறையும் முகன்அமர்ந்து
நல்விருந்து ஓம்புவான் இல்.
Goddess of fortune gladly dwells in that house
Where guests are greeted with smiling face.
Fortune smiles on the house of one who entertains
worthy guests with cheerful face.

85 வித்தும் இடல்வேண்டும் கொல்லோ விருந்துஓம்பி
மிச்சில் மிசைவான் புலம்.
Who feeds guests before he eats
Need not even sow his fields.
He who eats after entertaining guests will reap a
harvest even without sowing the fields.

86 செல்விருந்து ஓம்பி வருவிருந்து பார்த்துஇருப்பான்
நல்விருந்து வானத் தவர்க்கு.
Who hosts guests and waits for the next
Is, in heaven, an honoured guest.
He who receives guests one after another will be an
honoured guest in heaven.

87 இனைத்துணைத்து என்பதொன்று இல்லை விருந்தின்
துணைத்துணை வேள்விப் பயன்.
It's hard to assess the gains of hospitality
It lies in the worth of guests in reality.
The value of hospitality depends entirely on the value
of deserving guests.

88 பரிந்துஓம்பிப் பற்றற்றேம் என்பர் விருந்தோம்பி
வேள்வி தலைப்படா தார்.
Who shun the joy of hospitality will weep
'We hoarded and lost with none to help.'
Who never entertain guests are those who hoarded hard-
earned wealth and lost it with none to support.

89 உடைமையுள் இன்மை விருந்தோம்பல் ஓம்பா
மடமை மடவார்கண் உண்டு.
Poverty amidst plenty is to have no guests
Such stupidity belongs to idiots.
Lack of hospitality is poverty in prosperity. Such type
of foolishness is found only among fools.

90 மோப்பக் குழையும் அனிச்சம் முகந்திரிந்து
நோக்கக் குழையும் விருந்து.
*Anicham** withers when smelt**
Cold look withers the guest.
On seeing the cold look of the host, the face of the guest
withers like the *anicham* that withers when smelt.

---
* Anicham - a delicate sensitive flower

10. இனியவை கூறல்
SPEAKING SWEETLY

91   இன்சொலால் ஈரம் அளைஇப் படிறுஇலவாம்
செம்பொருள் கண்டார்வாய்ச் சொல்.

The words uttered by the righteous
Are sweet, kind and guileless.

The virtuous speak only sweet and tender words devoid
of deceit.

92   அகன்அமர்ந்து ஈதலின் நன்றே முகன்அமர்ந்து
இன்சொலன் ஆகப் பெறின்.

Kind words with a smiling face
Are better than gifts of grace.

It is better to speak nice words with a sweet smiling
face than giving gracious gifts.

93   முகத்தான் அமர்ந்துஇனிது நோக்கி அகத்தான்ஆம்
இன்சொ லினதே அறம்.

Smiling face, loving eyes and kind words —
Virtue lies in these signs.

Smiling face, loving eyes and sweet words are the signs
of virtue.

94   துன்புறூஉம் துவ்வாமை இல்லாகும் யார்மாட்டும்
இன்புறூஉம் இன்சொ லவர்க்கு.

Painful poverty will never embrace those
Who with sweet words cheer others.

Those who speak sweet words and delight everyone
will never suffer the agony of poverty.

95   பணிவுடையன் இன்சொலன் ஆதல் ஒருவற்கு
அணிஅல்ல மற்றுப் பிற.

Humility and sweet words are one's jewels
All others are not at all jewels.

Humility and sweet words alone are real jewels. All
others are not jewels.

96 அல்லவை தேய அறம்பெருகும் நல்லவை
நாடி இனிய சொலின்.
When fruitful words bubble with kindness
Evils diminish and virtue augments.
Useful words uttered with kindness reduce all evils
and increase virtue.

97 நயன்ஈன்று நன்றி பயக்கும் பயன்ஈன்று
பண்பின் தலைப்பிரியாச் சொல்.
Fruitful, polite and pleasant words
Beget happiness and fortunes.
Useful, courteous and pleasant words bring happiness
and prosperity.

98 சிறுமையுள் நீங்கிய இன்சொல் மறுமையும்
இம்மையும் இன்பம் தரும்.
Sweet words without meanness cheer
The life here and hereafter.
Sweet words without meanness delight this life and
the life in the other world.

99 இன்சொல் இனிதுஈன்றல் காண்பான் எவன்கொலோ
வன்சொல் வழங்கு வது.
Knowing well the pleasure of sweet words
Why cast bitter ones at others?
A man should not use harsh words knowing well that
sweet words give happiness.

100 இனிய உளவாக இன்னாத கூறல்
கனியிருப்பக் காய்கவர்ந் தற்று.
Using bitter words instead of pleasant words
Is like preferring unripe fruits to ripe ones.
Using bitter words in place of sweet ones is like
choosing unripe fruits instead of ripe ones.

11. செய்ந்நன்றி அறிதல்
GRATITUDE

101   செய்யாமல் செய்த உதவிக்கு வையகமும்
வானகமும் ஆற்ற லரிது.
Even heaven and earth will be a scant reward
For a help from one never rewarded.
Heaven and earth are not adequate for the help
received from one who has never been helped.

102   காலத்தி னால்செய்த நன்றி சிறிதுஎனினும்
ஞாலத்தின் மாணப் பெரிது.
A timely help though small in worth
Is greater than the earth.
A timely help, however small, is greater in worth than
the world.

103   பயன்தூக்கார் செய்த உதவி நயன்தூக்கின்
நன்மை கடலிற் பெரிது.
Help rendered without expecting benefits
Is greater than the sea in its goodness.
Help rendered without any expectation is greater than
the sea in its goodness.

104   தினைத்துணை நன்றி செயினும் பனைத்துணையாக்
கொள்வர் பயன்தெரி வார்.
Though the help received is millet small
The worthy deem it palm-tree tall.
Help received, though very small, is considered great
by the worthy.

105   உதவி வரைத்தன்று உதவி உதவி
செயப்பட்டார் சால்பின் வரைத்து.
Help given is not measured by its measure
It depends on the worth of the receiver.
The value of help depends not on the amount but on
the worth of the receiver.

106   மறவற்க மாசற்றார் கேண்மை துறவற்க
       துன்பத்துள் துப்பாயார் நட்பு.
       Never forget the friendship of the pure ones
       And never desert the timely helpers.
       People should neither forget the friendship of the blame-
       less nor desert those who helped them in distress.

107   எழுமை எழுபிறப்பும் உள்ளுவர் தங்கண்
       விழுமம் துடைத்தவர் நட்பு.
       The good will remember in all seven births
       Amity of those who dispelled their distress.
       The great will remember in all seven births the friendship
       of those who helped them in their distress.

108   நன்றி மறப்பது நன்றன்று நன்றல்லது
       அன்றே மறப்பது நன்று.
       Forgetting the good is no good but it's good
       To forget at once what is no good.
       It is improper to forget the good deeds done to us. But
       it is good to forget the wrong deeds at once.

109   கொன்றன்ன இன்னா செயினும் அவர்செய்த
       ஒன்றுநன்று உள்ளக் கெடும்.
       Even a death-like harm becomes nullified
       At the thought of one favour obtained.
       By remembering one help rendered, even a dreadful
       harm is forgotten.

110   எந்நன்றி கொன்றார்க்கும் உய்வுண்டாம் உய்வில்லை
       செய்ந்நன்றி கொன்ற மகற்கு.
       There is escape from sin even for virtue-killers
       But not for the gratitude-killers.
       There is scope even for those who have killed every
       virtue but not for those who have killed gratitude.

12. நடுவுநிலைமை
IMPARTIALITY

111   தகுதி எனஒன்று நன்றே பகுதியான்
பாற்பட்டு ஒழுகப் பெறின்.
Impartiality is indeed a virtue
If all men get their fair due.
Justice is a great virtue that gives impartial treatment
to everyone.

112   செப்பம் உடையவன் ஆக்கம் சிதைவுஇன்றி
எச்சத்திற்கு ஏமாப்பு உடைத்து.
An impartial man's wealth eternally helps
As a security to his race.
An impartial man's wealth is an imperishable security
to his future generations.

113   நன்றே தரினும் நடுவுஇகந்துஆம் ஆக்கத்தை
அன்றே ஒழிய விடல்.
Swiftly abandon wealth got thro' unjust means
Even though good it yields.
One should shun the wealth that comes through
unjust means whatever good it may bring.

114   தக்கார் தகவிலர் என்பது அவரவர்
எச்சத்தால் காணப் படும்.
The just and the unjust are understood
By what they leave behind.
Whether people are just or unjust is always known by
their deeds.

115   கேடும் பெருக்கமும் இல்லல்ல நெஞ்சத்துக்
கோடாமை சான்றோர்க்கு அணி.
Loss and gain are common; but equity in heart
Is the jewel of the perfect.
Loss and gain are quite natural in life. But a
balanced mind is the ornament of the great.

116 கெடுவல்யான் என்பது அறிகதன் நெஞ்சம்
நடுஒரீஇ அல்ல செயின்.
When the mind swerves from justice to sin
One should realize the impending ruin.
One who deviates from the path of justice and does evil
will certainly be ruined.

117 கெடுவாக வையாது உலகம் நடுவாக
நன்றிக்கண் தங்கியான் தாழ்வு.
A just and virtuous man's poverty
Is not seen as evil by humanity.
The world will not consider the poverty of an impartial
and virtuous man as an evil.

118 சமன்செய்து சீர்தூக்கும் கோல்போல் அமைந்துஒருபால்
கோடாமை சான்றோர்க்கு அணி.
Not being one-sided like an even balance
Is an ornament to the wise.
Being unbiased like an even balance is a jewel to
great men.

119 சொற்கோட்டம் இல்லது செப்பம் ஒருதலையா
உட்கோட்டம் இன்மை பெறின்.
Equity is words fully unbiased
Coming from a poised mind.
Equity means words without bias that come from a
firm and unbiased mind.

120 வாணிகம் செய்வார்க்கு வாணிகம் பேணிப்
பிறவும் தமபோல் செயின்.
Tending others' goods as his own
Is a merchant's best transaction.
Treating the goods of others as his own is a mark of
good trade.

13. அடக்கமுடைமை
SELF-CONTROL

121 அடக்கம் அமரருள் உய்க்கும் அடங்காமை
ஆரிருள் உய்த்து விடும்.
Self-control will place one among gods
Lack of it sinks one into a life of evils.
Self-control places one among gods. Lack of it throws
one into a life of miseries.

122 காக்க பொருளா அடக்கத்தை ஆக்கம்
அதனின்ஊஉங்கு இல்லை உயிர்க்கு.
Cherish and safeguard the wealth of self-control
No fortune is greater than that to a living soul.
One must cherish self-control as a great treasure, for
there is no greater wealth to man than that.

123 செறிவுஅறிந்து சீர்மை பயக்கும் அறிவுஅறிந்து
ஆற்றின் அடங்கப் பெறின்.
Self-control guided by wisdom
Fetches everlasting fame.
Self-controlled life guided by wisdom brings fame
that lasts forever.

124 நிலையில் திரியாது அடங்கியான் தோற்றம்
மலையினும் மாணப் பெரிது.
Who is firmly fixed in self-restraint
Is far greater than a mount.
A man who practises self-control is greater than the
greatness and firmness of a mountain.

125 எல்லார்க்கும் நன்றுஆம் பணிதல் அவருள்ளும்
செல்வர்க்கே செல்வம் தகைத்து.
Humility is surely a great virtue for one and all
To the wealthy it is another wealth above all.
Humility is certainly good for all. It is an added grace to
the wealthy.

126 ஒருமையுள் ஆமைபோல் ஐந்துஅடக்கல் ஆற்றின்
எழுமையும் ஏமாப்பு உடைத்து.
Restrain five senses in one birth like a tortoise
You'll be guarded in all seven births.
Those who control their five senses like a tortoise in
one birth are guarded in all seven births.

127 யாகாவார் ஆயினும் நாகாக்க காவாக்கால்
சோகாப்பர் சொல்லிழுக்குப் பட்டு.
Control your tongue if not anything; otherwise
A slip of the tongue brings evils.
Holding one's tongue is very important because a
slip of the tongue will bring sufferings.

128 ஒன்றானும் தீச்சொல் பொருட்பயன் உண்டாயின்
நன்றுஆகா தாகி விடும்.
A single harmful word uttered
Turns all good things bad.
Uttering even a single harmful word will surely spoil all
the goodness.

129 தீயினால் சுட்டபுண் உள்ளாறும் ஆறாதே
நாவினால் சுட்ட வடு.
Fire-burns will certainly heal inside
Tongue-burns won't but abide.
The wounds caused by fire will heal. But scars
caused by stinging words will never leave.

130 கதம்காத்துக் கற்றுஅடங்கல் ஆற்றுவான் செவ்வி
அறம்பார்க்கும் ஆற்றின் நுழைந்து.
Virtue seeks a chance to meet the soul
With no ire, but lore and self-control.
A man of learning and self-control who is free from
anger will be blessed by the god of virtue.

14. ஒழுக்கமுடைமை
DISCIPLINE

131   ஒழுக்கம் விழுப்பம் தரலான் ஒழுக்கம்
உயிரினும் ஓம்பப் படும்.
As discipline leads to dignity in life
Guard discipline above life.
Discipline brings honour. So, it should be cherished
more precious than life.

132   பரிந்துஓம்பிக் காக்க ஒழுக்கம் தெரிந்துஓம்பித்
தேரினும் அஃதே துணை.
Virtuous conduct is a man's prime aid
It's to be guarded with wary mind.
One should excel in good conduct and take pains to
cultivate and guard it.

133   ஒழுக்கம் உடைமை குடிமை இழுக்கம்
இழிந்த பிறப்பாய் விடும்.
Good conduct is the sign of noble birth
Bad conduct is the sign of low birth.
Discipline is a sign of noble birth. Indiscipline indicates
mean birth.

134   மறப்பினும் ஒத்துக் கொளலாகும் பார்ப்பான்
பிறப்பொழுக்கம் குன்றக் கெடும்.
The wise can learn the forgotten lore again
But loss of good conduct leads to ruin.
If the wise forget the past learning, they can learn it
again. But loss of discipline leads to ruin.

135   அழுக்காறு உடையான்கண் ஆக்கம்போன்று இல்லை
ஒழுக்கம் இலான்கண் உயர்வு.
Just as the jealous have no prosperity
The indecent have no dignity.
The envious do not prosper. Likewise, the indecent
never achieve greatness.

136   ஒழுக்கத்தின் ஒல்கார் உரவோர் இழுக்கத்தின்
ஏதம் படுபாக்கு அறிந்து.

Knowing well the disgrace of indiscipline
The stable waver not from discipline.

The disciplined will not deviate from virtues as they
know the evil effects of bad conduct.

137   ஒழுக்கத்தின் எய்துவர் மேன்மை இழுக்கத்தின்
எய்துவர் எய்தாப் பழி.

Good conduct ever brings great honour
Bad conduct ends in great dishonour.

Good conduct brings greatness and bad conduct brings
utter disgrace.

138   நன்றிக்கு வித்தாகும் நல்லொழுக்கம் தீயொழுக்கம்
என்றும் இடும்பை தரும்.

Noble character is the seed of righteousness
Ignoble character brings ills endless.

Good conduct is the seed of virtuous deeds. Bad
conduct leads to endless distress.

139   ஒழுக்க முடையவர்க்கு ஒல்லாவே தீய
வழுக்கியும் வாயால் சொலல்.

It's hard for men of virtuous conduct to utter
Even by a slip, words of evil nature.

Men of righteous conduct never utter evil words even by
a slip of the tongue.

140   உலகத்தோடு ஒட்ட ஒழுகல் பலகற்றும்
கல்லார் அறிவிலா தார்.

Who cannot live in harmony with the world
Though learned, are fools indeed.

Those who cannot live in harmony with the world are
fools though they are learned.

15. பிறனில் விழையாமை
NOT COVETING ANOTHER'S WIFE

141 பிறன்பொருளாள் பெட்டுஒழுகும் பேதைமை ஞாலத்து
அறம்பொருள் கண்டார்கண் இல்.

Who knows the laws of virtue and wealth in life
Won't do the folly of coveting another's wife.

A person who values virtue and wealth will not covet
another's wife.

142 அறன்கடை நின்றாருள் எல்லாம் பிறன்கடை
நின்றாரின் பேதையார் இல்.

Among those who deviate from virtue, no sinner
Is so silly as the one lurking at another's door.

Among those who deviate from virtue, none is so
foolish as the one who longs for another's wife.

143 விளிந்தாரின் வேறுஅல்லர் மன்ற தெளிந்தாரில்
தீமை புரிந்துஒழுகு வார்.

Who does evils and harms the wife of a friend
That trusts him is no different from the dead.

He who covets and does evil to the wife of a friend
who trusts him is not different from the dead.

144 எனைத்துணையர் ஆயினும் என்ஆம் திணைத்துணையும்
தேரான் பிறனில் புகல்.

However great one may be, one becomes nought
If one covets another's wife without thought.

However great a man may be, he loses his greatness
when he seeks another's wife.

145 எளிதுஎன இல்லிறப்பான் எய்தும்எஞ் ஞான்றும்
விளியாது நிற்கும் பழி.

One may treat coveting another's wife easily
But the guilt will stay endlessly.

One may consider coveting another's wife lightly. But
the disgrace will stay forever.

146   பகைபாவம் அச்சம் பழியென நான்கும்
         இகவாவாம் இல்இறப்பான் கண்.
Enmity, sin, fear and shame — these four in life
Leave not one who covets another's wife.
He who covets another's wife will always sink in enmity,
sin, fear and disgrace.

147   அறனியலான் இல்வாழ்வான் என்பான் பிறனியலாள்
         பெண்மை நயவா தவன்.
A family man who leads a virtuous life
Will not covet another's wife.
A family man leading a righteous life will not covet
another man's wife.

148   பிறன்மனை நோக்காத பேராண்மை சான்றோர்க்கு
         அறனொன்றோ ஆன்ற ஒழுக்கு.
Manly excellence of not eyeing another's wife
Is, to the great, a virtue and a code of life.
Noble manliness of not eyeing another's wife is a virtue
and also a discipline of the great.

149   நலக்குஉரியார் யாரெனின் நாமநீர் வைப்பின்
         பிறற்குஉரியாள் தோள்தோயா தார்.
Upright men in this sea-girt world are those
Who touch not arms of another's spouse.
Those who covet not another's wife get all blessings
in this sea-locked earth.

150   அறன்வரையான் அல்ல செயினும் பிறன்வரையாள்
         பெண்மை நயவாமை நன்று.
Even if one transgresses virtue's limit
Better covet not another's life-mate.
Whatever sin one may commit, one should not desire
for another man's wife.

16. பொறையுடைமை
TOLERANCE

151 அகழ்வாரைத் தாங்கும் நிலம்போலத் தம்மை
இகழ்வார்ப் பொறுத்தல் தலை.

Chief of virtues is to bear with revilers
Just as the earth bears its diggers.

Chief of all virtues is to tolerate the insults of others just
as the earth tolerates the diggers.

152 பொறுத்தல் இறப்பினை என்றும் அதனை
மறத்தல் அதனினும் நன்று.

To bear with others' evil is a good trait
Better it is to forget it.

Tolerance of intolerable wrongs is good. Forgetting
such deeds is definitely better.

153 இன்மையுள் இன்மை விருந்தொரால் வன்மையுள்
வன்மை மடவார்ப் பொறை.

To disregard hosting of guests is want of want
To endure fools is might of might.

Lack of hospitality is the worst form of poverty. To bear
with fools is the greatest strength.

154 நிறையுடைமை நீங்காமை வேண்டின் பொறையுடைமை
போற்றி ஒழுகப் படும்.

Practise and preserve patience
To retain one's perfectness.

One should always practise patience if he likes to
retain his perfectness.

155 ஒறுத்தாரை ஒன்றாக வையாரே வைப்பர்
பொறுத்தாரைப் பொன்போல் பொதிந்து.

Who punish the offenders are despised
Who forbear are esteemed like gold.

The world will not respect the avengers but regard the
tolerant as gold.

156   ஒறுத்தார்க்கு ஒருநாளை இன்பம் பொறுத்தார்க்குப்
       பொன்றும் துணையும் புகழ்.

Avenger's joy lasts only for one day
Forgiver's fame stays till Doomsday.

Retaliation gives only a momentary joy.But forbearance
gives everlasting glory.

157   திறன்அல்ல தற்பிறர் செய்யினும் நோநொந்து
       அறன்அல்ல செய்யாமை நன்று.

Though others do intolerable harm, pity them
And better it is to do no evil to them.

Even if others do the worst evil to one, it is better to
avoid doing evil to them.

158   மிகுதியான் மிக்கவை செய்தாரைத் தாம்தம்
       தகுதியான் வென்று விடல்.

Conquer men who do evils by arrogance
Simply by your tolerance.

With tolerance one should conquer those who do harm
due to their haughtiness.

159   துறந்தாரின் தூய்மை உடையர் இறந்தார்வாய்
       இன்னாச்சொல் நோற்கிற் பவர்.

Who forbear evil words of the unrighteous
Are far purer than the ascetics.

Those who tolerate the rude remarks of the unjust
are purer than the ascetics.

160   உண்ணாது நோற்பார் பெரியர் பிறர்சொல்லும்
       இன்னாச்சொல் நோற்பாரின் பின்.

Better are they who endure bitter insults
Than those who fast and do penance.

Those who endure insults are better than those who
do penance by fasting.

17. அழுக்காறாமை
NOT ENVYING

161 ஒழுக்காறாக் கொள்க ஒருவன்தன் நெஞ்சத்து
அழுக்காறு இலாத இயல்பு.

Value the unenvying nature of the heart
As the code of good conduct.

One should value the unenvying nature of the heart as
the disciplined way of life.

162 விழுப்பேற்றின் அஃதொப்பது இல்லையார் மாட்டும்
அழுக்காற்றின் அன்மை பெறின்.

Of all the goodness nothing can equal
Being free from envy of one and all.

Among all precious possessions nothing is equal to
the state of being free from envy.

163 அறன்ஆக்கம் வேண்டாதான் என்பான் பிறனாக்கம்
பேணாது அழுக்கறுப் பான்.

Who loves not virtue and wealth
Alone envies others' wealth.

One who does not desire virtue and wealth alone will
envy others' wealth.

164 அழுக்காற்றின் அல்லவை செய்யார் இழுக்காற்றின்
ஏதம் படுபாக்கு அறிந்து.

Who know that envy causes misery
Will do no wrong out of envy.

Those who know that envy causes sufferings will never
do evil out of envy.

165 அழுக்காறு உடையார்க்கு அதுசாலும் ஒன்னார்
வழுக்கியும் கேடூஎன் பது.

To the envious, their envy itself is enough
Tho' enemies fail, it will bring grief.

The envious need no other enemy. Even if their enemies
fail, their envy is enough to ruin them.

166 கொடுப்பது அழுக்கறுப்பான் சுற்றம் உடுப்பதூஉம்
உண்பதூஉம் இன்றிக் கெடும்.
Kin of those who envy charity to others
Perish without food and clothes.
The relatives of those who envy the act of charity
will perish without food and clothes.

167 அவ்வித்து அழுக்காறு உடையானைச் செய்யவள்
தவ்வையைக் காட்டி விடும்.
Fortune herself will desert the envious
And direct her sister to the envious.
Fortune, the goddess of wealth, deserts the jealous
and introduces the goddess of misfortune to the jealous.

168 அழுக்காறு எனஒரு பாவி திருச்செற்றுத்
தீயுழி உய்த்து விடும்.
Envy, the matchless sinner, ruins wealth
And leads one to eternal evil path.
Envy is a great sinner that destroys a person's wealth
and leads him to the evil path.

169 அவ்விய நெஞ்சத்தான் ஆக்கமும் செவ்வியான்
கேடும் நினைக்கப் படும்.
Wealth of the jealous and want of the just
Make enough food for thought.
It is worth pondering why good men suffer in poverty
while the envious prosper.

170 அழுக்கற்று அகன்றாரும் இல்லைஅஃது இல்லார்
பெருக்கத்தில் தீர்ந்தாரும் இல்.
No one has prospered through jealousy
Nor the unenvious have lost prosperity.
No one has prospered through envy and those who
are free from envy have never become poor.

18. வெஃகாமை
NOT COVETING OTHERS' WEALTH

171 நடுவுஇன்றி நன்பொருள் வெஃகின் குடிபொன்றிக்
குற்றமும் ஆங்கே தரும்.
Coveting honest wealth by unfair means
Ruins family and begets crimes.
Unjust coveting of the honest wealth of others results
in the ruin of one's own family and leads to crimes.

172 படுபயன் வெஃகிப் பழிப்படுவ செய்யார்
நடுவன்மை நாணு பவர்.
Who shrink from shame of injustice
Do no sinful deed of avarice.
Those who shun injustice will never commit any sin
out of greed.

173 சிற்றின்பம் வெஃகி அறன்அல்ல செய்யாரே
மற்றுஇன்பம் வேண்டு பவர்.
Who seek eternal happiness
For petty joys, do no evil acts.
People who seek eternal happiness will never stoop
to any sinful deeds for petty joys.

174 இலம்என்று வெஃகுதல் செய்யார் புலம்வென்ற
புன்மையில் காட்சி யவர்.
The spotless wise who've conquered five senses
Even in penury, won't covet others' riches.
Those who control five senses will never covet others'
wealth even in poverty.

175 அஃகி அகன்ற அறிவுஎன்னாம் யார்மாட்டும்
வெஃகி வெறிய செயின்.
Of what use is knowledge sharp and wide
If foolish deeds are done out of greed?
Deep and vast knowledge gained is of no use if one
madly covets another man's wealth.

176 அருள்வெஃகி ஆற்றின்கண் நின்றான் பொருள்வெஃகிப்
பொல்லாத சூழக் கெடும்.
Who follows the path of virtue and grace
Perishes if he plots evils out of avarice.
One who seeks the path of grace and virtue comes to
ruin, if one plots evil deeds of coveting others' wealth.

177 வேண்டற்க வெஃகிஆம் ஆக்கம் விளைவயின்
மாண்டற்கு அரிதாம் பயன்.
Covet not wealth gained through greed
For its fruits rarely do good.
One must avoid gaining others' wealth through greed,
for there is no good in it.

178 அஃகாமை செல்வத்திற்கு யாதெனின் வெஃகாமை
வேண்டும் பிறன்கைப் பொருள்.
The way to keep one's wealth undwindled
Is not to covet wealth in another's hand.
If one has to protect one's wealth, one should not
covet another's wealth.

179 அறன்அறிந்து வெஃகா அறிவுடையார்ச் சேரும்
திறன்அறிந்து ஆங்கே திரு.
Knowing their worth, Fortune stays with the wise
Who value virtue and covet not riches.
Knowing their worth, the goddess of wealth stays with
the wise who value virtue and do not covet riches.

180 இறல்ஈனும் எண்ணாது வெஃகின் விறல்ஈனும்
வேண்டாமை என்னுஞ் செருக்கு.
Thoughtless coveting leads to destruction
Greedless pride brings distinction.
Thoughtless coveting leads to ruin and greedless
pride leads to victory.

19. புறங்கூறாமை
NOT BACKBITING

181   அறம்கூறான் அல்ல செயினும் ஒருவன்
புறம்கூறான் என்றல் இனிது.

**Though one ignores virtue and does evils
It is good not to backbite others.**

Even if one is not virtuous and does evils, it is good
not to backbite.

182   அறன்அழீஇ அல்லவை செய்தலின் தீதே
புறன்அழீஇப் பொய்த்து நகை.

**Worse is to smile before and slander behind
Than to decry virtue and do deeds not good.**

Praising somebody in their presence and then backbiting are worse than decrying virtue and doing evils.

183   புறம்கூறிப் பொய்த்துடயிர் வாழ்தலின் சாதல்
அறம்கூறும் ஆக்கம் தரும்.

**Death is better than a life of backbiting
As death brings virtue's blessing.**

It is better to die than to live by backbiting, as death
brings fruits of virtue.

184   கண்நின்று கண்அறச் சொல்லினும் சொல்லற்க
முன்இன்று பின்நோக்காச் சொல்.

**You may utter heartless words to one's face
But backbite not ignoring after-effects.**

One may use harsh words in one's presence but
should not backbite disregarding after-effects.

185   அறம்சொல்லும் நெஞ்சத்தான் அன்மை புறம்சொல்லும்
புன்மையால் காணப் படும்.

**Who extols virtue openly but not in the heart
Is by mean backbiting exposed.**

A person may talk of virtue but his backbiting exposes
his meanness.

186 பிறன்பழி கூறுவான் தன்பழி யுள்ளும்
திறன்தெரிந்து கூறப் படும்.
One's worst faults will be sieved and revealed
If one gets others' faults exposed.
The worst flaws of a man will be searched out and
revealed if he backbites.

187 பகச்சொல்லிக் கேளிர்ப் பிரிப்பர் நகச்சொல்லி
நட்பாடல் தேற்றா தவர்.
Who cannot foster friends thro' pleasing words
Lose friendship thro' slandering ones.
Backbiters can never gain new friends but only lose their
friends.

188 துன்னியார் குற்றமும் தூற்றும் மரபினார்
என்னைகொல் ஏதிலார் மாட்டு.
If they trumpet faults of even close friends
What will they not do to strangers?
Those who backbite even dear friends will undoubtedly
do worse to strangers.

189 அறன்நோக்கி ஆற்றுங்கொல் வையம் புறன்நோக்கிப்
புன்சொல் உரைப்பான் பொறை.
Out of virtue the earth bears those
Who backbite with mean words.
The earth endures the burden of backbiters only with a
sense of virtue.

190 ஏதிலார் குற்றம்போல் தம்குற்றம் காண்கிற்பின்
தீதுஉண்டோ மன்னும் உயிர்க்கு.
If everyone sees his faults as he sees others'
Will any evil ever fall on living beings?
No evil will fall on living beings if everyone sees his
faults as he sees others' faults.

20. பயனில சொல்லாமை
NOT SPEAKING VAIN WORDS

191 பல்லார் முனியப் பயன்இல சொல்லுவான்
எல்லாரும் எள்ளப் படும்.
Who utters vain words displeasing all
Is despised by one and all.
He who utters empty words displeasing others will be
condemned by everyone.

192 பயன்இல பல்லார்முன் சொல்லல் நயன்இல
நட்டார்கண் செய்தலின் தீது.
Vain words spoken in public are worse
Than wrongs done to mates.
Useless speech in front of others is more harmful than
doing evil to friends.

193 நயன்இலன் என்பது சொல்லும் பயன்இல
பாரித்து உரைக்கும் உரை.
Long and vain speech trumpets
One's utter worthlessness.
Long and useless words expose the speaker's total
lack of virtue.

194 நயன்சாரா நன்மையின் நீக்கும் பயன்சாராப்
பண்பில்சொல் பல்லா ரகத்து.
One's vain and crude words before an assembly
Remove one's gains and goodness simply.
Empty and crude speech in public is fruitless and
devoid of virtue.

195 சீர்மை சிறப்பொடு நீங்கும் பயன்இல
நீர்மை உடையார் சொலின்.
Whenever the good speak useless words
All esteem and eminence they lose.
When men of dignity speak useless words, they lose
their greatness and esteem.

196 பயன்இல்சொல் பாராட்டு வானை மகன்எனல்
மக்கட் பதடி எனல்.
**Who speaks vain words call him not a man
Rather call him a chaff among men.**
He who indulges in empty words is not called a man
but a human chaff.

197 நயன்இல சொல்லினும் சொல்லுக சான்றோர்
பயன்இல சொல்லாமை நன்று.
**It's good for the perfect to utter not vain words
Even if they speak unjust words.**
The perfect may even utter unfair words but it is
good to avoid useless words.

198 அரும்பயன் ஆயும் அறிவினார் சொல்லார்
பெரும்பயன் இல்லாத சொல்.
**The wise who discern merit won't utter
Words that lack gains greater.**
Men of wisdom and reason will never utter useless
words.

199 பொருள்தீர்ந்த பொச்சாந்தும் சொல்லார் மருள்தீர்ந்த
மாசறு காட்சி யவர்.
**Men of clear wisdom and spotless vision
Even forgetfully utter not words in vain.**
Men of wisdom and vision will never utter silly words
even forgetfully .

200 சொல்லுக சொல்லின் பயனுடைய சொல்லற்க
சொல்லின் பயனிலாச் சொல்.
**Always utter fruitful words
Never utter futile words.**
One should always speak useful words but never
indulge in vain speech.

21. தீவினையச்சம்
FEAR OF DOING EVIL

201   தீவினையார் அஞ்சார் விழுமியார் அஞ்சுவர்
தீவினை என்னும் செருக்கு.
The wicked never fear the pride of evil
The good ever fear that evil.
The wicked never fear evil but the good always fear
the arrogance of sinful deeds.

202   தீயவை தீய பயத்தலால் தீயவை
தீயினும் அஞ்சப் படும்.
Evil is feared more than fire
As evil begets evil ever.
One must fear evil more than fire as one evil leads to
another evil.

203   அறிவினுள் எல்லாம் தலையென்ப தீய
செறுவார்க்கும் செய்யா விடல்.
Crown of wisdom is to shun evil
Even to foes who do evil.
Supreme wisdom is not to do evil in return even to
enemies who do evil.

204   மறந்தும் பிறன்கேடு சூழற்க சூழின்
அறம்சூழும் சூழ்ந்தவன் கேடு.
Never plot evil against others even forgetfully
Or else virtue will ruin you surely.
One must avoid plotting evil against others. Otherwise,
virtue will destroy one who plots others' ruin.

205   இலன்என்று தீயவை செய்யற்க செய்யின்
இலன்ஆகும் மற்றும் பெயர்த்து.
Plead not poverty for doing evil
For you'll become poorer still.
One should not do sinful deeds pleading poverty as it
will make one poorer.

206 தீப்பால தான்பிறர்கண் செய்யற்க நோய்ப்பால
தன்னை அடல்வேண்டா தான்.

Who desire to avoid evil for themselves
Should eschew doing evil to others.

Those who want to avoid evil for themselves must avoid
doing evil to others.

207 எனைப்பகை உற்றாரும் உய்வர் வினைப்பகை
வீயாது பின்சென்று அடும்.

One may escape from deadly enmity but still
Enmity of the evil will chase and kill.

One may escape from the ill effects of enmity but the
enmity of one's own sinful deeds will bring ruin to one.

208 தீயவை செய்தார் கெடுதல் நிழல்தன்னை
வீயாது அடிஉறைந் தற்று.

Destruction follows one who commits evil acts
Like the shadow following one's footsteps.

Ruin follows evil-doers like a man's shadow that
follows his footsteps.

209 தன்னைத்தான் காதலன் ஆயின் எனைத்தொன்றும்
துன்னற்க தீவினைப் பால்.

If you love yourself above all
Do no evil however small.

One who loves oneself should refrain from doing even
the smallest evil to others.

210 அருங்கேடன் என்பது அறிக மருங்கோடித்
தீவினை செய்யான் எனின்.

Who slips not from right path to do evils
Is guarded from all ills.

A person who stays away from doing evils will be free
from all evils.

22. ஒப்புரவறிதல்
DUTY TO SOCIETY

211   கைம்மாறு வேண்டா கடப்பாடு மாரிமாட்டு
என்ஆற்றும் கொல்லோ உலகு.

Duty expects not anything in return
Just as rain expects none.

Rain does not expect anything in return from the
world. Similarly, duty to society demands no return.

212   தாளாற்றித் தந்த பொருள்எல்லாம் தக்கார்க்கு
வேளாண்மை செய்தல் பொருட்டு.

All riches that tireless efforts fetch
Are to help those deserving much.

All the wealth earned by the benevolent by tireless
efforts is meant to serve the worthy men.

213   புத்தேள் உலகத்தும் ஈண்டும் பெறல்அரிதே
ஒப்புரவின் நல்ல பிற.

Even in heaven and earth it's rare to find
A better deed than serving mankind.

There is no better deed in heaven and earth than
serving the society.

214   ஒத்தது அறிவான் உயிர்வாழ்வான் மற்றையான்
செத்தாருள் வைக்கப் படும்.

He alone is alive who is in tune with the world
All others are deemed dead.

He who is in harmony with others alone lives while
the rest are considered dead.

215   ஊருணி நீர்நிறைந் தற்றே உலகவாம்
பேரறி வாளன் திரு.

The wealth of the truly wise is like
The brimming village tank.

The wealth of the wise who love humanity is beneficial
to all like the village tank full of water.

216 பயன்மரம் உள்ளூர்ப் பழுத்தற்றால் செல்வம்
நயனுடை யான்கண் படின்.
Abundant wealth of a benevolent person
Is like a fruit-laden tree in mid-town.
The wealth of a generous person serves like a fruit-
bearing tree in the middle of a town benefitting all.

217 மருந்தாகித் தப்பா மரத்தற்றால் செல்வம்
பெருந்தகை யான்கண் படின்.
Wealth of a generous man is like a herbal tree
That becomes an unfailing remedy.
The wealth of a generous man is like a herbal tree which
serves as medicine that cures without fail.

218 இடன்இல் பருவத்தும் ஒப்புரவிற்கு ஒல்கார்
கடன்அறி காட்சி யவர்.
The dutiful even with dwindled affluence
Won't slacken in benevolence.
Even in utter poverty the dutiful will never give up their
generosity.

219 நயன்உடையான் நல்கூர்ந்தான் ஆதல் செயும்நீர
செய்யாது அமைகலா வாறு.
One who is generous feels very poor
When unable to do any favour.
A generous person considers himself poor when he
is unable to help others.

220 ஒப்புரவி னால்வரும் கேடுஎனின் அஃதொருவன்
விற்றுக்கோள் தக்கது உடைத்து.
The ruin that comes out of doing charity
Is worth buying by getting into slavery.
Even ruin is worth buying by selling oneself if it comes
of doing charity.

23. ஈகை
CHARITY

221
வறியார்க்கொன்று ஈவதே ஈகைமற் றெல்லாம்
குறியெதிர்ப்பை நீரது உடைத்து.

Giving to the poor alone is real charity
All else aim at recompense only.

Helping the poor alone is called charity. All other gifts
seek only repayment.

222
நல்ஆறு எனினும் கொளல்தீது மேலுலகம்
இல்லெனினும் ஈதலே நன்று.

Receiving is bad even tho' for the cause of good
Giving is good though heaven is denied.

Receiving even for a good cause is evil. Giving is
good even if heaven is denied.

223
இலன்என்னும் எவ்வம் உரையாமை ஈதல்
குலன்உடையான் கண்ணே உள.

Giving before one pleads penury
Marks the man of nobility.

Giving even before one expresses one's poverty is
the quality found in a noble man.

224
இன்னாது இரக்கப் படுதல் இரந்தவர்
இன்முகம் காணும் அளவு.

Begging indeed is the most painful sight
Till one sees the beggar's face bright.

It is a most painful sight to see begging till the beggar's
face becomes bright on receiving.

225
ஆற்றுவார் ஆற்றல் பசிஆற்றல் அப்பசியை
மாற்றுவார் ஆற்றலின் பின்.

Great is the power of those who endure hunger
Greater is appeasing others' hunger.

The ability of a person to relieve others of hunger is
rated higher than the ability to endure hunger.

226 அற்றார் அழிபசி தீர்த்தல் அஃதொருவன்
பெற்றான் பொருள்வைப் புழி.

**Relieving the killing hunger of the needy
Is the safest treasury of the wealthy.**

By relieving the hunger of the poor, the rich find a good
place to store their wealth.

227 பாத்தூண் மரீஇ யவனைப் பசிஎன்னும்
தீப்பிணி தீண்டல் அரிது.

**Fiery disease of hunger seldom touches
Those who share their meals.**

The fiery hunger will never touch those who share their
food with others.

228 ஈத்துடவக்கும் இன்பம் அறியார்கொல் தாம்உடைமை
வைத்துஇழக்கும் வன்க ணவர்.

**The cruel who hoard and lose know not happiness
Of gladly helping the have-nots.**

Those who hoard and lose wealth do not know the joy
of gladdening the poor with charity.

229 இரத்தலின் இன்னாது மன்ற நிரப்பிய
தாமே தமியர் உணல்.

**Eating all alone merely for hoarding
Is more painful than begging.**

Eating alone for merely saving one's wealth is even more
painful than begging.

230 சாதலின் இன்னாதது இல்லை இனிதுஅதூஉம்
ஈதல் இயையாக் கடை.

**Nothing else is indeed so miserable as dying
But sweet it is when incapable of giving.**

Nothing else is as painful as death. But death is
pleasant when one is unable to give alms to the poor.

24. புகழ்
FAME

231 ஈதல் இசைபட வாழ்தல் அதுஅல்லது
ஊதியம் இல்லை உயிர்க்கு.

The only benefit in life is glory
That comes of charity.

The only asset in life is fame which comes through
acts of charity.

232 உரைப்பார் உரைப்பவை எல்லாம் இரப்பார்க்குஒன்று
ஈவார்மேல் நிற்கும் புகழ்.

Whatever spoken in the world in praise
Is the glory of alms-givers.

All the glory in the world is the glory of those who
give alms to the poor.

233 ஒன்றா உலகத்து உயர்ந்த புகழல்லால்
பொன்றாது நிற்பதுஒன்று இல்.

Nothing in the world remains undying
Except fame unique and towering.

Nothing remains everlasting in this world except
renowned fame.

234 நிலவரை நீள்புகழ் ஆற்றின் புலவரைப்
போற்றாது புத்தேள் உலகு.

Heaven will never acclaim even the gods
But men on earth with lasting laurels.

Heaven will not praise the gods but men on earth with
everlasting fame.

235 நத்தம்போல் கேடும் உளதுஆகும் சாக்காடும்
வித்தகர்க்கு அல்லால் அரிது.

Fame in fall and life in doom
Are only to men of wisdom.

Only the wise can convert loss into gain and death
into life of glory.

236 தோன்றின் புகழொடு தோன்றுக அஃதிலார்
தோன்றலின் தோன்றாமை நன்று.
Enter a field and build up repute
If not, it's better to enter not.
One must enter the chosen field and earn fame, or else
one should not enter.

237 புகழ்பட வாழாதார் தம்நோவார் தம்மை
இகழ்வாரை நோவது எவன்.
Why do the fameless blame the despisers
Rather than blaming themselves?
It is useless for the fameless to blame their despisers
instead of blaming themselves.

238 வசையென்ப வையத்தார்க்கு எல்லாம் இசையென்னும்
எச்சம் பெறாஅது விடின்.
To live without leaving a legacy of fame
Is to earn the whole world's blame.
It is a disgrace for all those on earth if they fail to leave
behind fame.

239 வசையிலா வண்பயன் குன்றும் இசையிலா
யாக்கை பொறுத்த நிலம்.
The land that bears inglorious bodies
Will diminish in blameless yields.
The earth bearing the burden of men without fame
loses its fertility and yields less.

240 வசையொழிய வாழ்வாரே வாழ்வார் இசையொழிய
வாழ்வாரே வாழா தவர்.
Those who are blameless alone really live
The fameless are not considered alive.
Life without blame alone is life and life without fame is
mere survival.

25. அருளுடைமை
COMPASSION

241   அருட்செல்வம் செல்வத்துள் செல்வம் பொருட்செல்வம்
பூரியார் கண்ணும் உள.

Wealth of wealth is the wealth of kindness
Worldly wealth even the mean possess.

Compassion is the greatest wealth. Even the worst of
men possess worldly wealth.

242   நல்லாற்றால் நாடி அருளாள்க பல்லாற்றால்
தேரினும் அஃதே துணை.

By fair means seek and secure grace
All codes proclaim it as assistance.

One should pursue the path of compassion. All faiths
prescribe it as a support for life.

243   அருள்சேர்ந்த நெஞ்சினார்க்கு இல்லை இருள்சேர்ந்த
இன்னா உலகம் புகல்.

Men of graceful heart would seldom pass
Into the world of darkness and distress.

The darkness and distress of hell are not for men of
kindness.

244   மன்னுயிர் ஓம்பி அருள்ஆள்வாற்கு இல்லென்ப
தன்உயிர் அஞ்சும் வினை.

Men of mercy who guard all beings
Are free from fear of evils.

Men of compassion protecting all beings on earth are
free from fear of evils.

245   அல்லல் அருள்ஆள்வார்க்கு இல்லை வளிவழங்கும்
மல்லல்மா ஞாலம் கரி.

Sorrows are not for those with merciful heart
This wind-blown world bears witness to it.

Men of graceful compassion suffer no pain. This world
bears witness to it.

246   பொருள்நீங்கிப் பொச்சாந்தார் என்பர் அருள்நீங்கி
      அல்லவை செய்துஒழுகு வார்.

**Who neglect virtue and life's purpose
Are graceless in their acts.**

Those who are not compassionate and do sinful deeds
lack virtue and purpose of life.

247   அருளில்லார்க்கு அவ்வுலகம் இல்லை பொருளில்லார்க்கு
      இவ்வுலகம் இல்லாகி யாங்கு.

**This world is not for the penniless
Nor is heaven for the graceless.**

This world is not for the poor and the heavenly world is
not for the unkind.

248   பொருள்அற்றார் பூப்பர் ஒருகால் அருள்அற்றார்
      அற்றார்மற்று ஆதல் அரிது.

**The poor may perhaps flourish some day
But the cruel prosper not any day.**

Men without money may prosper some day but those
without mercy will never flourish.

249   தெருளாதான் மெய்ப்பொருள் கண்டற்றால் தேரின்
      அருளாதான் செய்யும் அறம்.

**Who performs charity without sympathy
Is like an unwise man seeking reality.**

One who does charity without mercy is like an insensible
man seeking the profound truth.

250   வலியார்முன் தன்னை நினைக்கதான் தன்னின்
      மெலியார்மேல் செல்லும் இடத்து.

**Imagine yourself facing the stronger
While oppressing the weaker.**

While oppressing weaker persons a man should imagine
himself against the mightier ones.

26. புலால் மறுத்தல்
AVOIDING MEAT

251 தன்ஊன் பெருக்கற்குத் தான்பிறிது ஊன்உண்பான்
எங்ஙனம் ஆளும் அருள்.
How could one ever be compassionate
If one fattens on animal meat?
One who fattens himself feeding on the animal flesh can
never be kind to others.

252 பொருள்ஆட்சி போற்றாதார்க்கு இல்லை அருளாட்சி
ஆங்கில்லை ஊன்தின் பவர்க்கு.
Gains of wealth are not for spendthrifts
For meat-eaters no gains of grace.
The thriftless cannot have wealth and meat-eaters
cannot have kindness.

253 படைகொண்டார் நெஞ்சம்போல் நன்றூஉக்காது ஒன்றன்
உடல்சுவை உண்டார் மனம்.
Meat-eaters find no joy in good
Like weapon wielders' mind.
The meat-eaters do not find joy in grace like those who
carry murderous weapons.

254 அருளல்லது யாதெனில் கொல்லாமை கோறல்
பொருளல்லது அவ்வூன் தினல்.
Non-killing is indeed an act of kindness
Killing and eating it is unkindness.
Not killing a creature is an act of kindness. Killing and
eating its meat is unkindness.

255 உண்ணாமை உள்ளது உயிர்நிலை ஊன்உண்ண
அண்ணாத்தல் செய்யாது அளறு.
Eat not meat and life remains unhurt
Hell swallows men who eat meat.
By giving up meat-eating, lives are saved. Meat-eaters
cannot escape from going to hell.

256   தினல்பொருட்டால் கொல்லாது உலகெனின் யாரும்
       விலைப்பொருட்டால் ஊன்தருவார் இல்.
**If men refrain from killing for eating meat
There will be none to sell meat.**
If men do not kill animals for eating, there will be no
one to sell meat.

257   உண்ணாமை வேண்டும் புலாஅல் பிறிதுஒன்றன்
       புண்அது உணர்வார்ப் பெறின்.
**If one knows meat is but a sore
One won't eat it any more.**
If one knows that meat is only a sore of an animal,
one will refrain from eating it.

258   செயிரின் தலைப்பிரிந்த காட்சியார் உண்ணார்
       உயிரின் தலைப்பிரிந்த ஊன்.
**The undeluded wise will ever avoid meat
Which is but the flesh of a lifeless beast.**
Wise men who have clear mind will refrain from eating
the flesh of a lifeless animal.

259   அவிசொரிந்து ஆயிரம் வேட்டலின் ஒன்றன்
       உயிர்செகுத்து உண்ணாமை நன்று.
**Non-killing and not eating meat are ever
Better than limitless sacrificial fire.**
It is better to refrain from killing and eating meat than
numerous offerings of ghee on fire.

260   கொல்லான் புலாலை மறுத்தானைக் கைகூப்பி
       எல்லா உயிரும் தொழும்.
**All living beings on earth will lovingly salute
Him who kills not and eats not meat.**
He who gives up killing and eating meat will be adored
by one and all.

27. தவம்
PENANCE

261   உற்றநோய் நோன்றல் உயிர்க்குஉறுகண் செய்யாமை
      அற்றே தவத்திற்கு உரு.

To endure pain and to pain not others even once
Is the sign of good penance.

Real penance lies in enduring sufferings and not
causing sufferings to others.

262   தவமும் தவமுடையார்க்கு ஆகும் அவம்அதனை
      அஃதிலார் மேற்கொள் வது.

Penance befits only penance-doers
It is a fruitless effort for others.

Penance befits only those who do penance and it is a
useless effort for others.

263   துறந்தார்க்குத் துப்புரவு வேண்டி மறந்தார்கொல்
      மற்றை யவர்கள் தவம்.

Is it to provide sustenance to ascetics
That family men forget penance?

Family men refrain from penance in order to help those
who have renounced life.

264   ஒன்னார்த் தெறலும் உவந்தாரை ஆக்கலும்
      எண்ணின் தவத்தான் வரும்.

To ruin foes and advance mates
Penance alone has the force.

Penance has the power to destroy the enemies and
elevate the friends.

265   வேண்டிய வேண்டியாங்கு எய்தலால் செய்தவம்
      ஈண்டு முயலப் படும்.

Try to do hard penance here
To get your heart's desire.

People should try to do hard penance to achieve
what their hearts desire.

266 தவஞ்செய்வார் தம்கருமம் செய்வார்மற்று அல்லார்
அவஞ்செய்வார் ஆசையுள் பட்டு.

Ascetics accomplish their noble deeds
Others with greed do evil deeds.

Penance-doers achieve their noble ideals while the
greedy do only harmful deeds.

267 சுடச்சுடரும் பொன்போல் ஒளிவிடும் துன்பம்
சுடச்சுட நோற்கிற் பவர்க்கு.

Like gold that shines when heated in fire
Men enduring pain of penance glitter.

As fire refines gold and makes it brighter, sufferings of
penance make the ascetics purer.

268 தன்உயிர் தான்அறப் பெற்றானை ஏனைய
மன்னுயிர் எல்லாம் தொழும்.

All living beings on earth will show reverence
For men who rise above ego thro' penance.

Those who renounce ego and control the mind through
penance are worshipped by all living beings.

269 கூற்றம் குதித்தலும் கைகூடும் நோற்றலின்
ஆற்றல் தலைப்பட் டவர்க்கு.

Even conquering Death is a likely occurance
To men who possess the might of penance.

Whoever is strengthened with the power of penance
can conquer even the god of death.

270 இலர்பலர் ஆகிய காரணம் நோற்பார்
சிலர்பலர் நோலா தவர்.

Only a few are wealthy but many are not
For a few do penance and many do not.

A few are rich and many are poor, for only a few do
penance while many do not.

28. கூடா ஒழுக்கம்
IMPROPER CONDUCT

271   வஞ்ச மனத்தான் படிற்றொழுக்கம் பூதங்கள்
ஐந்தும் அகத்தே நகும்.

**Body's five elements laugh to themselves
At the lying conduct of pretenders.**

The five elements in the body will laugh at the pretensions
of a man of improper conduct.

272   வானுயர் தோற்றம் எவன்செய்யும் தன்நெஞ்சம்
தான்அறி குற்றப் படின்.

**What is the use of a man's grand saintly postures
If his mind is knowingly bent on evils?**

A man's saintly postures are of no use if his mind is
knowingly bent on evil thoughts.

273   வலிஇல் நிலைமையான் வல்லுருவம் பெற்றம்
புலியின்தோல் போர்த்துமேய்ந் தற்று.

**Boasting saintliness with weakness within
Is like a cow grazing in tiger's skin.**

The saintly appearance of a man without inner strength is
like a grazing cow clothed in a tiger's skin.

274   தவம்மறைந்து அல்லவை செய்தல் புதல்மறைந்து
வேட்டுவன் புள்சிமிழ்த் தற்று.

**Doing evil deeds disguised in saintly robes
Is like a fowler behind a bush to net birds.**

A sinning man disguised in saintly dress is like a bird-
hunter hiding behind a bush.

275   பற்றற்றேம் என்பார் படிற்றொழுக்கம் எற்றுஎற்றுஎன்று
ஏதம் பலவும் தரும்.

**Who claim they're saintly but sin secretly
Will bitterly cry in eternal misery.**

Men who claim sainthood but practise evil bring only
eternal misery upon themselves.

276

நெஞ்சில் துறவார் துறந்தார்போல் வஞ்சித்து
வாழ்வாரின் வன்கணார் இல்.

None is so cruel as a feigning hermit
Who lives by utter deceit.

None is so cruel as the one who pretends to be an
ascetic and deceives the world.

277

புறங்குன்றி கண்டனைய ரேனும் அகங்குன்றி
மூக்கில் கரியார் உடைத்து.

Like *the kunri**, red is some men's exterior
But black, like its nose, is their interior.

There are people who appear shining outwardly like
the *kunri berry* but black inwardly like its nose.

278

மனத்தது மாசுஆக மாண்டார்நீ ராடி
மறைந்துஒழுகு மாந்தர் பலர்.

Many spotted minds bathe in holy rivers
Concealing evil in saintly gaze.

There are many people who like ascetics clean their
body in holy water but hide their evil mind.

279

கணைகொடிது யாழ்கோடு செவ்விதுஆங் கன்ன
வினைபடு பாலால் கொளல்.

Judge men by deeds but not by mere looks
Straight arrow kills, curved lute delights.

A straight arrow kills but a bent lute charms. Likewise,
men must be judged only by their deeds.

280

மழித்தலும் நீட்டலும் வேண்டா உலகம்
பழித்தது ஒழித்து விடின்.

If one avoids what world condemns as smear
One needn't tonsure or grow long hair.

There is no need to tonsure or grow long hair if one
shuns evil deeds.

---

* kunri - a bright red seed with a black tip

29. கள்ளாமை
NOT STEALING

281 எள்ளாமை வேண்டுவான் என்பான் எனைத்துஒன்றும்
கள்ளாமை காக்கதன் நெஞ்சு.

One should guard the mind against theft
If one wants to escape contempt.

He who wants to avoid contempt should guard against
the very thought of stealing.

282 உள்ளத்தால் உள்ளலும் தீதே பிறன்பொருளைக்
கள்ளத்தால் கள்வேம் எனல்.

The very thought of robbing others' wealth
By fraud is a sin of stealth.

Even the thought of robbing others' wealth is a sin
and so it must be eschewed.

283 களவினால் ஆகிய ஆக்கம் அளவுஇறந்து
ஆவது-போலக் கெடும்.

Stolen wealth may appear to gain
But it will result in limitless ruin.

Stolen wealth seems to grow but actually it will result
in limitless ruin.

284 களவின்கண் கன்றிய காதல் விளைவின்கண்
வீயா விழுமம் தரும்.

Inordinate passion for thieving
Results in endless suffering.

Limitless desire to steal others' wealth will bring in
endless suffering.

285 அருள்கருதி அன்புடையர் ஆதல் பொருள்கருதிப்
பொச்சாப்புப் பார்ப்பார்கண் இல்.

Love and grace can never be found in those
With an eye on others' unguarded riches.

Those who covet the unguarded wealth of others have
no grace and love.

286   அளவின்கண் நின்றுஒழுகல் ஆற்றார் களவின்கண்
கன்றிய காத லவர்.

Who long to cherish stolen wealth
Tread not the righteous path.

Those who love stolen wealth will not stick to the
righteous path.

287   களவுஎன்னும் காரறி வாண்மை அளவுஎன்னும்
ஆற்றல் புரிந்தார்கண் இல்.

The blackest craft of basest fraud is not found
In men with measured wisdom sound.

The basest deed of stealing is not found in men of
profound righteousness.

288   அளவுஅறிந்தார் நெஞ்சத்து அறம்போல நிற்கும்
களவுஅறிந்தார் நெஞ்சில் கரவு.

In the hearts of the virtuous virtue reigns
In the hearts of thieves deceit remains.

Virtue lies in the thoughts of the virtuous and deceit
lies in the hearts of thieves.

289   அளவுஅல்ல செய்தாங்கே வீவர் களவல்ல
மற்றைய தேற்றா தவர்.

Who know nothing but thieving
Die by their endless evil doing.

Those who know nothing but stealing will perish by
their own wicked deeds.

290   கள்வார்க்குத் தள்ளும் உயிர்நிலை கள்ளார்க்குத்
தள்ளாது புத்தே ளுலகு.

Honest souls gain heavenly ecstasy
Thieves lose even their body.

Those who refrain from stealing gain heaven, whereas
thieves lose their life.

30. வாய்மை
TRUTHFULNESS

291   வாய்மை எனப்படுவது யாதுஎனின் யாதுஒன்றும்
தீமை இலாத சொலல்.

"What is truth?" if the question be
It's speech with words evil-free.

Truth is nothing but speaking without the least degree
of evil to others.

292   பொய்ம்மையும் வாய்மை இடத்த புரைதீர்ந்த
நன்மை பயக்கும் எனின்.

Even untruth has the stamp of truthfulness
If it brings good sans harmfulness.

Even a harmless lie can be considered as truth when it
brings benevolent results.

293   தன்நெஞ்சு அறிவது பொய்யற்க பொய்த்தபின்
தன்நெஞ்சே தன்னைச் சுடும்.

Do not speak falsehood knowingly
As conscience pricks woefully.

A man shall not utter falsehood deliberately as his
conscience will torment him afterwards.

294   உள்ளத்தால் பொய்யாது ஒழுகின் உலகத்தார்
உள்ளத்துள் எல்லாம் உளன்.

Who remains true to his conscience
Lives forever in all noble hearts.

He who is free from falsehood dwells in the hearts of
all good people.

295   மனத்தொடு வாய்மை மொழியின் தவத்தொடு
தானஞ்செய் வாரின் தலை.

Superior is one who speaks the truth earnestly
To those who do penance and charity.

He who speaks the truth is superior to those doing
penance and charity.

296　பொய்யாமை அன்ன புகழ்இல்லை எய்யாமை
எல்லா அறமும் தரும்.

No honour can ever equal truthfulness
As it yields every virtue sans efforts.

Nothing can match truthfulness which brings in without
effort every virtue along with fame.

297　பொய்யாமை பொய்யாமை ஆற்றின் அறம்பிற
செய்யாமை செய்யாமை நன்று.

If you observe non-lying and non-lying only
You needn't practise other virtues really.

He who speaks the truth and nothing but the truth need
not practise any other virtues.

298　புறந்தூய்மை நீரான் அமையும் அகந்தூய்மை
வாய்மையால் காணப் படும்.

Water provides only external purity
Truth reveals internal purity.

Water cleans the body. Likewise, truth enlightens
the soul.

299　எல்லா விளக்கும் விளக்கல்ல சான்றோர்க்குப்
பொய்யா விளக்கே விளக்கு.

All lamps are not lamps in wise men's sight
Truthfulness alone is deemed light.

All lamps are not real lamps. To the great, the lamp
of truth alone is the lamp.

300　யாம்மெய்யாக் கண்டவற்றுள் இல்லை எனைத்தொன்றும்
வாய்மையின் நல்ல பிற.

Of all good things that we have found
Nothing surpasses truth profound.

Of all the good things in the world there is no virtue
greater than truth.

31. வெகுளாமை
RESTRAINING ANGER

301 செல்இடத்துக் காப்பான் சினம்காப்பான் அல்இடத்துக்
காக்கின்என் காவாக்கால் என்.
Restrain anger where it would have effect
Elsewhere, curbed or not, it matters not.
Anger against the weak is wrong but it is useless
against the strong.

302 செல்லா இடத்துச் சினம்தீது செல்லிடத்தும்
இல்அதனின் தீய பிற.
Anger is bad before the powerful
Worse it is before the feeble.
Anger shown to the strong is bad and it is worse if it is
shown to the weak.

303 மறத்தல் வெகுளியை யார்மாட்டும் தீய
பிறத்தல் அதனான் வரும்.
Forget anger towards anyone
For it begets evil and pain.
A person must avoid anger towards all, for it brings him
all evils.

304 நகையும் உவகையும் கொல்லும் சினத்தின்
பகையும் உளவோ பிற.
Is there any greater foe than anger
Which kills joy and laughter?
There is no greater enemy than anger which kills one's
happiness and laughter.

305 தன்னைத்தான் காக்கின் சினம்காக்க காவாக்கால்
தன்னையே கொல்லும் சினம்.
To guard yourself, keep wrath at bay
Unchecked, ire will yourself slay.
A person must guard himself against anger or else it
will lead him to self-destruction.

306　சினம்என்னும் சேர்ந்தாரைக் கொல்லி இனம்என்னும்
ஏமப் புணையைச் சுடும்.

Fire of anger that guts all who draw near it
Burns kinship, the life-boat.

Anger destroys not only one who gets angry but also
one's relations who help them in times of danger.

307　சினத்தைப் பொருள்என்று கொண்டவன் கேடு
நிலத்தறைந்தான் கைபிழையா தற்று.

Ruin of men who see anger as their strength
Is like the hand getting hurt on hitting earth.

An angry man's ruin is as sure as the hand that strikes
the ground getting injured.

308　இணர்எரி தோய்வுஅன்ன இன்னா செயினும்
புணரின் வெகுளாமை நன்று.

One may torture you like the blazing fire
It's better to curb your ire.

Though tortured like scorching fire, it is better to control
one's anger.

309　உள்ளியது எல்லாம் உடன்எய்தும் உள்ளத்தால்
உள்ளான் வெகுளி எனின்.

All good wishes are obtained instantly
If one's thoughts are ire-free.

A man will attain everything he wants if his mind is
free from the thoughts of anger.

310　இறந்தார் இறந்தார் அனையர் சினத்தைத்
துறந்தார் துறந்தார் துணை.

The ire-fed are like the lifeless
The ire-free equal the ascetics.

Those who lose temper are like the dead and those
who renounce anger are like ascetics.

32. இன்னா செய்யாமை
NOT DOING HARM

311   சிறப்புஈனும் செல்வம் பெறினும் பிறர்க்குஇன்னா
       செய்யாமை மாசுஅற்றார் கோள்.

Code of the spotless is to hurt none
Tho' glory-yielding wealth is won.

The law of the pure is never to hurt others even if it
brings wealth that achieves fame.

312   கறுத்துஇன்னா செய்தவக் கண்ணும் மறுத்துஇன்னா
       செய்யாமை மாசுஅற்றார் கோள்.

Not to hurt others who do evil in ire
Is always the code of the pure.

It is the code of the pure-hearted never to hurt others even
when they do them harm in anger.

313   செய்யாமல் செற்றார்க்கும் இன்னாத செய்தபின்
       உய்யா விழுமம் தரும்.

Even taking vengeance on deliberate evil-doers
Will surely bring inescapable ills.

Even vengeance against planned evil-doers brings endless miseries inevitably.

314   இன்னாசெய் தாரை ஒறுத்தல் அவர்நாண
       நன்னயம் செய்து விடல்.

Punish those who have done great evils
By shaming them with good deeds.

The best way of punishing the evil-doers is to forget their
harmful deeds and do good to them.

315   அறிவினான் ஆகுவது உண்டோ பிறிதின்நோய்
       தம்நோய்போல் போற்றாக் கடை.

What good does a man of wisdom obtain
If he treats not others' woes as his own?

A man's knowledge is of no use if he does not regard
the sufferings of others as his own.

316   இன்னா எனத்தான் உணர்ந்தவை துன்னாமை
வேண்டும் பிறன்கண் செயல்.
What is felt painful by one
Shall be done to none.
What is considered by one as harmful should not be
done to others.

317   எனைத்தானும் எஞ்ஞான்றும் யார்க்கும் மனத்தான்ஆம்
மாணாசெய் யாமை தலை.
Hurting no one even in thought at any time
Even in small measure is virtue prime.
To refrain from hurting anyone wilfully in any manner
at any time even in thought is the chief virtue.

318   தன்உயிர்க்கு இன்னாமை தானறிவான் என்கொலோ
மன்னுயிர்க்கு இன்னா செயல்.
Why should one who knows the pain of evils
Do them to other human beings?
A man should never harm others when he himself
knows the sufferings of evils.

319   பிறர்க்குஇன்னா முற்பகல் செய்யின் தமக்குஇன்னா
பிற்பகல் தாமே வரும்.
If you do harm to others in the forenoon
Evil will follow in the afternoon.
If a man inflicts pain upon others, sorrows will afflict
him quickly.

320   நோய்எல்லாம் நோய்செய்தார் மேலவாம் நோய்செய்யார்
நோயின்மை வேண்டு பவர்.
Who want to be free from evils won't do evils
As all evils rebound on evil-doers.
Those who want to be free from sufferings will not do
wrong since all wrongs recoil on wrong-doers.

33. கொல்லாமை
NON-KILLING

321 அறவினை யாதெனின் கொல்லாமை கோறல்
பிறவினை எல்லாம் தரும்.

What is a virtuous deed? It is non-killing
Evils spring from killing.

Non-killing of creatures is a virtuous act. All sinful deeds
arise out of killing.

322 பகுத்துஉண்டு பல்லுயிர் ஓம்புதல் நூலோர்
தொகுத்தவற்றுள் எல்லாம் தலை.

Sharing one's food for guarding all beings
Is the prime virtue in all sayings.

Sharing one's food with others for protecting all lives
is the chief virtue, according to scholars.

323 ஒன்றாக நல்லது கொல்லாமை மற்றுஅதன்
பின்சாரப் பொய்யாமை நன்று.

Crown of all virtues is non-killing
Next to it ranks non-lying.

Non-killing is the supreme of all the virtues and non-
lying is next to it.

324 நல்லாறு எனப்படுவது யாதெனின் யாதொன்றும்
கொல்லாமை சூழும் நெறி.

What is the right path? It's only
. **The virtue of not killing any.**

Non-killing of any creature is considered to be the virtuous
way of life.

325 நிலைஅஞ்சி நீத்தாருள் எல்லாம் கொலைஅஞ்சிக்
கொல்லாமை சூழ்வான் தலை.

Of all who fear life and renounce the world
One who dreads killing is great indeed.

One who refrains from killing is greater than those
who have renounced the world fearing life.

326 கொல்லாமை மேற்கொண்டு ஒழுகுவான் வாழ்நாள்மேல்
செல்லாது உயிருண்ணும் கூற்று.

Life-devouring Death spares the breath
Of one who puts no life to death.

Even the god of death won't take away the life of one
who refrains from killing other beings.

327 தன்னுயிர் நீப்பினும் செய்யற்க தான்பிறிது
இன்னுயிர் நீக்கும் வினை.

Deprive not others' cherished life
Even if it costs your dear life.

One must certainly refrain from killing even if one's dear
life is in peril.

328 நன்றாகும் ஆக்கம் பெரிதெனினும் சான்றோர்க்குக்
கொன்றாகும் ஆக்கம் கடை.

Though killing may bring gain
The wise shun it as mean.

The wise despise the disgraceful act of killing, however
great its gains may be.

329 கொலைவினையர் ஆகிய மாக்கள் புலைவினையர்
புன்மை தெரிவா ரகத்து.

Those who live by killing are regarded
As men of mean deeds by the learned.

Those who live by killing are considered by the wise
as men of mean deeds.

330 உயிர்உடம்பின் நீக்கியார் என்ப செயிர்உடம்பின்
செல்லாத்தீ வாழ்க்கை யவர்.

Who lived by merciless killing of beings
Live in penury with acute diseases.

Those who once led their life by killing will live in
poverty with dreadful diseases.

34. நிலையாமை
IMPERMANENCE

331 நில்லாத வற்றை நிலையின என்றுஉணரும்
புல்லறி வாண்மை கடை.

To view the fleeting as everlasting
Is foolish and degrading.

It is utterly foolish and deplorable to mistake impermanence for permanence.

332 கூத்தாட்டு அவைக்குழாத் தற்றே பெருஞ்செல்வம்
போக்கும் அதுவிளிந் தற்று.

Wealth is like a gathering of play-goers
Slowly comes but quickly disperses.

The rise and fall of fortune is like the gathering and
dispersing of the crowd in a theatre.

333 அற்கா இயல்பிற்றுச் செல்வம் அதுபெற்றால்
அற்குப ஆங்கே செயல்.

Nature of wealth is indeed ever fleeting
Once gained, do things everlasting.

Wealth is impermanent. So one has to use it at
once on charitable deeds of lasting value.

334 நாள்என ஒன்றுபோல் காட்டி உயிர்ஈரும்
வாள்அது உணர்வார்ப் பெறின்.

A day to the wise is a sword
Hacking the life indeed.

The wise consider a day as a sword that cuts down
the life of a man.

335 நாச்செற்று விக்குள்மேல் வாரா/முன் நல்வினை
மேற்சென்று செய்யப் படும்.

Always hasten to do good and virtuous deeds
Before tongue fails and last hiccup comes.

One must do noble deeds without delay, for death
may come anytime.

336 நெருநல் உளன்ஒருவன் இன்றுஇல்லை என்னும்
பெருமை உடைத்துஇவ் வுலகு.

Alive was he yesterday, but not today
It is a marvel in the world's way.

Yesterday he was alive but today he is no more. This
impermanence is the strange way of the world.

337 ஒருபொழுதும் வாழ்வது அறியார் கருதுப
கோடியும் அல்ல பல.

Men cannot claim even a moment as theirs
Yet give themselves to countless plans.

Men are not sure of the next moment in their life. Yet
they think of millions of future plans.

338 குடம்பை தனித்துஒழியப் புள்பறந் தற்றே
உடம்போடு உயிரிடை நட்பு.

The bond between the body and the soul
Is like a bird leaving an egg-shell.

The soul quits the body any day like a bird coming out
of the egg-shell.

339 உறங்குவது போலும் சாக்காடு உறங்கி
விழிப்பது போலும் பிறப்பு.

Death is like falling into deep sleep
Birth is like waking up from sleep.

Death is like falling asleep. But birth is like waking up
from sleep.

340 புக்கில் அமைந்தின்று கொல்லோ உடம்பினுள்
துச்சில் இருந்த உயிர்க்கு.

The soul sheltered somewhere in this body takes
No place of permanence.

The soul has no permanent home of its own. It has taken
only a temporary shelter in the body.

35. துறவு
RENUNCIATION

341 யாதனின் யாதனின் நீங்கியான் நோதல்
அதனின் அதனின் இலன்.

From what from what a man is free
From that from that his griefs flee.

A man is free from all sufferings when he abstains from all desires.

342 வேண்டின்உண் டாகத் துறக்க துறந்தபின்
ஈண்டுஇயற் பால பல.

If you want real happiness, renounce in due time
After renunciation here ensues joy sublime.

If you want real happiness, renounce all your possessions. Then you will gain great happiness.

343 அடல்வேண்டும் ஐந்தன் புலத்தை விடல்வேண்டும்
வேண்டிய எல்லாம் ஒருங்கு.

To conquer desires of five senses
Renounce all temptations.

We must give up totally all our desires to control our five senses.

344 இயல்பாகும் நோன்பிற்குஒன்று இன்மை உடைமை
மயலாகும் மற்றும் பெயர்த்து.

True penance needs total renunciation
Possession leads only to confusion.

Renouncing everything is true penance. Possession of anything leads to delusion.

345 மற்றும் தொடர்ப்பாடு எவன்கொல் பிறப்புஅறுக்கல்
உற்றார்க்கு உடம்பும் மிகை.

Body also is a burden to those seeking no births
Why then do they have any attachments?

Even the body is a burden to those seeking no rebirths, so there should not be any worldly bonds.

346 யான்எனது என்னும் செருக்குஅறுப்பான் வானோர்க்கு
உயர்ந்த உலகம் புகும்.
Who destroy the pride of 'I' and 'mine'
Enter a world rare for gods to gain.
Those who curb the pride of 'I' and 'mine' enter the
heavenly world inaccessible even to gods.

347 பற்றி விடாஅ இடும்பைகள் பற்றினைப்
பற்றி விடாஅ தவர்க்கு.
Men clinging to bonds without losing hold
Will ever be held in sorrows' hold.
Sorrows and sufferings will grip those who hold on to the
worldly attachments.

348 தலைப்பட்டார் தீரத் துறந்தார் மயங்கி
வலைப்பட்டார் மற்றை யவர்.
Those who totally renounce obtain salvation
The rest are caught in world's delusion.
Only those who renounce everything attain bliss; others
are caught in the net of desires.

349 பற்றற்ற கண்ணே பிறப்புஅறுக்கும் மற்று
நிலையாமை காணப் படும்.
Attachments severed, rebirth ceases
Or else impermanence prevails.
Renunciation stops rebirth. Attachment brings death
and birth again and again.

350 பற்றுக பற்றற்றான் பற்றினை அப்பற்றைப்
பற்றுக பற்று விடற்கு.
Cling to the bond of God, who is free from ties
Cling to that bond to break all bonds.
Those attached to God, who is free from all ties, will be
free from all earthly attachments.

36. மெய்யுணர்தல்
REALIZING THE TRUTH

351 பொருள்அல்ல வற்றைப் பொருள்என்று உணரும்
மருளான்ஆம் மாணாப் பிறப்பு.
Delusion of taking untruth for truth
Results in ignoble birth.
Ignorance which takes unreality for reality results in
worthless birth and sufferings.

352 இருள்நீங்கி இன்பம் பயக்கும் மருள்நீங்கி
மாசுஅறு காட்சி யவர்க்கு.
Men of spotless vision free from delusions
Gain bliss eschewing sorrows.
Darkness of grief departs and bliss comes to those
with pure vision and clear mind.

353 ஐயத்தின் நீங்கித் தெளிந்தார்க்கு வையத்தின்
வானம் நணியது உடைத்து.
To men free from doubts with vision clear
Heaven is nearer than earthly sphere.
Heaven is nearer than the earth to those who are
free from doubts and have a clear vision.

354 ஐயுணர்வு எய்தியக் கண்ணும் பயம்இன்றே
மெய்உணர்வு இல்லா தவர்க்கு.
Controlling five senses is of no worth
Without realization of the truth.
Controlling five senses is useless if we do not realize
the profound inner truth.

355 எப்பொருள் எத்தன்மைத்து ஆயினும் அப்பொருள்
மெய்ப்பொருள் காண்பது அறிவு.
Whatever be the matter of whatever quality
True wisdom is to see its reality.
True mark of wisdom is to find the profound truth of
varied things.

356 கற்றூஉண்டு மெய்ப்பொருள் கண்டார் தலைப்படுவர்
மற்றூஉண்டு வாரா நெறி.
The learned who've seen here the truth
Will find the path of no birth.
If one understands the truth here on the earth, one will
find no rebirth.

357 ஓர்த்துஉள்ளம் உள்ளது உணரின் ஒருதலையாப்
பேர்த்துஉள்ள வேண்டா பிறப்பு.
Who has analysed and realized the truth
Has no need to think of rebirth.
There is no fear of rebirth if a person has analysed and
found out the truth firmly.

358 பிறப்புஎன்னும் பேதைமை நீங்கச் சிறப்புஎன்னும்
செம்பொருள் காண்பது அறிவு.
See the truth to avoid the folly of rebirth
It is true wisdom of real worth.
Wisdom is realization of the truth which removes the
folly of rebirth.

359 சார்புஉணர்ந்து சார்பு கெடஒழுகின் மற்றழித்துச்
சார்தரா சார்தரு நோய்.
Who seek the truth breaking bonds
Will be free from worldly ills.
Those who seek the truth by severing attachments will
be free from woes.

360 காமம் வெகுளி மயக்கம் இவைமூன்றன்
நாமம் கெடக்கெடும் நோய்.
If lust, wrath and delusion cease
All pains end without trace.
All pains and sorrows will disappear if lust, anger and
confusion are given up.

73

37. அவா அறுத்தல்
CURBING DESIRES

361
அவாஎன்ப எல்லா உயிர்க்கும்எஞ் ஞான்றும்
தவாஅப் பிறப்புஈனும் வித்து.
Desire is the seed of ceaseless births
For all living things at all times.
Craving is the cause of endless births to all living
beings at all times.

362
வேண்டுங்கால் வேண்டும் பிறவாமை மற்றுஅது
வேண்டாமை வேண்ட வரும்.
If you desire for anything, desire for no births
Rebirth comes not if you give up desires.
If one has any desire, it should be only for freedom
from births. It is achieved by renouncing desires.

363
வேண்டாமை அன்ன விழுச்செல்வம் ஈண்டில்லை
யாண்டும் அஃதுஒப்பது இல்.
No other greater fortune is here or there
Than the fortune of having no desire.
There is no greater wealth either in this world or in heaven
than the wealth of desirelessness.

364
தூஉய்மை என்பது அவாவின்மை மற்றுஅது
வாஅய்மை வேண்ட வரும்.
Lack of desire is indeed the mind's purity
Which comes while seeking veracity.
Purity of mind is freedom from yearning and it comes
while seeking the truth.

365
அற்றவர் என்பார் அவாஅற்றார் மற்றையார்
அற்றாக அற்றது இலர்.
Who renounce are free from desires
Others are not free from desires.
Only those who totally give up desires enjoy freedom
from all desires.

366 அஞ்சுவது ஒரும் அறனே ஒருவனை
வஞ்சிப்பது ஒரும் அவா.
Virtue lies in fear of desire
As desire is the deceiver.
Fearing the bond of desires is a great virtue as desires
have the power to deceive.

367 அவாவினை ஆற்ற அறுப்பின் தவாவினை
தான்வேண்டும் ஆற்றான் வரும்.
Who completely roots out all his desires
Achieves good deeds as he desires.
If a man destroys all his desires completely, he will
easily achieve noble deeds.

368 அவாஇல்லார்க்கு இல்லாகும் துன்பம் அஃதுஉண்டேல்
தவாஅது மேன்மேல் வரும்.
No sufferings are for those without yearnings
Endless grief is for those with yearnings.
There are no sufferings for those without desires. There
is endless grief for those having desires.

369 இன்பம் இடையறாது ஈண்டும் அவாவென்னும்
துன்பத்துள் துன்பம் கெடின்.
When desire, the woe of woes, dies
Eternal bliss ensues.
There is an eternal flow of happiness when desire, the
evil of evils, leaves.

370 ஆரா இயற்கை அவாநீப்பின் அந்நிலையே
பேரா இயற்கை தரும்.
Give up your insatiable desires
And gain eternal joys.
If a person leaves out desires that can never be fulfilled,
he will gain eternal joys.

38. ஊழ்
FATE

371   ஆகுஊழால் தோன்றும் அசைவின்மை கைப்பொருள்
போகுஊழால் தோன்றும் மடி.

Fate of gain brings perseverance
Fate of loss brings indolence.

Fate of wealth brings tireless efforts and fate of loss brings
laziness.

372   பேதைப் படுக்கும் இழவுஊழ் அறிவகற்றும்
ஆகல்ஊழ் உற்றக் கடை.

Adverse fate makes us fools
Friendly fate makes us wise.

Evil fate makes us fools and benevolent fate makes
us all wise.

373   நுண்ணிய நூல்பல கற்பினும் மற்றும்தன்
உண்மை அறிவே மிகும்.

Whatever a man may deeply learn
Only natural wisdom will remain.

However deep a person's learning be, only his native
wisdom will prevail.

374   இருவேறு உலகத்து இயற்கை திருவேறு
தெள்ளியர் ஆதலும் வேறு.

Twofold is earthly life's natural form
They are wealth and wisdom.

Wealth and wisdom mark the two different natures of
worldly life due to fate.

375   நல்லவை எல்லாஅம் தீயவாம் தீயவும்
நல்லவாம் செல்வம் செயற்கு.

In pursuit of wealth, fate may turn good
Into bad and bad into good.

In making wealth, it is possible that fate turns all good
things into evil and all evil things into good.

376 பரியினும் ஆகாவாம் பால்அல்ல உய்த்துச்
சொரியினும் போகா தம.

What's not fated, though guarded, remains not
What's fated, even when poured, leaves not.

Things not ordained to a man are not his. Things ordained
to him, even when drained, are not lost.

377 வகுத்தான் வகுத்த வகையல்லால் கோடி
தொகுத்தார்க்கும் துய்த்தல் அரிது.

Men amass wealth in crores but enjoy it
Only as ordained by fate.

Though men amass wealth, they can enjoy it only as
destined by fate.

378 துறப்பார்மன் துப்புர வில்லார் உறற்பால
ஊட்டா கழியும் எனின்.

The penniless will become ascetics
If fate relieves them of their griefs.

The poor will renounce all desires if fate does not
trouble them.

379 நன்றுஆம்கால் நல்லவாக் காண்பவர் அன்றுஆம்கால்
அல்லற் படுவது எவன்.

When good things come, men see them as gain
When evils come, why complain?

When men consider good fortune as gain, they should
not feel disturbed when they are troubled.

380 ஊழிற் பெருவலி யாவுள மற்றொன்று
சூழினும் தான்முந் துறும்.

What is stronger than destiny? It is a power
That prevails over human endeavour.

Destiny is the greatest power which will overcome all
human efforts.

II

பொருட்பால்

WEALTH

39. இறைமாட்சி
REGAL DIGNITY

381 படைகுடி கூழ்அமைச்சு நட்புஅரண் ஆறும்
உடையான் அரசருள் ஏறு.

Army, subjects, wealth, ministers, allies, forts —
Who has these six is a lion among monarchs.

An ideal king shall possess army, people, wealth,
council of ministers, friends and forts.

382 அஞ்சாமை ஈகை அறிவூக்கம் இந்நான்கும்
எஞ்சாமை வேந்தற்கு இயல்பு.

Unfailing courage, charity, wisdom and zeal —
These four are qualities regal.

Courage, charity, wisdom and zeal are the four good
qualities of a king.

383 தூங்காமை கல்வி துணிவுடைமை இம்மூன்றும்
நீங்கா நிலன்ஆள் பவர்க்கு.

Vigilance, learning and courage — these three
Shall never leave the ruler of a country.

A king should always have the three virtues, namely,
vigilance, learning and bravery.

384 அறன்இழுக்காது அல்லவை நீக்கி மறன்இழுக்கா
மானம் உடையது அரசு.

Who fails not in virtue, avoids evils and is bold
Is a king honourable and dignified.

A noble king avoids vices; he is a man of virtue,
boldness and dignity.

385 இயற்றலும் ஈட்டலும் காத்தலும் காத்த
வகுத்தலும் வல்லது அரசு.

Acquiring, gaining, saving and sharing treasure—
Efficiency in these marks an able ruler.

Acquiring, storing, protecting and distributing wealth
are the duties of an able king.

386 காட்சிக்கு எளியன் கடுஞ்சொல்லன் அல்லனேல்
மீக்கூறும் மன்னன் நிலம்.
The world extols the land of the ruler
With easy access and words sweeter.
The world praises a king who is accessible to his
subjects and free from harsh words.

387 இன்சொலால் ஈத்துஅளிக்க வல்லார்க்குத் தன்சொலால்
தான்கண் டனைத்துஇவ் வுலகு.
The world surely extols and obeys the words
Of one who kindly speaks, gives and guards.
The world praises and obeys the king who is soft-
spoken and generous in giving.

388 முறைசெய்து காப்பாற்றும் மன்னவன் மக்கட்கு
இறையென்று வைக்கப் படும்.
People regard the king as god
For just rule and guard.
If a king administers justice and protects his subjects,
he will be regarded as god.

389 செவிகைப்பச் சொற்பொறுக்கும் பண்புடை வேந்தன்
கவிகைக்கீழ்த் தங்கும் உலகு.
The world lives under the sway of a ruler
Who endures words bitter to the ear.
If a king bears with bitter criticisms, the world will
prosper under his reign.

390 கொடைஅளி செங்கோல் குடிஓம்பல் நான்கும்
உடையான்ஆம் வேந்தர்க்கு ஒளி.
Bounty, mercy, justice and love for the subjects —
Who has all these is a light among monarchs.
A king is regarded as a light to other kings, when he
is benevolent, gracious, just and caring.

40. கல்வி
LEARNING

391   கற்க கசடறக் கற்பவை கற்றபின்
நிற்க அதற்குத் தக.

Learn well whatever is worthy of learning
Then act according to that learning.

One should learn thoroughly what is worth learning
and then act in accordance with it.

392   எண்என்ப ஏனை எழுத்துஎன்ப இவ்விரண்டும்
கண்என்ப வாழும் உயிர்க்கு.

Numbers and letters, according to scholars
Are the two eyes of all human beings.

Science and arts are considered to be the two eyes
of human beings.

393   கண்ணுடையர் என்பவர் கற்றோர் முகத்திஇரண்டு
புண்ணுடையர் கல்லா தவர்.

The learned ones alone have real eyes
Others have two sores on their faces.

The educated are considered to have real eyes but
the illiterates have only two sores on their faces.

394   உவப்பத் தலைக்கூடி உள்ளப் பிரிதல்
அனைத்தே புலவர் தொழில்.

To meet with joy and part with sweet thought
Of meeting again is learned men's habit.

It is very common for the learned people to meet with
joy and part with the fond hope of meeting again.

395   உடையார்முன் இல்லார்போல் ஏக்கற்றும் கற்றார்
கடையரே கல்லா தவர்.

Who learn like the poor before the rich
Are great; the rest are low very much.

Those who learn by humbling themselves like the poor
before the rich are great. Others are very low.

396   தொட்டனைத்து ஊறும் மணற்கேணி மாந்தர்க்குக்
கற்றனைத்து ஊறும் அறிவு.

Dig deeper the sand-well, more water flows
Read deeper, more wisdom grows.

The deeper we dig the well, the more water we get. The
more we learn, the more wisdom we acquire.

397   யாதானும் நாடாமால் ஊராமால் என்ஒருவன்
சாந்துணையும் கல்லாத வாறு.

Why should a man fail to learn till he dies
As it makes all lands and towns his?

The learned man makes all lands and towns his own.
So, one should learn well till one's death.

398   ஒருமைக்கண் தான்கற்ற கல்வி ஒருவற்கு
எழுமையும் ஏமாப்பு உடைத்து.

The learning of a man in one birth
Helps him up to his seventh birth.

The learning acquired in one birth helps a man in all his
seven births.

399   தாம்இன் புறுவது உலகுஇன் புறக்கண்டு
காமுறுவர் கற்றறிந் தார்.

Finding the world rejoicing at their learning
The learned long for more learning.

Learned men want to learn more, when they find
deeper learning delights others.

400   கேடுஇல் விழுச்செல்வம் கல்வி ஒருவற்கு
மாடுஅல்ல மற்றை யவை.

Learning is supreme imperishable wealth
Other things are not real wealth.

Learning is supreme and everlasting wealth. No other
wealth is real wealth.

41. கல்லாமை
ILLITERACY

401   அரங்குஇன்றி வட்டுஆடி யற்றே நிரம்பிய
       நூல்இன்றிக் கோட்டி கொளல்.
       To address the learned assembly unprepared
       Is like playing dice without a board.
       Addressing the learned without extensive study is
       like playing dice without a board.

402   கல்லாதான் சொல்கா முறுதல் முலைஇரண்டும்
       இல்லாதாள் பெண்காமுற் றற்று.
       Longing of an unlearned man for public speaking
       Is like a breastless maid's desire for loving.
       The unlearned man's desire for public speaking is like
       a breastless woman's longing for sex.

403   கல்லா தவரும் நனிநல்லர் கற்றார்முன்
       சொல்லாது இருக்கப் பெறின்.
       The unlearned seem to be men of excellence
       If before the wise they keep silence.
       Even the unlearned are deemed wise if they keep quiet
       before the learned.

404   கல்லாதான் ஓட்பம் கழியநன்று ஆயினும்
       கொள்ளார் அறிவுடை யார்.
       Unlettered man's wit, though rarely fine,
       Is not accepted by the learned men.
       The wise will not accept even the occasional flash of
       intelligence of an illiterate.

405   கல்லா ஒருவன் தகைமை தலைப்பெய்து
       சொல்லாடச் சோர்வு படும்.
       The pride of an unlettered man fades
       As he converses with the scholars.
       The pride of an illiterate gets exposed when he
       interacts with the learned.

406 உளர்என்னும் மாத்திரையர் அல்லால் பயவாக்
களர்அனையர் கல்லா தவர்.
Just alive are the unlettered but as useless
As the fallow land that remains fruitless.
The unlettered are as useless as the wasteland and
they simply exist.

407 நுண்மாண் நுழைபுலம் இல்லான் எழில்நலம்
மண்மாண் புனைபாவை யற்று.
Beauty of one sans subtle and penetrating mind
Is like the beauty of a clay doll adorned.
The beauty of an illiterate wihout a keen mind is like
the beauty of a doll made of clay.

408 நல்லார்கண் பட்ட வறுமையின் இன்னாதே
கல்லார்கண் பட்ட திரு.
Worse is the illiterates' prosperity
Than the learned's poverty.
The wealth of the unlearned is more harmful than the
poverty of the learned.

409 மேற்பிறந்தார் ஆயினும் கல்லாதார் கீழ்ப்பிறந்தும்
கற்றார் அனைத்திலர் பாடு.
The unlearned are not great tho' high-born
But great are the learned low-born.
Though the unlearned are high-born, they are not so
great as the learned who are low-born.

410 விலங்கொடு மக்கள் அனையர் இலங்குநூல்
கற்றாரோடு ஏனை யவர்.
As beasts to men, the unlearned are more
To the learned in splendid lore.
There is much difference between the learned and the
ignorant as between mankind and animals.

42. கேள்வி
LISTENING

411   செல்வத்துள் செல்வம் செவிச்செல்வம் அச்செல்வம்
செல்வத்துள் எல்லாம் தலை.

Listening is the wealth of wealth
It is the crown of all wealth.

Wealth acquired by listening is the wealth of wealth
and it is the greatest of all wealth.

412   செவிக்குணவு இல்லாத போழ்து சிறிது
வயிற்றுக்கும் ஈயப் படும்.

Whenever food for the ear is deferred
Some food for the stomach is offered.

When there is no food for the ear, some food will be
given to the stomach.

413   செவிஉணவிற் கேள்வி யுடையார் அவிஉணவின்
ஆன்றாரோடு ஒப்பர் நிலத்து.

Men whose ears receive food thro' listening
Resemble gods served with offering.

Men who find listening as food for their ears are like
gods served with sacred offering.

414   கற்றிலன் ஆயினும் கேட்க அஃதொருவற்கு
ஒற்கத்தின் ஊற்றாம் துணை.

Though unlettered, one should heed
It is a prop in hours of need.

Even the unlearned man should listen to the learned.
It will serve as a support in times of need.

415   இழுக்கல் உடையுழி ஊற்றுக்கோல் அற்றே
ஒழுக்கம் உடையார்வாய்ச் சொல்.

The counsel of the righteous, when heeded
Serves as a stick on slippery land.

The advice of the righteous is like a stick that helps
one on a marshy ground.

416 எனைத்தானும் நல்லவை கேடக அனைத்தானும்
ஆன்ற பெருமை தரும்.
Listen to wise words, however little
That much it elevates you still.
One should listen to good words, however brief. Even
those few words will bring greater dignity.

417 பிழைத்துஉணர்ந்தும் பேதைமை சொல்லார் இழைத்துணர்ந்து
ஈண்டிய கேள்வி யவர்.
Even if the wise understand incorrectly
They never speak foolishly.
Even if scholars do not grasp correctly, they will not
speak foolishly.

418 கேட்பினும் கேளாத் தகையவே கேள்வியால்
தோட்கப் படாத செவி.
The ears not attuned to good listening
Tho' open, are impaired of hearing.
The ears, not in the habit of listening to good things, are
considered deaf, though they can hear sounds.

419 நுணங்கிய கேள்வியர் அல்லார் வணங்கிய
வாயினர் ஆதல் அரிது.
Those not heeding to men of keen speeches
Rarely speak humble words.
Humility in speech cannot be attained by men who
never listen to the discourse of the wise.

420 செவியின் சுவையுணரா வாயுணர்வின் மாக்கள்
அவியினும் வாழினும் என்.
Some have joys of the mouth but not the ear
What matters if they live or expire?
It does not matter if the men whose taste is in their
tongues and not ears, live or die.

43. அறிவுடைமை
WISDOM

421   அறிவற்றம் காக்கும் கருவி செறுவார்க்கும்
உள்ளழிக்கல் ஆகா அரண்.

Wisdom is a weapon to guard against ruin
And a fort indestructible by hostile men.

Wisdom is a weapon to guard against destruction; it is
a fort which no enemy can destroy.

422   சென்ற இடத்தால் செலவிடா தீதுஒரீஇ
நன்றின்பால் உய்ப்பது அறிவு.

Wisdom restrains the wayward mind
And leads it from evil to good.

Wisdom curbs the wandering mind and directs it from
evil to good.

423   எப்பொருள் யார்யார்வாய்க் கேட்பினும் அப்பொருள்
மெய்ப்பொருள் காண்பது அறிவு.

Whatsoever is heard, from whomsoever
To discern the truth is wisdom clear.

To perceive the truth is wisdom, whatever be the
matter and whosoever utters it.

424   எண்பொருள வாகச் செலச்சொல்லித் தான்பிறர்வாய்
நுண்பொருள் காண்பது அறிவு.

Wisdom is to speak in terms simple and clear
And grasp even subtle matter.

To speak clearly to impress all and draw subtle truths
from others' utterances is wisdom.

425   உலகம் தழீஇயது ஒட்பம் மலர்தலும்
கூம்பலும் இல்லது அறிவு.

Friendship of the great without wax or wane
Is wisdom true and sane.

Befriending the great and keeping their friendship
stable and steady is worldly wisdom.

426 எவ்வது உறைவது உலகம் உலகத்தோடு
அவ்வது உறைவது அறிவு.

Wisdom is to live in tune with the mode
Of the changing world.

To live in harmony with the fast changing world is
true wisdom.

427 அறிவுடையார் ஆவது அறிவார் அறிவிலார்
அஃதுஅறி கல்லா தவர்.

The wise discern what is in store
But fools lack in that lore.

The wise foresee what is going to happen but the
unwise lack knowledge to predict this.

428 அஞ்சுவது அஞ்சாமை பேதைமை அஞ்சுவது
அஞ்சல் அறிவார் தொழில்.

Not to fear what to be feared is absolutely folly
To fear what to be feared is wise men's duty.

It is foolish not to fear what is to be feared; it is wise
to fear what is to be feared.

429 எதிரதாக் காக்கும் அறிவினார்க்கு இல்லை
அதிர வருவதோர் நோய்.

The wise who foresee pain of crisis
Guard against surprise shocks.

There is no terrifying shock to the wise who have the
foresight to guard themselves against the coming evil.

430 அறிவுடையார் எல்லாம் உடையார் அறிவிலார்
என்னுடைய ரேனும் இலர்.

Those with wisdom have everything
Fools with everything have nothing.

The wise possess everything but the unwise possess
nothing even if they have everything.

44. குற்றங்கடிதல்
AVOIDING FAULTS

431 செருக்கும் சினமும் சிறுமையும் இல்லார்
     பெருக்கம் பெருமித நீர்த்து.
Great indeed is the wealth of those men
Who aren't proud, angry and mean.
The wealth of those who are free from arrogance, anger
and petty-mindedness is really great.

432 இவறலும் மாண்புஇறந்த மானமும் மாணா
     உவகையும் ஏதம் இறைக்கு.
Miserliness, mean pride and excessive pleasures
Are indeed the faults of rulers.
Stinginess, low pride and excessive pleasures are the
pitfalls of rulers.

433 தினைத்துணையாம் குற்றம் வரினும் பனைத்துணையாக்
     கொள்வர் பழிநாணு வார்.
Even though a fault may seem millet small
Men fearing disgrace deem it palm tall.
Men who fear blame will consider even their small
fault as a great blunder.

434 குற்றமே காக்க பொருளாகக் குற்றமே
     அற்றம் தரூஉம் பகை.
As offence is a foe causing destruction
Guard against it with all caution.
As a precaution, one should be free from any grave
fault which is the enemy leading to ruin.

435 வருமுன்னர்க் காவாதான் வாழ்க்கை எரிமுன்னர்
     வைத்தூறு போலக் கெடும்.
A life not guarded against future blame
Is like a heap of straw before flame.
A life that is not guarded against future faults is like a
heap of straw before fire.

436 தன்குற்றம் நீக்கிப் பிறர்குற்றம் காண்கிற்பின்
என்குற்ற மாகும் இறைக்கு.

How can a king be faulted if he removes
First his faults, then looks into others'?

No fault will remain with the king who first corrects his
own faults and then sees others' faults.

437 செயற்பால செய்யாது இவறியான் செல்வம்
உயற்பாலது அன்றிக் கெடும்.

The wealth of a niggard who leaves undone
What is to be done will come to total ruin.

The wealth of the miser who leaves unfinished what is
to be finished, will come to destruction.

438 பற்றுள்ளம் என்னும் இவறன்மை எற்றுள்ளும்
எண்ணப் படுவதொன்று அன்று.

Clinging greed of a niggard's heart
Stands out as a greater fault.

The gripping greed of a miser is a unique flaw; it is
worse than all other offences.

439 வியவற்க எஞ்ஞான்றும் தன்னை நயவற்க
நன்றி பயவா வினை.

Never indulge in self-praise in any mood
Nor desire deeds bringing no good,

One should neither revel in self-boasting nor desire for
empty deeds.

440 காதல காதல் அறியாமை உய்க்கிற்பின்
ஏதில ஏதிலார் நூல்.

Enjoy what you long for in guarded secret
Plots of foes will face defeat.

If a person plans and acts on his desires secretly, the
evil designs of his enemies will fail.

45. பெரியாரைத் துணைக்கோடல்
SEEKING THE HELP OF THE GREAT

441 அறன்அறிந்து மூத்த அறிவுடையார் கேண்மை
திறன்அறிந்து தேர்ந்து கொளல்.

Value merit of men with morals and sagacity
And secure their amity.

One should analyse the value of men of virtue and
wisdom, and gain their friendship.

442 உற்றநோய் நீக்கி உறாஅமை முற்காக்கும்
பெற்றியார்ப் பேணிக் கொளல்.

Who cure ills now and save from future ills
Must be cherished as friends.

One should seek the friendship of those who will
remove present ills and protect from future evils.

443 அரியவற்றுள் எல்லாம் அரிதே பெரியாரைப்
பேணித் தமராக் கொளல்.

The rarest of all the rare gifts known
Is cherishing great men as our own.

To have great men as our relatives is the rarest of all
rare blessings in the world.

444 தம்மின் பெரியார் தமரா ஒழுகுதல்
வன்மையுள் எல்லாம் தலை.

To have men greater than oneself as relatives
And follow them is the chief of powers.

Cultivating intimate relationship with the worthy and
following their noble ideals is the greatest strength.

445 சூழ்வார்கண் ணாக ஒழுகலான் மன்னவன்
சூழ்வாரைச் சூழ்ந்து கொளல்.

A king must choose with prudence his ministers
As they act as his eyes.

As ministers are a king's eyes, they should be
selected with great care and wisdom.

446 தக்கார் இனத்தனாய்த் தான்ஒழுக வல்லானைச்
    செற்றார் செயக்கிடந்தது இல்.
    **Who has fit counsellors and does right deeds
    Has nothing to fear from foes.**
    One who has worthy men as guides and does right
    deeds need not fear the enemies.

447 இடிக்கும் துணையாரை ஆள்வாரை யாரே
    கெடுக்கும் தகைமை யவர்.
    **No enemy can bring any ruin to him
    Who has friends to rebuke him.**
    No enemy can destroy a man who has friends to censure
    him when he errs.

448 இடிப்பாரை இல்லாத ஏமரா மன்னன்
    கெடுப்பார் இலானுங் கெடும்.
    **A guardless sovereign with none to caution
    Even without foes will come to ruin.**
    The king without men to rebuke and guard him will
    perish even without enemies to destroy him.

449 முதல்இலார்க்கு ஊதியம் இல்லை மதலையாம்
    சார்புஇலார்க்கு இல்லை நிலை.
    **Without capital there is no profit
    And no stability without support.**
    There is no gain without capital in a trade and there is
    no stability without proper support.

450 பல்லார் பகைகொளலின் பத்தடுத்த தீமைத்தே
    நல்லார் தொடர்கை விடல்.
    **Ten times worse is to lose good friends
    Than to face countless foes.**
    To abandon good friends is far worse than facing a great
    number of enemies.

46. சிற்றினம் சேராமை
AVOIDING MEAN COMPANY

451 சிற்றினம் அஞ்சும் பெருமை சிறுமைதான்
சுற்றமாச் சூழ்ந்து விடும்.
The great dread mean-minded men
Only the mean regard them as kin.
The noble fear the friendship of the ignoble; only
mean men regard the ignoble as relatives.

452 நிலத்துஇயல்பால் நீர்திரிந்து அற்றாகும் மாந்தர்க்கு
இனத்துஇயல்பது ஆகும் அறிவு.
As water changes with the nature of the soil
Men's nature changes with friends' circle.
Water changes according to the soil; similarly men's
nature changes according to their friendship.

453 மனத்தான்ஆம் மாந்தர்க்கு உணர்ச்சி இனத்தான்ஆம்
இன்னான் எனப்படும் சொல்.
Man's wisdom comes from the mind
His worth rests on his friend.
Man's wisdom depends upon the mind and his
character depends upon his company.

454 மனத்து உளதுபோலக் காட்டி ஒருவற்கு
இனத்துஉள தாகும் அறிவு.
Wisdom appears to flow from the mind
But it really comes from a friend.
Man's wisdom appears to reside in his mind; but it
really emerges from the company of his friends.

455 மனம்தூய்மை செய்வினை தூய்மை இரண்டும்
இனம்தூய்மை தூவா வரும்.
Pure thoughts and pure deeds
Emerge from good friends.
Purity of thought and deed develops according to the
pure conduct of one's friends.

456 மனந்தூயார்க்கு எச்சம்நன் றாகும் இனந்தூயார்க்கு
இல்லைநன்று ஆகா வினை.

Those with spotless mind leave good progeny
Good deeds spring from good company.

The pure-minded bring forth good progeny as pure
friendship brings forth good deeds.

457 மனநலம் மன்னுயிர்க்கு ஆக்கம் இனநலம்
எல்லாப் புகழும் தரும்.

Goodness of mind brings souls prosperity
Good company brings them all glory.

Purity of mind brings wealth to souls; the company of
good friends brings them glory.

458 மனநலம் நன்குடைய ராயினும் சான்றோர்க்கு
இனநலம் ஏமாப்பு உடைத்து.

Though wise men have goodness of mind
Good company gives strength indeed.

Though good in mind, the wise find a tower of strength in
good company.

459 மனநலத்தின் ஆகும் மறுமைமற் றஃதும்
இனநலத்தின் ஏமாப் புடைத்து.

Pure mind surely leads to heavenly bliss
Good company adds strength to this.

A mind without a blemish leads to heavenly bliss; pure
friendship adds strength to it.

460 நல்லினத்தின் ஊங்கும் துணையில்லை தீயினத்தின்
அல்லற் படுப்பதூஉம் இல்.

No support is better than good company
No misery is worse than bad company.

There is no better help than good friendship and no
greater misery than bad friendship.

47. தெரிந்து செயல்வகை
ACTING WITH DELIBERATION

461   அழிவதூஉம் ஆவதூஉம் ஆகி வழிபயக்கும்
      ஊதியமும் சூழ்ந்து செயல்.

Act only after taking into account
The input, output and result.

One should first weigh the investment, expenditure
and income, and then proceed.

462   தெரிந்த இனத்தொடு தேர்ந்துஎண்ணிச் செய்வார்க்கு
      அரும்பொருள் யாதொன்றும் இல்.

Nothing is ever impossible for those who act
After wise counsel and careful thought.

One should consult chosen friends, deliberate with
the wise and act; then nothing becomes difficult.

463   ஆக்கம் கருதி முதல்இழக்கும் செய்வினை
      ஊக்கார் அறிவுடை யார்.

Men of wisdom won't embark on anything
And lose their capital to gain something.

Wise men in quest of gain will not do anything that
would ruin the capital itself.

464   தெளிவு இலதனைத் தொடங்கார் இளிவுஎன்னும்
      ஏதப்பாடு அஞ்சு பவர்.

Who dread doing disgraceful errors
Won't go in for doubtful ventures.

Those who fear committing shameful errors will not
begin any work not clear to them.

465   வகையறச் சூழாது எழுதல் பகைவரைப்
      பாத்திப் படுப்போர் ஆறு.

Waging a war without well thought out plans
Is to rear the foes in fertile fields.

Fighting against enemies without proper planning
will only strengthen the enemy.

466   செய்தக்க அல்ல செயக்கெடும் செய்தக்க
செய்யாமை யானும் கெடும்.
It's ruinous to do what is not worth doing
And also not to do what's worth doing.
Doing unfit things leads to ruin. Not doing fit things
also results in ruin.

467   எண்ணித் துணிக கருமம் துணிந்தபின்
எண்ணுவம் என்பது இழுக்கு.
Think first and then venture on an act
To venture and then think is a fault.
It is good to think first and then act; it is wrong to
act first and then think.

468   ஆற்றின் வருந்தா வருத்தம் பலர்நின்று
போற்றினும் பொத்துப் படும்.
Any deed without proper efforts and methods
Fails despite so many supporters.
Any work without proper efforts and methods will fail
despite the support of many.

469   நன்றுஆற்ற லுள்ளும் தவறுஉண்டு அவரவர்
பண்பறிந்து ஆற்றாக் கடை.
Do the deeds according to the nature of people
Or else even doing good may lead to evil.
Even a good deed may go wrong when it is not done
befitting the nature and disposition of men.

470   எள்ளாத எண்ணிச் செயல்வேண்டும் தம்மொடு
கொள்ளாத கொள்ளாது உலகு.
Deliberate and do what the world will approve
Or else your act the world won't approve.
As the world approves only what is acceptable, one
should do deeds without incurring ridicule.

48. வலியறிதல்
ASSESSING THE STRENGTH

471　வினைவலியும் தன்வலியும் மாற்றான் வலியும்
　　　துணைவலியும் தூக்கிச் செயல்.

Weigh the act, your own might, foes' might
And allies' might and proceed straight.

A person should weigh the act, his strength and that
of his foes and friends before venturing.

472　ஒல்வது அறிவது அறிந்ததன் கண்தங்கிச்
　　　செல்வார்க்குச் செல்லாதது இல்.

Nothing is impossible to those who understand
The nature and means of the deed.

Nothing is impossible to those who know the ways
and means of the task.

473　உடைத்தம் வலிஅறியார் ஊக்கத்தின் ஊக்கி
　　　இடைக்கண் முரிந்தார் பலர்.

Who know not their own power begin zealously
But perish midway woefully.

Many who do not know their strength, enthusiastically
begin an act but fail in the middle.

474　அமைந்தாங்கு ஒழுகான் அளவுஅறியான் தன்னை
　　　வியந்தான் விரைந்து கெடும்.

Who adapts not, knows not his limitation
And boasts will be damned to perdition.

He who does not adapt but praises himself without
knowing his limitation will quickly perish.

475　பீலிபெய் சாகாடும் அச்சுஇறும் அப்பண்டம்
　　　சால மிகுத்துப் பெயின்.

Tho' a cart carries light peacock feathers
Its axle breaks if the load exceeds.

The axle of a cart breaks if the cart is overloaded
even with light peacock feathers.

476   நுனிக்கொம்பர் ஏறினார் அஃதுஇறந்து ஊக்கின்
உயிர்க்குஇறுதி யாகி விடும்.

Climbing a tree beyond the tip of a branch
Will be the end of life very much.

One who attempts to climb the tree beyond the tip of
the branch will lose one's life.

477   ஆற்றின் அளவறிந்து ஈக அதுபொருள்
போற்றி வழங்கும் நெறி.

Donate within your means and worth
It's the way to guard your wealth.

A person should know his limit and give within his
means. That is the only way to save his wealth.

478   ஆகுஆறு அளவுஇட்டிது ஆயினும் கேடுஇல்லை
போகுஆறு அகலாக் கடை.

It matters not even if income is limited
As long as expenditure is restricted.

It is no harm even if the income is small as long as
the expenditure is within means.

479   அளவுஅறிந்து வாழாதான் வாழ்க்கை உளபோல
இல்லாகித் தோன்றாக் கெடும்.

Lavish life of one who lives not within means
Though grand, perishes without traces.

A man's life seems to be wealthy but it perishes if
he does not live within the bounds.

480   உளவரை தூக்காத ஒப்புரவு ஆண்மை
வளவரை வல்லைக் கெடும்.

One's wealth gained swiftly depletes
If bounty exceeds the limits.

One's wealth will quickly vanish if one's generosity
exceeds the limits.

49. காலம் அறிதல்
CHOOSING PROPER TIME

481   பகல்வெல்லும் கூகையைக் காக்கை இகல்வெல்லும்
வேந்தர்க்கு வேண்டும் பொழுது.

A crow can conquer even an owl in daylight
A king needs apt time to put foes to flight.

A crow can defeat an owl in daytime; likewise, a king
needs suitable time to conquer his enemies.

482   பருவத்தோடு ஒட்ட ஒழுகல் திருவினைத்
தீராமை ஆர்க்கும் கயிறு.

A well-timed action is the sure cord
That binds the fortune indeed.

A timely action is a cord that holds unstable wealth
together forever.

483   அருவினை என்ப உளவோ கருவியான்
காலம் அறிந்து செயின்.

Is there any task not possible for those
Who choose right time and means?

Nothing is impossible for those who act with the right
means at the right time.

484   ஞாலம் கருதினும் கைகூடும் காலம்
கருதி இடத்தால் செயின்.

The whole world is his who acts
At the right time and place.

Even the world can be conquered, if one acts at the
right time and right place.

485   காலம் கருதி இருப்பர் கலங்காது
ஞாலம் கருது பவர்.

Who aim to conquer the world
Wait for apt time undeterred.

Those who want to conquer the world should wait
patiently for the appropriate time.

486   ஊக்கம் உடையான் ஒடுக்கம் பொருதகர்
தாக்கற்குப் பேரும் தகைத்து.
The man of zeal keeps himself quiet
Like a ram retreating for a fight.
A ram retreats only to fight fiercely. Likewise, the
man with enthusiasm keeps himself restrained.

487   பொள்ளென ஆங்கே புறம்வேரார் காலம்பார்த்து
உள்வேர்ப்பர் ஒள்ளி யவர்.
The wise hide anger's outward fire
Biding their time with inward ire.
The wise do not burn with anger. They restrain and wait
for the right time to act.

488   செறுநரைக் காணின் சுமக்க இறுவரை
காணின் கிழக்காம் தலை.
Bear with your foes when you meet them
Cut down their heads at fateful time.
A person should bear with his enemies till the time
is appropriate to destroy them.

489   எய்தற்கு அரியது இயைந்தக்கால் அந்நிலையே
செய்தற்கு அரிய செயல்.
When rare and ripe opportunity arrives
Venture at once into rare deeds.
When the rare chance arrives, one should do rare
deeds immediately.

490   கொக்கொக்க கூம்பும் பருவத்து மற்றுஅதன்
குத்துஒக்க சீர்த்த இடத்து.
Just like a stork, bide your time
Act with might at right time.
One should wait like a stork for the right moment. When
the time is ripe, one should act firmly.

50. இடன் அறிதல்
ASSESSING THE PLACE

491   தொடங்கற்க எவ்வினையும் எள்ளற்க முற்றும்
       இடம்கண்ட பின்அல் லது.

Begin not any task and despise not your enemies
Till you find a right place to attack from all sides.

One should neither start any task nor scorn the foes,
till one finds the right place for action.

492   முரண்சேர்ந்த மொய்ம்பி னவர்க்கும் அரண்சேர்ந்துஆம்
       ஆக்கம் பலவும் தரும்.

Even to men of might and varied strength
A strong fort gives added strength.

It is a great advantage even to the men of mighty
power to have a strong fort.

493   ஆற்றாரும் ஆற்றி அடுப இடன்அறிந்து
       போற்றார்கண் போற்றிச் செயின்.

Even the weak can win if they select a right place
For strong defence and offence.

Even the less powerful can conquer their foes if they
choose the proper place for defence and offence.

494   எண்ணியார் எண்ணம் இழப்பர் இடன்அறிந்து
       துன்னியார் துன்னிச் செயின்.

If the brave fight from the vantage point
Foes will abandon the winning thought.

A careful approach by the brave from the right place
will outwit the enemy.

495   நெடும்புனலுள் வெல்லும் முதலை அடும்புனலின்
       நீங்கின் அதனைப் பிற.

In deep water a crocodile will win
Out of water others win.

The crocodile is all-powerful in deep water. But on
land other animals defeat it.

496 கடல்ஓடா கால்வல் நெடுந்தேர் கடல்ஓடும்
நாவாயும் ஓடா நிலத்து.

Strong wheeled chariots cannot run on the seas
Nor can ships sail on the shores.

As ships cannot sail on land, the wheeled chariots
cannot run on the seas.

497 அஞ்சாமை அல்லால் துணைவேண்டா எஞ்சாமை
எண்ணி இடத்தால் செயின்.

They require no ally but fearless might
If a right field they choose to fight.

If a right place is selected for the fight, no other help is
needed except his own fearless courage.

498 சிறுபடையான் செல்லிடம் சேரின் உறுபடையான்
ஊக்கம் அழிந்து விடும்.

A king in a right place even with a small army
Will spoil the grit of a king with a big army.

A small army in a safer place can defeat even a big
courageous army.

499 சிறைநலனும் சீரும் இலர்எனினும் மாந்தர்
உறைநிலத்தோடு ஒட்டல் அரிது.

It's hard to attack enemies in their place
Tho' they lack fort and force.

It is difficult to manage foes on their own soil, even
though they have no fort and enough strength.

500 கால்ஆழ் களரில் நரிஅடும் கண்அஞ்சா
வேலாள் முகத்த களிறு.

Even a jackal can kill a war tusker
Got stuck in the deep mire.

Even a jackal can kill a war elephant entangled in a
marshy ground.

51. தெரிந்து தெளிதல்
TESTING AND TRUSTING

501   அறம்பொருள் இன்பம் உயிர்அச்சம் நான்கின்
திறம்தெரிந்து தேறப் படும்.

Virtue, wealth, delight and fear of life —
Analyse these four and choose the chief.

One should choose a person on the basis of his
virtue, wealth, joy and fear of life.

502   குடிப்பிறந்து குற்றத்தின் நீங்கி வடுப்பரியும்
நாண்உடையான் கட்டே தெளிவு

Choose those noble-born of spotless fame
Who shrink from sin and have shame.

The ruler must choose men of noble birth who shun
faults and feel ashamed of doing evils.

503   அரியகற்று ஆசுஅற்றார் கண்ணும் தெரியுங்கால்
இன்மை அரிதே வெளிறு.

Even great scholars free from vice
Are seldom free from ignorance.

Even great scholars who are free from faults are not
totally free from ignorance.

504   குணம்நாடிக் குற்றமும் நாடி அவற்றுள்
மிகைநாடி மிக்க கொளல்.

Analyse good and bad qualities
Strike a balance and choose.

The ruler should weigh the merits and demerits of the
people and judge them accordingly by merit.

505   பெருமைக்கும் ஏனைச் சிறுமைக்கும் தம்தம்
கருமமே கட்டளைக் கல்.

For the greatness or the meanness of men
Their deeds are the touchstone.

The deeds of men are the real touchstone for their
nobility or meanness.

506 அற்றாரைத் தேறுதல் ஓம்புக மற்றுஅவர்
பற்றிலர் நாணார் பழி.
Select not men without kin and attachment
For any blame they fear not.
The ruler should not select men who have no attachment
and relatives, for they do not fear social blame.

507 காதன்மை கந்தா அறிவுஅறியார்த் தேறுதல்
பேதைமை எல்லாம் தரும்.
Choosing persons of incompetence
Out of love brings all ignorance.
Choosing fools as advisers out of love will lead to
utter foolishness and confusion.

508 தேரான் பிறனைத் தெளிந்தான் வழிமுறை
தீரா இடும்பை தரும்.
Believing untested and unknown persons
Fetches one's progeny endless woes.
Trusting strangers without testing them will bring
endless evils to one's progeny.

509 தேறற்க யாரையும் தேராது தேர்ந்தபின்
தேறுக தேறும் பொருள்.
Never choose men without judging
Assign apt work after choosing.
One should choose men after testing them and then
give them suitable work .

510 தேரான் தெளிவும் தெளிந்தான்கண் ஐயுறவும்
தீரா இடும்பை தரும்.
Trusting sans testing and doubting the tested
Will lead to great woes without end.
To trust men without any test and suspect those
already tested will lead to endless troubles.

52. தெரிந்து வினையாடல்
EVALUATING AND EMPLOYING

511 நன்மையும் தீமையும் நாடி நலம்புரிந்த
தன்மையான் ஆளப் படும்.
Choose and use those who comprehend
Good and bad, and love to do good.
One should choose and employ men who can weigh
good and bad, and love to do only positive things.

512 வாரி பெருக்கி வளம்படுத்து உற்றவை
ஆராய்வான் செய்க வினை.
Employ one who widens revenue sources
Promotes wealth and removes hurdles.
One should employ men who can enlarge the sources
of income, increase wealth and prevent hurdles.

513 அன்புஅறிவு தேற்றம் அவாஇன்மை இந்நான்கும்
நன்குடையான் கட்டே தெளிவு.
Affinity, wit, clarity and desirelessness —
Trust only those with these four traits.
One should employ men of virtues who are kind, wise,
clear-headed and contented.

514 எனைவகையான் தேறியக் கண்ணும் வினைவகையான்
வேறுஆகும் மாந்தர் பலர்.
Men may pass all tests, yet they vary
In their ways of discharging duty.
Though tested and found fit, men may differ in their
ways of executing a task.

515 அறிந்துஆற்றிச் செய்கிற்பாற்கு அல்லால் வினைதான்
சிறந்தான்என்று ஏவற்பாற் நன்று.
Employ not favourites but only who knows ways
To achieve things overcoming all hurdles.
One should not employ favourites but those who know
how to get things done.

516 செய்வானை நாடி வினைநாடிக் காலத்தோடு
எய்த உணர்ந்து செயல்.
Weigh well the man, the act and the time
Before assigning any work to him.
One should choose the right person, right deed and right
time, and then entrust the work to him.

517 இதனை இதனால் இவன்முடிக்கும் என்றுஆய்ந்து
அதனை அவன்கண் விடல்.
This deed, by these means, if he can perform
Test him; if convinced, assign it to him.
Only after evaluating the task, the means and the person
to do it, the task should be assigned to him.

518 வினைக்குஉரிமை நாடிய பின்றை அவனை
அதற்குஉரிய னாகச் செயல்.
After examining one's fitness for the deed
Employ him for that deed.
Only after having decided that a man is fit for the task,
one should employ him.

519 வினைக்கண் வினையுடையான் கேண்மைவேறு ஆக
நினைப்பானை நீங்கும் திரு.
Fortune forsakes one who disbelieves
Loyalty of diligent workers.
Fortune deserts one who doubts the loyalty of hard-
working persons.

520 நாள்தோறும் நாடுக மன்னன் வினைசெய்வான்
கோடாமை கோடாது உலகு.
Let the king be always alert to keep his men
Loyal and the world will be upright then.
The ruler should always be alert in keeping his workforce
faithful so as to make the world all right.

53. சுற்றந்தழால்
CHERISHING RELATIVES

521   பற்றற்ற கண்ணும் பழைமைபா ராட்டுதல்
      சுற்றத்தார் கண்ணே உள.

One may lose all wealth and be in penury
Still kin alone admire one's past glory.

A person may lose all his wealth; yet his relatives praise
his glorious past.

522   விருப்புஅறாச் சுற்றம் இயையின் அருப்புஅறா
      ஆக்கம் பலவும் தரும்.

Gift of loving kinship surely nurtures
Endless fortune in great measures.

Fortune will be ever increasing if one has the gift of
loving relatives.

523   அளவளாவு இல்லாதான் வாழ்க்கை குளவளாக்
      கோடுஇன்றி நீர்நிறைந் தற்று.

Kinless life is like a brimming tank
Which remains without a bank.

The life of a man without loving relatives is like a full-
flooded tank without a bank.

524   சுற்றத்தால் சுற்றப் படஒழுகல் செல்வம்தான்
      பெற்றத்தால் பெற்ற பயன்.

The fruits of prosperity are found
In bringing kinsmen around.

To live with the relatives around is the benefit of a happy
and prosperous life.

525   கொடுத்தலும் இன்சொலும் ஆற்றின் அடுக்கிய
      சுற்றத்தால் சுற்றப் படும்.

Generosity and sweet words enable one
To be circled by multitude of kin.

A large number of relatives gather around the man who
is generous and soft-spoken.

526 பெரும்கொடையான் பேணான் வெகுளி அவனின்
மருங்குஉடையார் மாநிலத்து இல்.
None but the generous and rageless in the world
Gain numerous kindred around.
Only men who are generous and wrathless in this world
gain countless relatives around them.

527 காக்கை கரவா கரைந்துஉண்ணும் ஆக்கமும்
அன்னநீ ரார்க்கே உள.
Crows hide not their food but call and share
Wealth accrues to men of such nature.
Crows invite their friends and share their food. Fortune
remains with men of similar nature.

528 பொதுநோக்கான் வேந்தன் வரிசையா நோக்கின்
அதுநோக்கி வாழ்வார் பலர்.
A king who views not all alike but on merit
Will have several relatives on that count.
A king with proper discretion will always have countless
relatives.

529 தமராகித் தன்துறந்தார் சுற்றம் அமராமைக்
காரணம் இன்றி வரும்.
Estranged relatives will return and stay
When cause for division fades away.
Once the cause for discord is removed, the deserted
relatives will come back and stay.

530 உழைப்பிரிந்து காரணத்தின் வந்தானை வேந்தன்
இழைத்துஇருந்து எண்ணிக் கொளல்.
When a deserter returns with a motive
King should help, ponder and receive.
The ruler should help, examine carefully and then admit
the deserter who returns with a cause.

54. பொச்சாவாமை
NOT FORGETTING DUTY

531 இறந்த வெகுளியின் தீதே சிறந்த
உவகை மகிழ்ச்சியின் சோர்வு.
Forgetting one's duty in excessive happiness
Is worse than wrath in excess.
Forgetting one's duty in overwhelming joy is worse than
excessive anger.

532 பொச்சாப்புக் கொல்லும் புகழை அறிவினை
நிச்ச நிரப்புக்கொன் றாங்கு.
As incessant want destroys wisdom
Forgetfulness in duty ruins fame.
Forgetfulness in one's duty ruins one's name and fame
just as constant poverty destroys wisdom.

533 பொச்சாப்பார்க்கு இல்லை புகழ்மை அதுஉலகத்து
எப்பால்நூ லோர்க்கும் துணிவு.
Forgetful men ever fail to fetch fame
All learned men uphold the same.
Those who are forgetful can never achieve glory. It is
the accepted view of all learned men.

534 அச்ச முடையார்க்கு அரண்இல்லை ஆங்கில்லை
பொச்சாப்பு உடையார்க்கு நன்கு.
As no fortress is fruitful for the fearful
No fortune is useful for the forgetful.
The fearful have no use of their fort. Likewise, the
forgetful have no use of their fortune.

535 முன்னுறக் காவாது இழுக்கியான் தன்பிழை
பின்ஊறு இரங்கி விடும்.
Who forget to guard against woes in advance
Will later deplore their faults.
Those who fail to protect themselves in advance will
repent for their faults later.

536 இழுக்காமை யார்மாட்டும் என்றும் வழுக்காமை
வாயின் அதுஒப்பது இல்.
Excellent it is beyond compare
To be ever with wakeful care.
To work with ever-wakeful care at all times is excellent
beyond comparison.

537 அரியஎன்று ஆகாத இல்லைபொச் சாவாக்
கருவியால் போற்றிச் செயின்.
Pursue work with unforgetful mind
And nothing hard you will find.
When we do a thing focusing our mind on it, nothing
will be difficult for us.

538 புகழ்ந்தவை போற்றிச் செயல்வேண்டும் செய்யாது
இகழ்ந்தார்க்கு எழுமையும் இல்.
Pursue what the wise praise as excellence
If not, there's no gain in all seven births.
One should pursue excellence praised by the wise;
or else there will be no gain in all seven births.

539 இகழ்ச்சியின் கெட்டாரை உள்ளுக தாம்தம்
மகிழ்ச்சியின் மைந்துறும் போழ்து.
Think of those ruined by forgetfulness
When filled with vain happiness.
When one is extremely proud and happy, one should
remember those who are ruined through forgetfulness.

540 உள்ளியது எய்தல் எளிதுமன் மற்றும்தான்
உள்ளியது உள்ளப் பெறின்.
All goals are easily achieved by him
Whose mind is set on them.
A person should set his mind upon his goals and then
act; only then can they be easily achieved.

55. செங்கோன்மை
JUST RULE

541 ஓர்ந்துகண் ணோடாது இறைபுரிந்து யார்மாட்டும்
     தேர்ந்துசெய் வஃதே முறை.

Enquiring, favouring no one, being impartial,
Consulting and rendering justice is just rule.

Just rule is to probe, favour none, be unbiased,
deliberate and render justice.

542 வான்நோக்கி வாழும் உலகெல்லாம் மன்னவன்
     கோல்நோக்கி வாழும் குடி.

As the whole world looks to the sky for rainfall
All subjects look to the king for just rule.

The world depends on rain for life. Likewise, the
citizens depend on the king for justice.

543 அந்தணர் நூற்கும் அறத்திற்கும் ஆதியாய்
     நின்றது மன்னவன் கோல்.

For virtue and the wise men's texts
The king's sceptre is the basis.

The king's just rule provides the basis for holy
scriptures and right conduct.

544 குடிதழீஇக் கோல்ஓச்சும் மாநில மன்னன்
     அடிதழீஇ நிற்கும் உலகு.

The world is at the feet of the benevolent ruler
Who reigns with love for people's welfare.

The world respects the king who rules justly for the
welfare of the people.

545 இயல்புளிக் கோல்ஓச்சும் மன்னவன் நாட்ட
     பெயலும் விளையுளும் தொக்கு.

Rains and grains together bless the land
Of the king who reigns by moral code.

Seasonal rains and yields are plenty in the land ruled
by a just king.

546   வேல்அன்று வென்றி தருவது மன்னவன்
கோல்அதூஉம் கோடாது எனின்.
Not lance but sceptre swayed with equity
Alone gives the king victory.
It is not the spear but only the sceptre of justice that
brings success to the king.

547   இறைகாக்கும் வையகம் எல்லாம் அவனை
முறைகாக்கும் முட்டாச் செயின்.
World's safety depends on the ruler
Just rule defends his honour.
The king protects all his people. His own just rule
protects his dignity.

548   எண்பதத்தான் ஓரா முறைசெய்யா மன்னவன்
தண்பதத்தான் தானே கெடும்.
The inaccessible and unrighteous chief
Perishes in disgraceful grief.
An inaccessible and unjust king will surely bring
destruction on himself.

549   குடிபுறங் காத்துஓம்பிக் குற்றம் கடிதல்
வடுஅன்று வேந்தன் தொழில்.
Guarding subjects and curbing crimes
Are not faults but king's duties.
The duties of a king are protecting his subjects from
enemies and punishing the wrong-doers.

550   கொலையிற் கொடியாரை வேந்துஒறுத்தல் பைங்கூழ்
களைகட் டதனொடு நேர்.
Passing death sentence on cruel murderers
Is like removing weeds from green fields.
Passing death sentence on ruthless killers is like
removing weeds from the land under crop.

56. கொடுங்கோன்மை
TYRANNICAL RULE

551 கொலைமேற்கொண் டாரிற் கொடிதே அலைமேற்கொண்டு
அல்லவை செய்துஒழுகும் வேந்து.

More cruel than a professional killer
Is the oppressive tyrannical ruler.

The king who harasses his subjects is worse than a
cruel murderer by trade.

552 வேலொடு நின்றான் இடுஎன் றதுபோலும்
கோலொடு நின்றான் இரவு.

A king extracting money from the citizens
Is like an armed man robbing travellers.

A cruel king's demand for money from his subjects is
like an armed man robbing helpless travellers.

553 நாள்தொறும் நாடி முறைசெய்யா மன்னவன்
நாள்தொறும் நாடு கெடும்.

A king who renders not justice every day
Loses his land day by day.

The king who fails to render justice regularly will lose
his country gradually.

554 கூழும் குடியும் ஒருங்குஇழக்கும் கோல்கோடிச்
சூழாது செய்யும் அரசு.

A thoughtless tyrant will completely lose
Both his wealth and citizens.

If the king abuses his authority, he will lose both his
wealth and the support of the people.

555 அல்லற்பட்டு ஆற்றாது அழுதகண் ணீர்அன்றே
செல்வத்தைத் தேய்க்கும் படை.

The unbearable tears shed by the oppressed
Are files to wear out the wealth amassed.

The unbearable tears of the oppressed are weapons
that destroy the wealth of a king.

556 மன்னர்க்கு மன்னுதல் செங்கோன்மை அஃதின்றேல்
மன்னாவாம் மன்னர்க்கு ஒளி.
Just rule brings a king everlasting fame
Without it, he has no esteem.
Just rule brings everlasting glory to a king. Unjust rule
dims his name.

557 துளியின்மை ஞாலத்திற்கு எற்றுஅற்றே வேந்தன்
அளியின்மை வாழும் உயிர்க்கு.
Just as beings in the world suffer without rain
People languish under a ruthless reign.
As all beings on earth suffer without rain, people suffer
under an unkind king.

558 இன்மையின் இன்னாது உடைமை முறைசெய்யா
மன்னவன் கோல்கீழ்ப் படின்.
Possessing is worse than not possessing
Under the sceptre of an unjust king.
Possession of wealth causes more distress than poverty
to those living under a merciless ruler.

559 முறைகோடி மன்னவன் செய்யின் உறைகோடி
ஒல்லாது வானம் பெயல்.
If a king abuses his reign for gains
Clouds won't give seasonal rains.
When a king fails to render justice, even seasons will
change and rains will fail.

560 ஆபயன் குன்றும் அறுதொழிலோர் நூல்மறப்பர்
காவலன் காவான் எனின்.
When a ruler guards not justly, cows yield less
And men of six duties forget texts.
If the king fails to protect his country, cows will yield
less milk and the priests will forget scriptures.

57. வெருவந்த செய்யாமை
AVOIDING OPPRESSION

561   தக்காங்கு நாடித் தலைச்செல்லா வண்ணத்தால்
ஒத்தாங்கு ஒறுப்பது வேந்து.

Call him a king who probes and punishes
Suitably to prevent offences.

A king examines thoroughly before giving suitable
punishment to prevent further evils.

562   கடிதுஓச்சி மெல்ல எறிக நெடிதுஆக்கம்
நீங்காமை வேண்டு பவர்.

Lift the rod firmly but strike very gently
It ensures long stay of prosperity.

The king must appear to be harsh but he must be
really kind. This will ensure long-lasting gains.

563   வெருவந்த செய்துஒழுகும் வெங்கோலன் ஆயின்
ஒருவந்தம் ஒல்லைக் கெடும்.

A ruthless sceptred-king's dreadful act
Surely hastens his ruin in fact.

An unkind ruler who is a terror to his people will
quickly perish.

564   இறைகடியன் என்றுஉரைக்கும் இன்னாச்சொல் வேந்தன்
உறைகடுகி ஒல்லைக் கெடும்.

"Our king is cruel," when subjects complain
His life and wealth shall swiftly decline.

When the subjects complain that the king is cruel, he
will soon lose his life and wealth.

565   அருஞ்செவ்வி இன்னா முகத்தான் பெருஞ்செல்வம்
பேஎய்கண் டன்னது உடைத்து.

Wealth of an inaccessible king with looks cruel
Is like the treasure guarded by the devil.

The cruel-faced king's wealth is no better than a
devil's treasure.

566 கடுஞ்சொல்லன் கண்ணிலன் ஆயின் நெடுஞ்செல்வம்
நீடின்றி ஆங்கே கெடும்.

If a king is harsh in speech and without mercies
Fast perish his vast riches.

The king who is harsh in speech and unsympathetic
soon loses his vast wealth.

567 கடுமொழியும் கைஇகந்த தண்டமும் வேந்தன்
அடுமுரண் தேய்க்கும் அரம்.

Unkind speech and excessive penalties
Erode king's winning power like files.

Bitter words and excessive punishments are the files
that wear out the conquering power of the king.

568 இனத்துஆற்றி எண்ணாத வேந்தன் சினத்துஆற்றிச்
சீரின் சிறுகும் திரு.

A king furious and indifferent to ministers
Will gradually lose all his fortunes.

A king burning with anger and not heeding the advice of
the wise will gradually lose all his wealth.

569 செருவந்த போழ்தில் சிறைசெய்யா வேந்தன்
வெருவந்து வெய்து கெடும்.

The ruler who possesses not proper safeguards
Dreads foes in wars and swiftly perishes.

The king without strong forts lives in fear of foes and
gets ruined.

570 கல்லார்ப் பிணிக்கும் கடுங்கோல் அதுவல்லது
இல்லை நிலக்குப் பொறை.

No greater burden is borne by the world
Than a tyrant bound by the unlearned.

There is no greater burden to the earth than the tyrant
surrounded by the council of illiterates.

58. கண்ணோட்டம்
BENIGN LOOK

571   கண்ணோட்டம் என்னும் கழிபெருங் காரிகை
உண்மையான் உண்டுஇவ் வுலகு.

In benign look with boundless beauty
The world exists really.

The world survives on limitless beauty found in the
compassion of the people.

572   கண்ணோட்டத்து உள்ளது உலகியல் அஃதிலார்
உண்மை நிலக்குப் பொறை.

Benign look is truly the way of life on earth
Men sans mercy are burden to earth.

The world survives on men of compassion and those
without mercy are burden to the earth.

573   பண்என்னாம் பாடற்கு இயைபின்றேல் கண்என்னாம்
கண்ணோட்டம் இல்லாத கண்.

Songs without music are indeed useless
Eyes sans benign look have no use.

Songs without tunes are of no use. Eyes without
benign look are of no use either.

574   உளபோல் முகத்துஉளவன் செய்யும் அளவினால்
கண்ணோட்டம் இல்லாத கண்.

Of what use are the seeming eyes to the face
If they have no sufficient grace?

Eyes are of no use to one's face if they show no
kindness in sufficient measure.

575   கண்ணிற்கு அணிகலம் கண்ணோட்டம் அஃதின்றேல்
புண்ணென்று உணரப் படும்.

Benign look is the jewel of the eyes
Without it they are but sores.

The jewel of the eyes is benign look; without it the
eyes are only sores.

576 மண்ணோடு இயைந்த மரத்தனையர் கண்ணோடு
     இயைந்துகண் ணோடா தவர்.
Men with no graceful eyes
Exist on earth like trees.
Men without benign look remain just like trees rooted
to the ground.

577 கண்ணோட்டம் இல்லவர் கண்ணிலர் கண்ணுடையார்
     கண்ணோட்டம் இன்மையும் இல்.
Men bereft of benign look have no real eyes
Men with real eyes lack not love for others.
Men without kindness have no real eyes. Men with eyes
are not without kind-heartedness.

578 கரும்ம் சிதையாமல் கண்ணோட வல்லார்க்கு
     உரிமை உடைத்துஇவ் வுலகு.
The whole world surely belongs to those
Who are benign and aware of duties.
The entire world belongs to those who are kind to
others and sincere in their duties.

579 ஒறுத்துஆற்றும் பண்பினார் கண்ணும்கண் ணோடிப்
     பொறுத்துஆற்றும் பண்பே தலை.
Showing kindness and patience even to those
Who hurt is the chief of virtues.
It is excellent to be kind and patient even to those
who hurt us.

580 பெயக்கண்டும் நஞ்சுஉண்டு அமைவர் நயத்தக்க
     நாகரிகம் வேண்டு பவர்.
The benign take even poison given by a companion
And yet calm and courteous they remain.
Benign people will take even the poison given by their
friends and yet remain cool and gracious.

59. ஒற்றாடல்
ESPIONAGE

581   ஒற்றும் உரைசான்ற நூலும் இவைஇரண்டும்
தெற்றெங்க மன்னவன் கண்.

Able spies and popular books on morals —
These two are a king's eyes.

The secret services and the books on morals are the
two eyes of a king.

582   எல்லார்க்கும் எல்லாம் நிகழ்பவை எஞ்ஞான்றும்
வல்லறிதல் வேந்தன் தொழில்.

King's duty is to learn from spies promptly
All happenings to his subjects daily.

The king should know promptly whatever happens to
his subjects every day.

583   ஒற்றினான் ஒற்றிப் பொருள்தெரியா மன்னவன்
கொற்றம் கொளக்கிடந்தது இல்.

Ways of victories are unknown to a king
Who knows not the benefits of spying.

A king who does not know the benefits of spying can
never achieve victory.

584   வினைசெய்வார் தம்சுற்றம் வேண்டாதார் என்றாங்கு
அனைவரையும் ஆராய்வது ஒற்று.

A spy is the one who spies on king's officials
His own relatives and enemies.

A good spy is the one who observes the conduct of
the king's employees, his relatives and enemies.

585   கடாஅ உருவொடு கண்அஞ்சாது யாண்டும்
உகாஅமை வல்லதே ஒற்று.

Unsuspected appearance, undaunted eyes
And keeping secrets mark the spies.

Able spies are those who have unsuspected appearance and fearlessness, and guard secrets.

586 துறந்தார் படிவத்தர் ஆகி இறந்துஆராய்ந்து
என்செயினும் சோர்வுஇலது ஒற்று.
Garbed as an ascetic, a spy gathers secrets
And remains tireless despite threats.
A spy guised as an ascetic works tirelessly and collects
information unmindful of threats.

587 மறைந்தவை கேட்கவற்று ஆகி அறிந்தவை
ஐயப்பாடு இல்லதே ஒற்று.
A spy is one who searches others' secrets out
And confirms them beyond doubt.
A spy collects the secrets of others and confirms them
beyond doubt.

588 ஒற்றுஒற்றித் தந்த பொருளையும் மற்றுமோர்
ஒற்றினால் ஒற்றிக் கொளல்.
Confirm not merely on one spy's report
But verify it with another's report.
The report of one spy must be verified with that of
another to confirm it.

589 ஒற்றுஒற்று உணராமை ஆள்க உடன்மூவர்
சொல்தொக்க தேறப் படும்.
Engage spies but not known to one another
Credit them if reports of three concur.
The spies should not know one another. The king should
believe and act if reports of three spies agree.

590 சிறப்புஅறிய ஒற்றின்கண் செய்யற்க செய்யின்
புறப்படுத்தான் ஆகும் மறை.
Never honour the spy in others' sight
If done, secrets will come to light.
A spy should not be honoured in public; if honoured,
it will expose the secrets to the public.

60. ஊக்கம் உடைமை
ZEAL

591   உடையர் எனப்படுவது ஊக்கம்அஃது இல்லார்
      உடையது உடையரோ மற்று.

**Who possess zeal alone have indeed everything
Who possess all but zeal have nothing.**

Only those with zeal have real wealth; those without
zeal have nothing, though they may have everything.

592   உள்ளம் உடைமை உடைமை பொருள்உடைமை
      நில்லாது நீங்கி விடும்.

**Possession of zeal alone is everlasting wealth
Material possessions are fleeting wealth.**

Possession of zeal is long-lasting wealth. Material
possessions are fleeting in nature.

593   ஆக்கம் இழந்தேம்என்று அல்லாவார் ஊக்கம்
      ஒருவந்தம் கைத்துஉடை யார்.

**Those with enduring zeal won't lament
The loss of wealth possessed.**

People with tireless zeal do not bother about the loss
of worldly wealth.

594   ஆக்கம் அதர்வினாய்ச் செல்லும் அசைவிலா
      ஊக்கம் உடையா னுழை.

**Wealth will ask and find the way to him
Who has unshaken enthusiasm.**

Good fortune enquires and enters the path of a person
who has abundant zeal.

595   வெள்ளத்து அனைய மலர்நீட்டம் மாந்தர்தம்
      உள்ளத்து அனையது உயர்வு.

**Stem length of lily depends on water level
Men's greatness depends on zeal.**

A lily rises according to the water level and men's
greatness rises according to their zeal.

596 உள்ளுவது எல்லாம் உயர்வுள்ளல் மற்றுஅது
தள்ளினும் தள்ளாமை நீர்த்து.
Let your thoughts be high and lofty always
You may fail but your zeal stays.
Men should always think high and noble. Even if they
fail, they should have the zeal forever.

597 சிதைவுஇடத்து ஒல்கார் உரவோர் புதையம்பின்
பட்டுப்பாடு ஒன்றும் களிறு.
The strong-willed never flinch at failures
Like braving tuskers smitten by arrows.
Strong-minded people are always firm even in defeat
like the brave elephants pierced by arrows.

598 உள்ளம் இலாதவர் எய்தார் உலகத்து
வள்ளியம் என்னும் செருக்கு.
Men without strong mind cannot take pride
In being liberal-minded in the world.
Men without a strong will cannot boast that they are
very generous to others.

599 பரியது கூர்ங்கோட்டது ஆயினும் யானை
வெருஉம் புலிதாக் குறின்.
Even a huge and sharp-tusked elephant fears
When a tiger with zeal charges.
Though the elephant is huge and sharp-tusked, it is
afraid of a tiger attacking it with ferocity.

600 உரம்ஒருவற்கு உள்ள வெறுக்கைஅஃது இல்லார்
மரம்மக்கள் ஆதலே வேறு.
Resolute mind alone is the real strength of men
Lacking it, they are trees in the form of men.
A firm mind is the real strength of men. Without it,
they are but trees in human form.

61. மடியின்மை
NOT BEING LAZY

601 குடிஎன்னும் குன்றா விளக்கம் மடிஎன்னும்
மாசூர மாய்ந்து கெடும்.

The eternal lamp of ancestry dims
When darkness of sloth rises.

The light of family honour will die due to the dark
smoke of laziness.

602 மடியை மடியா ஒழுகல் குடியைக்
குடியாக வேண்டு பவர்.

Always keep sloth at bay and be busy
To uphold the prestige of the family.

Those who aim at enhancing the prestige of the family
should give up laziness.

603 மடிமடிக் கொண்டுஒழுகும் பேதை பிறந்த
குடிமடியும் தன்னினும் முந்து.

A foolish man who lives with ruinous sloth
Ruins his family before his death.

A fool with deadly idleness causes the downfall of his
family before his death.

604 குடிமடிந்து குற்றம் பெருகும் மடிமடிந்து
மாண்ட உளுற்றி லவர்க்கு.

The lazy lacking zeal ruin their homes
And go on multiplying their crimes.

The lazy men without effort bring ruin to their families
and increase their sins.

605 நெடுநீர் மறவி மடிதுயில் நான்கும்
கெடுநீரார் காமக் கலன்.

Procrastination, forgetfulness, sloth and sleep
Are boats that the self-doomed love to keep.

Delay, forgetfulness, laziness and sleep are the
coveted vehicles of those prone to ruin.

606   படியுடையார் பற்றுஅமைந்தக் கண்ணும் மடியுடையார்
மாண்பயன் எய்தல் அரிது.
The slothful seldom gain greater benefits
Though endowed with regal gifts.
The lazy cannot achieve great gains even if they
enjoy royal benefits.

607   இடிபுரிந்து எள்ளும்சொல் கேட்பர் மடிபுரிந்து
மாண்ட உஞற்றி லவர்.
Who love indolence without dignified effort
Must endure others' words of contempt.
Those who love laziness lacking noble efforts will have
to face scornful words.

608   மடிமை குடிமைக்கண் தங்கின்தன் ஒன்னார்க்கு
அடிமை புகுத்தி விடும்.
If sloth dwells in a man of noble family
It will enslave him to his enemy.
If laziness remains in a man of nobility, it will make
him the slave of his enemy.

609   குடிஆண்மை யுள்வந்த குற்றம் ஒருவன்
மடிஆண்மை மாற்றக் கெடும்.
Disgrace on one's race and manliness stops
The moment one sheds laziness.
Freedom from laziness removes shame and disgrace
on one's family and manliness.

610   மடிஇலா மன்னவன் எய்தும் அடிஅளந்தான்
தாஅயது எல்லாம் ஒருங்கு.
The slothless king shall gain at once
All the worlds trod by God apace.
A king who is not lazy can gain all the worlds mea-
sured by God's great strides.

62. ஆள்வினை உடைமை
PERSEVERANCE

611   அருமை உடைத்துஎன்று அசாவாமை வேண்டும்
பெருமை முயற்சி தரும்.

Get not discouraged saying 'It's hard'.
Efforts will bring due regard.

Nothing is difficult to achieve. Strenuous efforts will
bring due honour.

612   வினைக்கண் வினைகெடல் ஓம்பல் வினைக்குறை
தீர்ந்தாரின் தீர்ந்தன்று உலகு.

As the world deserts those who midway shirk
Do not give up your task.

One should never give up a task in the middle, for the
world will abandon such people.

613   தாளாண்மை என்னும் தகைமைக்கண் தங்கிற்றே
வேளாண்மை என்னும் செருக்கு.

The pride of serving the humanity
Rests on excellence of industry.

The glory of benevolence depends on the excellence
of perseverance.

614   தாளாண்மை இல்லாதான் வேளாண்மை பேடிகை
வாள்ஆண்மை போலக் கெடும்.

An idle man's intent of charity is like a sword
Remaining in a eunuch's hand.

The thought of charity in a lazy man is useless like
the sword in a eunuch's hand.

615   இன்பம் விழையான் வினைவிழைவான் தன்கேளிர்
துன்பம் துடைத்துஊன்றும் தூண்.

Who shuns delight and delights in labour alone
Comforts kin and props like a pillar-stone.

One who loves work, but not pleasure and removes the
sufferings of his relatives is like a supporting pillar.

616 முயற்சி திருவினை ஆக்கும் முயற்றின்மை
இன்மை புகுத்தி விடும்.
Perseverance leads to prosperity
Effortlessness results in poverty.
Strenuous effort brings wealth and laziness brings only
poverty.

617 மடிஉளாள் மாமுகடி என்ப மடியிலான்
தாள்உளாள் தாமரையி னாள்.
Goddess of misfortune dwells with indolence
Goddess of prosperity abides with deligence.
Misfortune lives with the lazy and Fortune lives with
the industrious.

618 பொறியின்மை யார்க்கும் பழிஅன்று அறிவுஅறிந்து
ஆள்வினை இன்மை பழி.
Bad luck is not at all a fault of anyone
But lack of lore and effort brings stain.
Bad luck is never blamed. What is blamed is lack of
knowledge and effort.

619 தெய்வத்தான் ஆகாது எனினும் முயற்சிதன்
மெய்வருத்தக் கூலி தரும்.
Destiny may not favour one's achievement
Yet hard labour brings due payment.
Though fate may not be favourable, strenuous effort
will yield its reward.

620 ஊழையும் உப்பக்கம் காண்பர் உலைவுஇன்றித்
தாழாது உஞற்று பவர்.
Men overcome even the relentless destiny
With their ceaseless industry.
Those with untiring and unfailing efforts will conquer
even the unyielding fate.

63. இடுக்கண் அழியாமை
FORTITUDE

621   இடுக்கண் வருங்கால் நகுக அதனை
அடுத்துஊர்வது அஃதொப்பது இல்.
Laugh away the trouble when it comes
Nothing equals it to conquer pains.
Adversity can be overcome by taking it lightly. So
smiling is the easy way to overcome it.

622   வெள்ளத்து அனைய இடும்பை அறிவுடையான்
உள்ளத்தின் உள்ளக் கெடும்.
Even though misfortune may rise like a flood
A wise man overcomes it by thoughts bold.
A wise man with a determined mind will conquer even a
flood of troubles.

623   இடும்பைக்கு இடும்பை படுப்பர் இடும்பைக்கு
இடும்பை படாஉ தவர்.
Who, in grief, do not grieve
Make grief itself grieve.
The resolute will never allow grief to overcome them
but will make even grief itself grieve.

624   மடுத்தவாய் எல்லாம் பகடுஅன்னான் உற்ற
இடுக்கண் இடர்ப்பாடு உடைத்து.
Trouble is troubled by him who is relentless
Like a bull pulling a cart thro' all blocks.
Trouble itself is troubled if it confronts a man with
bull-like efforts.

625   அடுக்கி வரினும் அழிவுஇலான் உற்ற
இடுக்கண் இடுக்கண் படும்.
A man of fortitude troubles the troubles
In spite of successive troubles.
A strong-willed man, who boldly faces sufferings,
drives away all sorrows.

626 அற்றேம்என்று அல்லல் படுபவோ பெற்றேம்என்று
ஓம்புதல் தேற்றா தவர்.

Who guard not and gloat not in plenty
Seldom fret and fume in penury.

Those who are neither miserly nor elated in prosperity
will never grieve in poverty.

627 இலக்கம் உடம்புஇடும்பைக்கு என்று கலக்கத்தைக்
கையாறாக் கொள்ளாதாம் மேல்.

As the body is but the butt of sorrows
The wise never care for woes.

The wise do not take sorrows to heart as they know
that the body is subject to suffering.

628 இன்பம் விழையான் இடும்பை இயல்புஎன்பான்
துன்பம் உறுதல் இலன்.

Who seeks not joy but takes woes as natural
Hardly ever regrets the ordeal.

A person who does not seek pleasure and takes
sufferings as natural will never be prone to grief.

629 இன்பத்துள் இன்பம் விழையாதான் துன்பத்துள்
துன்பம் உறுதல் இலன்.

Who never seeks joy of joys
Has no pain of sorrows.

A person who does not long for joy will never be upset
by the pain of sorrows.

630 இன்னாமை இன்பம் எனக்கொளின் ஆகும்தன்
ஒன்னார் விழையும் சிறப்பு.

Who finds joy even in woes
Is admired even by foes.

Even enemies will hail the glory of a person who takes
pain as pleasure.

64. அமைச்சு
MINISTRY

631   கருவியும் காலமும் செய்கையும் செய்யும்
அருவினையும் மாண்டது அமைச்சு.
Means, time, mode and rare deeds ——
A minister is efficient in these.
A wise minister is one who is efficient in choosing the
right means, time, manner and rare ventures.

632   வன்கண் குடிகாத்தல் கற்றறிதல் ஆள்வினையோடு
ஐந்துடன் மாண்டது அமைச்சு.
Firmness, nobility, concern, lore and efforts ——
An ideal minister has these five traits.
An ideal minister excels in firmness, nobility, concern,
knowledge and efforts.

633   பிரித்தலும் பேணிக் கொளலும் பிரிந்தார்ப்
பொருத்தலும் வல்லது அமைச்சு.
An able minister is one who divides foes' allies,
Keeps friends and binds parted ones.
A minister is one who is able to divide enemies' allies,
cherish friends and unite the parted ones.

634   தெரிதலும் தேர்ந்து செயலும் ஒருதலையாச்
சொல்லலும் வல்லது அமைச்சு.
Enquiry, deliberate action and firm counsel
Should mark the minister able.
An able minister is one who deeply enquires, decides
on the ways of execution and boldly advises.

635   அறன்அறிந்து ஆன்றுஅமைந்த சொல்லான்எஞ் ஞான்றும்
திறன்அறிந்தான் தேர்ச்சித் துணை.
Choose as minister an able man who is virtuous,
Capable of wise counsel and executing tacts.
A king should choose as minister one known for virtue,
wise words and efficient execution.

636 மதிநுட்பம் நூலோடு உடையார்க்கு அதிநுட்பம்
யாஉள முன்நிற் பவை.

What can withstand the innate brain
Combined with learning's gain?

Nothing can withstand a minister's inherent intelligence
combined with his acquired knowledge.

637 செயற்கை அறிந்தக் கடைத்தும் உலகத்து
இயற்கை அறிந்து செயல்.

However well-versed in performing a deed
One should tread the way of the world.

Although one knows all subtle techniques, one should
act in tune with the world.

638 அறிகொன்று அறியான் எனினும் உறுதி
உழைஇருந்தான் கூறல் கடன்.

An indifferent and ignorant king may reject
But a minister's duty is to advise aright.

An ignorant and reluctant ruler may ignore the advice.
But a minister's duty is to advise him rightly.

639 பழுதுஎண்ணும் மந்திரியின் பக்கத்துள் தெவ்வோர்
எழுபது கோடி உறும்.

A king's numerous enemies are better certainly
Than a minister guiding him wrongly.

Millions of open enemies of a king are better than a
minister who gives him wrong guidance.

640 முறைப்படச் சூழ்ந்தும் முடிவுஇலவே செய்வர்
திறப்பாடு இலாஅ தவர்.

An inefficient minister will always fail
To finish even a plan designed well.

An inefficient minister will never finish even a well-
planned scheme.

65. சொல்வன்மை
POWER OF SPEECH

641 நாநலம் என்னும் நலனுடைமை அந்நலம்
யாநலத்து உள்ளதூஉம் அன்று.
The gift of the gab is the best of the gifts
And forms not part of other gifts.
Power of speech is a rare gift. There is no other gift
rarer than that.

642 ஆக்கமும் கேடும் அதனால் வருதலால்
காத்துஓம்பல் சொல்லின்கண் சோர்வு.
Gain or loss depends on one's words
So guard against slip in words.
Words can bring either gain or ruin. So we must guard
against a slip of the tongue.

643 கேட்டார்ப் பிணிக்கும் தகையவாய்க் கேளாரும்
வேட்ப மொழிவதாம் சொல்.
What holds the audience spellbound and reach
Others and make them long for, is a speech.
A speech should captivate the audience and appeal
even to those who have not heard it.

644 திறன்அறிந்து சொல்லுக சொல்லை அறனும்
பொருளும் அதனின்ஊஉங்கு இல்.
Weigh and utter your words very well
Thai no virtue and wealth can excel.
One should choose and use words that even virtue and
wealth cannot excel.

645 சொல்லுக சொல்லைப் பிறிதுஓர்சொல் அச்சொல்லை
வெல்லும்சொல் இன்மை அறிந்து.
Select and speak only such words
Not excelled by other words.
One should use such words which are not excelled by
any other words.

646 வேட்பத்தாம் சொல்லிப் பிறர்சொல் பயன்கோடல்
மாட்சியின் மாசுஅற்றார் கோள்.

**Code of spotless men is to say what is desirable
And grasp from others what is useful.**

The code of great men is to speak sweet words that
attract others and take merit in others' speech.

647 சொலல்வல்லன் சோர்வுஇலன் அஞ்சான் அவனை
இகல்வெல்லல் யார்க்கும் அரிது.

**An efficient, tireless and fearless speaker
Is hard for anyone to conquer.**

No one can defeat a speaker who is good, tireless and
bold in a debate.

648 விரைந்து தொழில்கேட்கும் ஞாலம் நிரந்துஇனிது
சொல்லுதல் வல்லார்ப் பெறின்.

**The world will always be quick to execute
The words that are sweetly well-set.**

The world will quickly carry out the sweet and well-set
words of eloquent speakers.

649 பலசொல்லக் காமுறுவர் மன்றமாசு அற்ற
சிலசொல்லல் தேற்றா தவர்.

**Who cannot speak brief and flawless words
Are fond of uttering too many words.**

Those who can never be brief and faultless use too
many words in their speech.

650 இணர்ஊழ்த்தும் நாறா மலர்அனையர் கற்றது
உணர விரித்துஉரையா தார்.

**Who cannot express their lore to others
Are like a bunch of scentless flowers.**

Those who are unable to express what they have
learnt are like flowers without fragrance.

66. வினைத்தூய்மை
PURITY IN ACTION

651   துணைநலம் ஆக்கம் தரூஉம் வினைநலம்
வேண்டிய எல்லாம் தரும்.

Good company brings a man worldly riches
Good deeds fulfil all his wishes.

Good company brings wealth to a person, but goodness of action fulfils all his desires.

652   என்றும் ஒருவுதல் வேண்டும் புகழொடு
நன்றி பயவா வினை.

Better avoid always deeds that lead not
To great fame and benefit.

Acts that do not bring glory and gain must always
be shunned.

653   ஓஓதல் வேண்டும் ஒளிமாழ்கும் செய்வினை
ஆஅதும் என்னு மவர்.

Who aspires to grow up in wordly esteem
Should shun deeds that dim one's fame.

One who seeks future greatness or fame should avoid
deeds that stain one's name.

654   இடுக்கண் படினும் இளிவந்த செய்யார்
நடுக்கற்ற காட்சி யவர்.

Men with clear vision avoid mean action
Even in great affliction.

Men with foresight will do nothing shameful even in
extreme distress.

655   எற்றுஎன்று இரங்குவ செய்யற்க செய்வானேல்
மற்றுஅன்ன செய்யாமை நன்று.

Never do what you will later regret
If you do so, do not ever repeat.

One should not do anything that one will regret later.
If done, one should not repeat the mistake.

656 ஈன்றாள் பசிகாண்பான் ஆயினும் செய்யற்க
சான்றோர் பழிக்கும் வினை.
Do no deeds that noble souls do not approve
Even on seeing mother starve.
One should not do anything that will be condemned
by the great even to feed one's starving mother.

657 பழிமலைந்து எய்திய ஆக்கத்தின் சான்றோர்
கழிநல் குரவே தலை.
Better is the woeful poverty of the perfect
Than the wealth got through evil act.
The pinching poverty of the wise is far better than the
ill-gotten wealth.

658 கடிந்த கடிந்துஒரார் செய்தார்க்கு அவைதாம்
முடிந்தாலும் பீழை தரும்.
Those daring to do deeds forbidden
May gain but meet with affliction.
Those who do deeds shunned by the learned may
win initially but will grieve later.

659 அழக்கொண்ட எல்லாம் அழப்போம் இழப்பினும்
பிற்பயக்கும் நற்பா லவை.
What's gained by others' tears is lost in tears
Well-earned wealth, though lost, returns.
Wealth got through other's sufferings will not last.
Earnings by fair means, though lost, are regained.

660 சலத்தால் பொருள்செய்துஎம் ஆர்த்தல் பசுமண்
கலத்துள்நீர் பெய்துஇரீஇ யற்று.
To hoard wealth gained through means evil
Is like storing water in unbaked clay vessel.
Hoarding ill-gotten wealth is like keeping water in an
unbaked clay pot.

67. வினைத்திட்பம்
FIRMNESS IN ACTION

661 வினைத்திட்பம் என்பது ஒருவன் மனத்திட்பம்
மற்றைய எல்லாம் பிற.

Firmness in action is but robust mind
All others are not of that kind.

Strength of action depends on the firmness of the mind;
all other abilities are not of this nature.

662 ஊறுஒரால் உற்றபின் ஒல்காமை இவ்விரண்டின்
ஆறுஎன்பர் ஆய்ந்தவர் கோள்.

Avoiding barriers and losing not heart if hindered
Are the two aims of the learned.

The two principles of the wise are to avert hurdles
and overcome if obstacles come.

663 கடைக்கொட்கச் செய்தக்கது ஆண்மை இடைக்கொட்கின்
எற்றா விழுமம் தரும்.

True manliness is to execute and then reveal
As woes ensue if exposed in the middle.

Success of an action should be revealed only at the
end as endless sufferings follow if revealed midway.

664 சொல்லுதல் யார்க்கும் எளிய அரியஆம்
சொல்லிய வண்ணம் செயல்.

It is always easy to preach something
But hard to practise the same thing.

It is always easy to preach but difficult to follow what
has been preached.

665 வீறுஎய்தி மாண்டார் வினைத்திட்பம் வேந்தன்கண்
ஊறுஎய்தி உள்ளப் படும்.

One's firmness in action that achieves fame
And reaches the king, will win esteem.

The achievement of fame through firmness of action
reaches the king and it is praised by all.

666 எண்ணிய எண்ணியாங்கு எய்துப எண்ணியார்
திண்ணியர் ஆகப் பெறின்.

Whatever people desire, they get as desired
If only they have firmness of mind.

Men of resolute mind will surely achieve whatever they
wish for.

667 உருவுகண்டு எள்ளாமை வேண்டும் உருள்பெருந்தேர்க்கு
அச்சுஆணி அன்னார் உடைத்து.

Despise not one by appearance, for there are
Men like the linchpin of a huge rolling car.

Appearance of a man does not matter. He may be as
important as the linchpin of a rolling chariot.

668 கலங்காது கண்ட வினைக்கண் துளங்காது
தூக்கம் கடிந்து செயல்.

Waver not on acts resolved but act firmly,
Fearlessly and wakefully.

An act must be executed firmly and boldly without delay
and with alertness.

669 துன்பம் உறவரினும் செய்க துணிவுஆற்றி
இன்பம் பயக்கும் வினை.

With whatever hardships you are beset
Boldly do deeds that bring delight.

Despite initial sufferings, one must do with firmness
the deeds that bring delight in the end.

670 எனைத்திட்பம் எய்தியக் கண்ணும் வினைத்திட்பம்
வேண்டாரை வேண்டாது உலகு.

The world will esteem no other power
But the will power to do whatever.

The world will not respect a man, whatever abilities he
may have, unless he has will power.

68. வினைசெயல்வகை
MODE OF ACTION

671
சூழ்ச்சி முடிவு துணிவெய்தல் அத்துணிவு
தாழ்ச்சியுள் தங்குதல் தீது.
As the end of deliberation is decision
It is harmful to delay execution.
After taking a well-considered decision, it is extremely
harmful to delay the action.

672
தூங்குக தூங்கிச் செயற்பால தூங்கற்க
தூங்காது செய்யும் வினை.
Delay only the deeds that merit delay
Delay not deeds that merit no delay.
Only those acts which deserve delay should be delayed.
Other acts should not be delayed.

673
ஒல்லும்வாய் எல்லாம் வினைநன்றே ஒல்லாக்கால்
செல்லும்வாய் நோக்கிச் செயல்.
Better do deeds whenever feasible, or else
Act after finding proper time and place.
When it is possible, it is good to act. Otherwise, one
should find out the right time and place to act.

674
வினைபகை என்றுஇரண்டின் எச்சம் நினையும்கால்
தீஎச்சம் போலத் தெறும்.
Duty and enmity left incomplete
Ruin like fire partly put out.
Unfinished action and ignored enmity lead to ruin like
unextinguished fire that flares up.

675
பொருள்கருவி காலம் வினைஇடனொடு ஐந்தும்
இருள்தீர எண்ணிச் செயல்.
Resources, means, time, place and deed —
Examine these five before you proceed.
One must consider resources, ways, time, place and
nature of the deed before carrying out an act.

676 முடிவும் இடையூறும் முற்றியாங்கு எய்தும்
படுபயனும் பார்த்துச் செயல்.

Judge the mode of completion, hurdles and gain
Before you plunge into an action.

Mode of completion, obstacles and profit should be
measured well before venturing into an action.

677 செய்வினை செய்வான் செயல்முறை அவ்வினை
உள்ளறிவான் உள்ளம் கொளல்.

Learning the tactics from an expert
Is the best way to do an act.

The best way to perform a deed is learning the
techniques from an expert.

678 வினையால் வினையாக்கிக் கோடல் நனைகவுள்
யானையால் யானையாத் தற்று.

Doing one deed by another deed similar
Is like luring one tusker by another.

One should use one act to achieve another, just as a
trained elephant is used to capture another elephant.

679 நட்டார்க்கு நல்ல செயலின் விரைந்ததே
ஒட்டாரை ஒட்டிக் கொளல்.

More immediate is to befriend foes
Than doing good to friends.

It is more urgent to make friends with foes than doing
good to friends.

680 உறைசிறியார் உள்நடுங்கல் அஞ்சிக் குறைபெறின்
கொள்வர் பெரியார்ப் பணிந்து.

A weak ruler who fears great internal uproar
Bows to mighty foe and accepts peace-offer.

Peace is the only means for the survival of a weak
king against a mighty enemy.

69. தூது
ENVOY

681   அன்புடைமை ஆன்ற குடிப்பிறத்தல் வேந்துஅவாம்
பண்புடைமை தூதுஉரைப்பான் பண்பு.

Kindness, noble birth and courteous qualities
That please the king, make good envoys.

Love, noble birth and courteous qualities that please
the king are the essentials of efficient ambassadors.

682   அன்புஅறிவு ஆராய்ந்த சொல்வன்மை தூதுஉரைப்பார்க்கு
இன்றி யமையாத மூன்று.

Kindness, intelligence and astute eloquence
These three are an envoy's essential traits.

Kindness, intelligence and power of expression are the
three essential qualities of an ambassador.

683   நூலாருள் நூல்வல்லன் ஆகுதல் வேலாருள்
வென்றி வினையுரைப்பான் பண்பு.

A scholar among scholars tells another ruler
The deeds that caused success to his leader.

The envoy, the greatest among scholars, can relate
to another ruler the causes for his king's success.

684   அறிவுஉரு ஆராய்ந்த கல்விஇம் மூன்றன்
செறிவுடையான் செல்க வினைக்கு.

A person with sense, scholarship and personality
Is fit enough to go as an emissary.

A person who has intelligence, good looks and deep
learning is fit to become an envoy.

685   தொகச்சொலலித் தூவாத நீக்கி நகச்சொல்லி
நன்றி பயப்பதாம் தூது.

An envoy is he who briefs in pleasing vein
Unoffending and earning greater gain.

A good envoy should speak precisely, pleasantly and
humbly to bring gain to his king.

686 கற்றுக்கண் அஞ்சான் செலச்சொல்லிக் காலத்தால்
தக்கது அறிவதாம் தூது.

Deep learning, fearlessness, persuasive way
And rising to the occasion make an envoy.

A good envoy is one who is well-read and bold, speaks
convincingly and acts according to the situation.

687 கடன்அறிந்து காலம் கருதி இடன்அறிந்து
எண்ணி உரைப்பான் தலை.

Knowing the duty, suitable time and place
The best envoy thinks before he speaks.

The best envoy knows his duty, the right time and place,
and he deliberates before conveying the message.

688 தூய்மை துணைமை துணிவுடைமை இம்மூன்றின்
வாய்மை வழியுரைப்பான் பண்பு.

Purity, keeping wise company and boldness —
These three are truly an envoy's traits.

An envoy should possess honesty, company of wise
men and courage.

689 விடுமாற்றம் வேந்தர்க்கு உரைப்பான் வடுமாற்றம்
வாய்சோரா வன்க ணவன்.

The envoy conveys the king's exact news
In flawless, unfaltering and firm words.

The envoy conveys the king's exact message to another
king in a firm and faultless language.

690 இறுதி பயப்பினும் எஞ்சாது இறைவற்கு
உறுதி பயப்பதாம் தூது.

Even risking his life, a fearless ambassador
Conveys the message benefitting his ruler.

A good envoy fearlessly conveys the message
benefitting his ruler even at the cost of his life.

70. மன்னரைச் சேர்ந்தொழுகல்
ASSOCIATING WITH RULERS

691   அகலாது அணுகாது தீக்காய்வார் போல்க
இகல்வேந்தர்ச் சேர்ந்தொழுகு வார்.

Move with a moody king as with fire
Neither too far nor too near.

Men around a wavering ruler, like those before the fire,
should go neither too far from him nor too near him.

692   மன்னர் விழைப விழையாமை மன்னரால்
மன்னிய ஆக்கம் தரும்.

Covet not things which the king cherishes
This fetches lasting royal riches.

If men do not crave for what the king desires, they will
gain abiding wealth.

693   போற்றின் அரியவை போற்றல் கடுத்தபின்
தேற்றுதல் யார்க்கும் அரிது.

Guard yourself against grave wrongs
Or you can't clear king's misgivings.

One should be careful and avoid blunders. Otherwise,
it is very difficult to clear the king's suspicions.

694   செவிச்சொல்லும் சேர்ந்த நகையும் அவித்தொழுகல்
ஆன்ற பெரியா ரகத்து.

Avoid whispering and laughing
In the presence of a great king.

Whispers and exchange of smiles should be avoided in
the presence of the king.

695   எப்பொருளும் ஓரார் தொடராா்மற்று அப்பொருளை
விட்டக்கால் கேட்க மறை.

Neither overhear nor pursue the king's secret
But learn only when he reveals it.

One should not overhear or show interest in learning
the king's secret till it is disclosed by him.

696   குறிப்புஅறிந்து காலம் கருதி வெறுப்புஇல
        வேண்டுப வேட்பச் சொலல்.

Watch his good mood and time, and then utter
What the king shuns not and likes better.

Take into account the king's mood and time, and speak
to him what he likes to listen to.

697   வேட்பன சொல்லி வினையில எஞ்ஞான்றும்
        கேட்பினும் சொல்லா விடல்.

Ever utter things desired by the rulers
Tho' pressed, utter not vain things.

One should always speak pleasant things to the king
and never speak useless things even if compelled.

698   இளையர் இனமுறையர் என்றுஇகழார் நின்ற
        ஒளியோடு ஒழுகப் படும்.

Despise not the king as kin or junior
But treat him with due honour.

The ruler should not be scorned as a relative or a junior.
He should be given due honour.

699   கொளப்பட்டேம் என்றுஎண்ணிக் கொள்ளாத செய்யார்
        துளக்கற்ற காட்சி யவர்.

Men with vision do no undesirable things
Thinking they have the king's blessings.

The wise will not do anything unacceptable to the king,
thinking that they enjoy the king's favour.

700   பழையம் எனக்கருதிப் பண்புஅல்ல செய்யும்
        கெழுதகைமை கேடு தரும்.

To presume old friendship and to venture
On unworthy deeds lead to disaster.

Taking the king's intimacy for granted and doing
unworthy acts may lead to destruction.

71. குறிப்பறிதல்
MIND-READING

701   கூறாமை நோக்கிக் குறிப்பறிவான் எஞ்ஞான்றும்
மாறாநீர் வைய்க்கு அணி.
Whoever can read another's unspoken mind
Is a jewel of the sea-locked world.
One who reads another's thoughts from his appearance
is a jewel of the world surrounded by the seas.

702   ஐயப் படாஅது அகத்தது உணர்வானைத்
தெய்வத்தோடு ஒப்பக் கொளல்.
Esteem him who reads another's mind
Beyond doubt, as equal to god.
The person who is able to read another person's mind
correctly is regarded as equal to god.

703   குறிப்பின் குறிப்புணர் வாரை உறுப்பினுள்
யாது கொடுத்தும் கொளல்.
Secure the man who reads others' minds
By giving him whatever the price is.
A ruler should at any cost secure the services of the
man who reads others' minds from their looks.

704   குறித்தது கூறாமைக் கொள்வாரோடு ஏனை
உறுப்புழார் அனையரால் வேறு.
Mind-readers differ from others mentally
Tho' in limbs they resemble closely.
Those who read others' minds without being revealed
resemble others physically but differ mentally.

705   குறிப்பின் குறிப்புணரா ஆயின் உறுப்பினுள்
என்ன பயத்தவோ கண்.
Of what use are the eyes among all organs
If they can't see and read others' minds?
The chief function of the eyes is to read the minds of
others by merely looking at their faces.

706 அடுத்தது காட்டும் பளிங்குபோல் நெஞ்சம்
கடுத்தது காட்டும் முகம்.
Face is the clear index of the mind
As crystal reflects things around.
As a crystal reflects things around it, the face shows
one's likes and dislikes.

707 முகத்தின் முதுக்குறைந்தது உண்டோ உவப்பினும்
காயினும் தான்முந் துறும்.
Is there anything more sensible than the face
To tell one's own joy or ire in advance?
There could be no better index than the face that
shows the joy or the anger of the mind.

708 முகம்நோக்கி நிற்க அமையும் அகம்நோக்கி
உற்றது உணர்வார்ப் பெறின்.
It's enough to stand and look at the face
Of those who can read others' thoughts.
For those endowed with the power of reading the mind,
it is enough if others stand before them.

709 பகைமையும் கேண்மையும் கண்ணுரைக்கும் கண்ணின்
வகைமை உணர்வார்ப் பெறின்.
Who can read the varying looks of others
Finds enmity or amity from their eyes.
One who can read the mind by looking at the eyes of
others can say whether they are foes or friends.

710 நுண்ணியம் என்பார் அளக்கும்கோல் காணும்கால்
கண்அல்லது இல்லை பிற.
The true measuring rod of discerning minds
Is none but the eye finding all subtleties.
Eye alone is the apt measuring rod of the wise who
can read others' minds.

72. அவை அறிதல்
KNOWING THE ASSEMBLY

711   அவையறிந்து ஆராய்ந்து சொல்லுக சொல்லின்
தொகையறிந்த தூய்மை யவர்.

Those with pure mind and studied eloquence
Should use words that suit the audience.

Men of clear mind and powerful speech should use
words that suit the audience.

712   இடைதெரிந்து நன்குஉணர்ந்து சொல்லுக சொல்லின்
நடைதெரிந்த நன்மை யவர்.

Men of eloquence judge and speak words
To suit the time and listeners' moods.

Good men with eloquence should use right words to
suit the time and the nature of the audience.

713   அவையறியார் சொல்லல்மேற் கொள்பவர் சொல்லின்
வகையறியார் வல்லதூஉம் இல்.

Who speak unmindful of the audience
Lack diction and eloquence.

Those who speak without minding the audience lack
choice of words and oratorical skill.

714   ஒளியார்முன் ஒள்ளியர் ஆதல் வெளியார்முன்
வான்சுதை வண்ணம் கொளல்.

Be brilliant ever before the bright
Before the dull, be chalk white.

An orator should be brilliant before the bright but act as
a stupid before the dull.

715   நன்றுஎன்ற வற்றுள்ளும் நன்றே முதுவருள்
முந்து கிளவாச் செறிவு.

Holding back before the wise
Is the best of all virtues.

Best of all virtues is modesty which controls one's
tongue before the wise.

716 ஆற்றின் நிலைதளர்ந் தற்றே வியன்புலம்
ஏற்றுஉணர்வார் முன்னர் இழுக்கு.

Blunder in speech in the assembly of the wise
Is like stumbling in virtue's ways.

Committing mistakes in speech in a learned assembly
is slipping from the path of virtue.

717 கற்றறிந்தார் கல்வி விளங்கும் கசடறச்
சொல்தெரிதல் வல்லார் அகத்து.

Erudition of scholars will surely shine bright
Before scholars who value words aright.

Greatness of scholars can be brought out only in an
assembly of the wise.

718 உணர்வது உடையார்முன் சொல்லல் வளர்வதன்
பாத்தியுள் நீர்சொரிந் தற்று.

Speaking before a receptive audience
Is like watering fertile crops.

Speaking to an attentive audience is like watering a
field of fertile crops.

719 புல்லவையுள் பொச்சாந்தும் சொல்லற்க நல்லவையுள்
நன்கு செலச்சொல்லு வார்.

Who speak good things well in a learned council
Speak not even forgetfully before the ignoble.

Those who speak persuasively before the wise should
never talk so to the mean even by a slip.

720 அங்கணத்துள் உக்க அமிழ்தற்றால் தம்கணத்தர்
அல்லார்முன் கோட்டி கொளல்.

Wasting words on men not of your calibre
Is like spilling divine nectar in the gutter.

Speech addressed to fools is like throwing divine
nectar in the sewer.

73. அவை அஞ்சாமை
NOT FEARING THE ASSEMBLY

721 வகைஅறிந்து வல்லவை வாய்சோரார் சொல்லின்
தொகைஅறிந்த தூய்மை யவர்.

Knowing the word power and the council's mood
Men of purity speak not anything absurd.

Pure-minded orators knowing the quality of audience
and the power of words never falter in their speech.

722 கற்றாருள் கற்றார் எனப்படுவர் கற்றார்முன்
கற்ற செலச்சொல்லு வார்.

Who binds the learned with lore acquired
Is a learned among the learned.

The orator who makes the learned spellbound with
his scholarship is a scholar among scholars.

723 பகையகத்துச் சாவார் எளியர் அரியர்
அவையகத்து அஞ்சா தவர்.

Many face death in the field of the enemy
But a few fearlessly face the assembly.

Many face the foes and die in the battlefield. But only
a few face the assembly with boldness.

724 கற்றார்முன் கற்ற செலச்சொல்லித் தாம்கற்ற
மிக்காருள் மிக்க கொளல்.

Impress the scholars with your learned lore
From greater scholars learn still more.

An orator should impress the scholars with his scholarship and learn more from greater scholars.

725 ஆற்றின் அளவுஅறிந்து கற்க அவைஅஞ்சா
மாற்றம் கொடுத்தல் பொருட்டு.

Learn grammar and logic diligently
To retort boldly in an assembly.

The orator should master oratorical skills essential to
counter the arguments of his foes bravely.

726 வாளொடுஎன் வன்கண்ணர் அல்லார்க்கு நூலொடுஎன்
நுண்ணவை அஞ்சு பவர்க்கு.
Of what use is a sword to one who is cowardly
Or lore to the learned fearing assembly?
To one who dreads an assembly, learning is as useless
as a sword in the hands of a coward.

727 பகையகத்துப் பேடிகை ஒள்வாள் அவையகத்து
அஞ்சு மவன்கற்ற நூல்.
Among the wise the lore of the tongue-tied
Is like a sword in the eunuch's hand.
The scholarship of those who fear speaking in an assembly
is as useless as a sword in the eunuch's hand.

728 பல்லவை கற்றும் பயம்இலரே நல்லவையுள்
நன்கு செலச்சொல்லா தார்.
Who speak not good things clearly in an assembly
Of the good, tho' learned are useless surely.
Those who cannot effectively speak good things in an
assembly are useless, however educated they are.

729 கல்லா தவரின் கடையென்ப கற்றுஅறிந்தும்
நல்லார் அவைஅஞ்சு வார்.
The scholar who dreads an august assembly
Is inferior to the ignorant certainly.
The learned man who fears to face an assembly of the
good is inferior even to the illiterates.

730 உள்ளெனினும் இல்லாரொடு ஒப்பர் களன்அஞ்சிக்
கற்ற செலச்சொல்லா தார்.
Who fear to tell the assembly their lore boldly
Though alive are equal to the dead really.
Those who fear the assembly and cannot express
convincingly resemble the dead.

74. நாடு
COUNTRY

731   தள்ளா விளையுளும் தக்காரும் தாழ்வுஇலாச்
செல்வரும் சேர்வது நாடு.
That alone is a country which has unfailing yields
Men of virtue and men of great riches.
An ideal country should possess farmers with unfailing
harvests, virtuous scholars and wealthy men.

732   பெரும்பொருளால் பெட்டக்க தாகி அருங்கேட்டால்
ஆற்ற விளைவது நாடு.
Vast alluring wealth, absence of calamity
And bountiful yield make a country.
Abundant wealth, absence of calamity and never-failing
harvests make a good country.

733   பொறைஒருங்கு மேல்வருங்கால் தாங்கி இறைவற்கு
இறைஒருங்கு நேர்வது நாடு.
Bearing burdens and paying taxes willingly
Are the hallmarks of an ideal country.
An ideal country is the one where people gladly bear all
burdens and pay all taxes.

734   உறுபசியும் ஓவாப் பிணியும் செறுபகையும்
சேராது இயல்வது நாடு.
Flourishes the country which is free
From hunger, plague and enmity.
A country which is free from excessive hunger,
epidemics and dreaded enemies prospers.

735   பல்குழுவும் பாழ்செய்யும் உட்பகையும் வேந்துஅழைக்கும்
கொல்குறும்பும் இல்லது நாடு.
Factions, internal strife and seditious chieftains —
A country should be free from these.
Absence of divisions, hidden enmity and troublesome
chieftains make an ideal country.

736 கேடுஅறியாக் கெட்ட இடத்தும் வளங்குன்றா
நாடுஎன்ப நாட்டின் தலை.
A land of lands knows not ruin by enemies
Even if ruined, riches won't freeze.
An ideal country will not be ruined by foes. Even if
ruined, it will remain prosperous forever.

737 இருபுனலும் வாய்ந்த மலையும் வருபுனலும்
வல்லரணும் நாட்டிற்கு உறுப்பு.
Twofold waters, fertile hills with rivers
And forts are a country's limbs.
Water from rain and springs, hills with rivers and strong
forts are the vital aspects of a good country.

738 பிணியின்மை செல்வம் விளைவுஇன்பம் ஏமம்
அணிஎன்ப நாட்டிற்குஇவ் வைந்து.
Health, wealth, yield, joy and defence
Are a country's five ornaments.
The five ornaments of a country are health, wealth,
crops, happiness and security.

739 நாடுஎன்ப நாடா வளத்தன நாடுஅல்ல
நாட வளம்தரும் நாடு.
A land that prospers even without hard labour
Is a country; not the one demanding labour.
An ideal country is the one that grows with its natural
resources without hard labour.

740 ஆங்குஅமைவு எய்தியக் கண்ணும் பயமின்றே
வேந்துஅமை வில்லாத நாடு.
If a land lacks love between king and subjects
All its blessings are worthless.
All the above gifts of a country are quite useless if there
is no harmony between the king and the subjects.

75. அரண்
FORT

741   ஆற்று பவர்க்கும் அரண்பொருள் அஞ்சித்தன்
போற்று பவர்க்கும் பொருள்.

**A fort is vital for those who launch attacks
And those who fear and seek defence.**

The fort is very important both for the aggressors and
the defenders alike.

742   மணிநீரும் மண்ணும் மலையும் அணிநிழல்
காடும் உடையது அரண்.

**Clear water, open land, mounts and forests
With cool shade form a good fortress.**

A good fort has clear water, vast area, mountains and
forests with cool shade.

743   உயர்வுஅகலம் திண்மை அருமைஇந் நான்கின்
அமைவுஅரண் என்றுஉரைக்கும் நூல்.

**A fort should be tall, wide, strong and secure
Science of war testifies to these four sure.**

A fort should have enough height, breadth, strength
and safety from enemies' reach.

744   சிறுகாப்பின் பேரிடத்த தாகி உறுபகை
ஊக்கம் அழிப்பது அரண்.

**A spacious fort with a small spot to be guarded
When besieged, baffles even foes bold.**

A fort with large space within and with a small area to
defend will demoralize even bold foes.

745   கொளற்குஅரிதாய்க் கொண்டகூழ்த் தாகி அகத்தார்
நிலைக்குஎளிதாம் நீரது அரண்.

**A good fort is one that is suited to those within
Well-provisioned and hard to win.**

A good fort is the one which is unconquerable, amply
provisioned and well-suited for its inmates to live in.

746 எல்லாப் பொருளும் உடைத்தாய் இடத்துஉதவும்
நல்ஆள் உடையது அரண்.
A fortress contains all provisions required
With heroes to defend in times of need.
A good fort should contain necessary provisions and
smart warriors to defend it in times of need.

747 முற்றியும் முற்றாது எறிந்தும் அறைப்படுத்தும்
பற்றற்கு அரியது அரண்.
Unconquerable by siege, assault
Or treachery is a good fort.
A good fort is the one which withstands blockade, direct
attack and treachery.

748 முற்றுஆற்றி முற்றி யவரையும் பற்றுஆற்றிப்
பற்றியார் வெல்வது அரண்.
A good fort defends itself and braves
The attacks of the besieging foes.
A fort should have the ability to defend itself and win
by defying the attacks of the enemies.

749 முனைமுகத்து மாற்றலர் சாய வினைமுகத்து
வீறுஎய்தி மாண்டது அரண்.
A fort gains glory by strategy of soldiers inside
For defeating foes outside in the battlefield.
A fort gains reputation by the planning of its soldiers
inside to destroy the enemies in the battlefield.

750 எனைமாட்சித்து ஆகியக் கண்ணும் வினைமாட்சி
இல்லார்கண் இல்லது அரண்.
A fortress is of no use, however grand
If it lacks men of action to defend.
Even a grand fort is useless if the forces are not able to
defend it.

76. பொருள் செயல்வகை
EARNING WEALTH

751 பொருள்அல் லவரைப் பொருளாகச் செய்யும்
பொருள்அல்லது இல்லை பொருள்.
There is nothing as good as money
That makes the worthless worthy.
There is nothing precious like wealth which converts
worthless men worthy.

752 இல்லாரை எல்லாரும் எள்ளுவர் செல்வரை
எல்லாரும் செய்வர் சிறப்பு.
The poor are despised by all
The rich are praised by all.
The poor are despised though they are worthy but the
rich are honoured by all though they are unworthy.

753 பொருளென்னும் பொய்யா விளக்கம் இருள்அறுக்கும்
எண்ணிய தேயத்துச் சென்று.
Wealth, the unfailing light, enters desired lands
And darkness of malice it dispels.
Wealth, the everlasting light, drives away enmity from
all lands.

754 அறன்ஈனும் இன்பமும் ஈனும் திறன்அறிந்து
தீதுஇன்றி வந்த பொருள்.
The wealth earned through means fair
Is a source of virtue and pleasure.
Wealth acquired through fair means brings virtue and
happiness.

755 அருளொடும் அன்பொடும் வாராப் பொருள்ஆக்கம்
புல்லார் புரள விடல்.
Wealth not earned with love and grace
Must be eschewed as evil at once.
One must give up the wealth earned without kindness
and goodness as evil.

756 உறுபொருளும் உல்கு பொருளும்தன் ஒன்னார்த்
தெறுபொருளும் வேந்தன் பொருள்.
Unclaimed wealth, tolls and tributes of foes
Constitute a king's revenues.
Unclaimed wealth, taxes and compensation for war
damages form a king's revenues.

757 அருள்என்னும் அன்புஈன் குழவி பொருள்என்னும்
செல்வச் செவிலியால் உண்டு.
The love-born baby called grace grows
With its foster mother called riches.
Wealth, the foster mother, nurses the child of love
called grace.

758 குன்றுஎறி யானைப்போர் கண்டற்றால் தன்கைத்தொன்று
உண்டாகச் செய்வான் வினை.
Doing a business with enough finance in hand
Is like watching a tusker-fight from a mound.
Doing a business with enough money in hand is as
safe as watching an elephant-fight from a hill.

759 செய்க பொருளைச் செறுநர் செருக்கறுக்கும்
எஃகுஅதனின் கூரியது இல்.
Gain wealth to destroy enemies' pride
No sharper steel is found.
One should earn wealth as there is no sharper
weapon than that to ruin the arrogance of foes.

760 ஒண்பொருள் காழ்ப்ப இயற்றியார்க்கு எண்பொருள்
ஏனை இரண்டும் ஒருங்கு.
Who gain vast wealth through fair means
Will gain both virtue and joy with ease.
Those who gather wealth through fair means will
gain both virtue and joy easily.

77. படைமாட்சி
GREATNESS OF AN ARMY

761 உறுப்புஅமைந்து ஊறுஅஞ்சா வெல்படை வேந்தன்
வெறுக்கையுள் எல்லாம் தலை.

An army well-organized, bold and conquering
Is the greatest wealth of a king.

A fearless, well-organized and successful army is the
most important wealth of a ruler.

762 உலைவுஇடத்து ஊறுஅஞ்சா வன்கண் தொலைவுஇடத்துத்
தொல்படைக்கு அல்லால் அரிது.

Forces with traditional might alone can fight
Braving the wounds in danger and defeat.

A traditional army alone can brave a mighty enemy
even ignoring the setbacks.

763 ஒலித்தக்கால் என்ஆம் உவரி எலிப்பகை
நாகம் உயிர்ப்பக் கெடும்.

A hostile pack of rats may make sea-like noises
But they vanish when a cobra hisses.

A pack of rats disappears before a hissing cobra.
Likewise, a weak army vanishes before a brave army.

764 அழிவுஇன்று அறைபோகாது ஆகி வழிவந்த
வன்க ணதுவே படை.

Only a force unmarred by defeat and treachery
With its inherited valour is an army.

A force unaffected by defeat and treachery with its
hereditary courage is an army.

765 கூற்றுஉடன்று மேல்வரினும் கூடி எதிர்நிற்கும்
ஆற்ற லதுவே படை.

That alone is the army with great strength
Which can together defy even Death.

That alone is a strong army which can jointly challenge
even Yama, the god of death.

766

மறம்மானம் மாண்ட வழிச்செலவு தேற்றம்
எனநான்கே ஏமம் படைக்கு.

Valour, honour, tradition and loyalty
Are the defence of an army.

Valour, honour, glorious tradition and loyalty are the
safeguards of a powerful army.

767

தார்தாங்கிச் செல்வது தானை தலைவந்த
போர்தாங்கும் தன்மை அறிந்து.

An able army marches ahead to root out the foes
Knowing already the enemy's strategies.

An able army finds the tactics of the enemies in
advance and proceeds to destroy them.

768

அடல்தகையும் ஆற்றலும் இல்எனினும் தானை
படைத்தகையால் பாடு பெறும்.

An army gains renown by its appearance
Though weak in defence and offence.

An army may be weak in defence and offence. But it
should impress by its big show and gain fame.

769

சிறுமையும் செல்லாத் துனியும் வறுமையும்
இல்லாயின் வெல்லும் படை.

An army will surely triumph when it is free
From desertion, aversion and penury.

An army will win when there are no desertions, incurable
hatred and poverty.

770

நிலைமக்கள் சால உடைத்துஎனினும் தானை
தலைமக்கள் இல்வழி இல்.

An army without great generals has no praise
'ïho' it has very many experienced soldiers.

Though the army has numerous able and experienced
soldiers, it is of no use without dynamic generals.

78. படைச் செருக்கு
MILITARY MIGHT

771   என்றுமுன் நில்லன்மின் தெவ்விர் பலர்என்று
முன்நின்று கல்நின் றவர்.

Dare not stand before my chief, O foes!
Those who dared, stand as *stones*.

The enemies who dared to oppose the chief have
become *hero-stones*.

772   கான முயல்எய்த அம்பினில் யானை
பிழைத்தவேல் ஏந்தல் இனிது.

Better hold a spear that missed a standing tusker
Than an arrow that killed a running hare.

It is sweeter to hold a spear that missed a motionless
elephant than an arrow that kiiled a running hare.

773   பேராண்மை என்ப தறுகண்ஒன்று உற்றக்கால்
ஊராண்மை மற்றுஅதன் எஃகு.

Great manliness is to fight the battle fiercely
Its edge is to help the fallen enemy.

The great manliness is to fight the battle with courage.
But it's better to show mercy to the humbled enemies.

774   கைவேல் களிற்றொடு போக்கி வருபவன்
மெய்வேல் பறியா நகும்.

Hero who hurls the spear at a war-elephant
Smiles and draws another from his chest.

The hero who throws the spear at an elephant smiles and
draws another from his chest.

775   விழித்தகண் வேல்கொண்டு எறிய அழித்துஇமைப்பின்
ஒட்டன்றோ வன்க ணவர்க்கு.

Even winking at the hurling of spears
Is a defeat to the heroes.

Even winking at the hurling of lances by enemies is
counted as defeat to the heroes.

---

* monuments in stones to commemorate dead warriors

776 விழுப்புண் படாதநாள் எல்லாம் வழுக்கினுள்
வைக்கும்தன் நாளை எடுத்து.
The valiant count as futile all their days
With no war wounds.
The warriors count their days without receiving
glorious war wounds as fruitless days.

777 சுழலும் இசைவேண்டி வேண்டா உயிரார்
கழல்யாப்புக் காரிகை நீர்த்து.
Who seek all-pervasive fame but not safety
Of their life wear heroic anklets for beauty.
Those who seek universal glory but not their safety
wear heroic anklets to add beauty.

778 உறின்உயிர் அஞ்சா மறவர் இறைவன்
செறினும்சீர் குன்றல் இலர்.
Heroes with daring spirit, despite king's ire
Shrink not in valour.
Even when the king disapproves, the soldiers who
are ready to die will remain undaunted.

779 இழைத்தது இகவாமைச் சாவாரை யாரே
பிழைத்தது ஒறுக்கிற் பவர்.
Who can find fault with those
Who die to fulfil their vows?
None blames those soldiers who pledge to win but
lose their lives.

780 புரந்தார்கண் நீர்மல்கச் சாகிற்பின் சாக்காடு
இரந்துகோள் தக்கது உடைத்து.
The death that causes tears of their king
Is worth seeking even by begging.
The death which invites the grief of the ruler is
most welcome to true soldiers.

79. நட்பு
FRIENDSHIP

781 செயற்குஅரிய யாவுள நட்பின் அதுபோல்
விணைக்குஅரிய யாவுள காப்பு.

**What is rarer than friendship indeed
That saves one from foe's deed?**

It is quite rare to get the friendship that guards a
person against all actions of enemies.

782 நிறைநீர நீரவர் கேண்மை பிறைமதிப்
பின்நீர பேதையார் நட்பு.

**Like waxing moon wise men's friendship grows
Like waning moon fools' friendship fades.**

Friendship of the wise grows like the waxing moon
but that of fools decreases like the waning moon.

783 நவில்தொறும் நூல்நயம் போலும் பயில்தொறும்
பண்புடை யாளர் தொடர்பு.

**Close amity of the noble brings more delight
As repeated reading brings more insight.**

As repeated reading brings better understanding,
friendship of the noble brings deeper delight.

784 நகுதல் பொருட்டன்று நட்டல் மிகுதிக்கண்
மேற்சென்று இடித்தல் பொருட்டு.

**True friendship is not for mere enjoyment
But to reprove faults of one's mate.**

Friendship is not meant for petty joy but to point out
a friend's faults when he goes astray.

785 புணர்ச்சி பழகுதல் வேண்டா உணர்ச்சிதான்
நட்புஆம் கிழமை தரும்.

**True friendship is not in constant meetings
But its rights are in mutual feelings.**

True friendship is not in frequent meetings. Mutual
feelings will yield the rights of friendship.

786 முகம்நக நட்பது நட்பன்று நெஞ்சத்து
அகம்நக நட்பது நட்பு.
Friendship lies not in smiling faces
From smiling hearts it flows.
True friendship is not a mere smile on the face but it
is something felt deep within the heart.

787 அழிவின் அவைநீக்கி ஆறுஉய்த்து அழிவின்கண்
அல்லல் உழப்பதாம் நட்பு.
Amity rescues from ruin, shows good paths
And shares pains in times of crisis.
Good friendship saves one from ruin, shows the right
paths and shares the distress.

788 உடுக்கை இழந்தவன் கைபோல ஆங்கே
இடுக்கண் களைவதுஆம் நட்பு.
Friendship hastens to save friends in distress
Like hands quickly restoring slipping dress.
Friendship is one which rescues the friends in distress
like one's own hands setting right the slipping dress.

789 நட்பிற்கு வீற்றிருக்கை யாதெனில் கொட்புஇன்றி
ஒல்லும்வாய் ஊன்றும் நிலை.
Friendship lies in unwavering ways
And helps in all possible times.
Friendship lies in consistency and provides support
on all possible occasions.

790 இனையர் இவர்எமக்கு இன்னம்யாம் என்று
புனையினும் புல்என்னும் நட்பு.
To boast 'He is beloved to me as I am to him'
Puts such friendship in low esteem.
It is only mean friendship which proclaims that the
friends are so close to each other.

80. நட்பாராய்தல்
CHOOSING FRIENDS

791 நாடாது நட்டலின் கேடுஇல்லை நட்டபின்
வீடுஇல்லை நட்பாள் பவர்க்கு.
Nothing is more ruinous than rash friendship
Once formed it can't be given up.
Nothing is worse than thoughtless friendship, for
once formed it cannot be abandoned.

792 ஆய்ந்துஆய்ந்து கொள்ளாதான் கேண்மை கடைமுறை
தான்சாம் துயரம் தரும்.
Friendship formed without repeated testing
Will surely bring in deadly suffering.
Untested friendship will certainly lead to grievous
pain and death.

793 குணனும் குடிமையும் குற்றமும் குன்றா
இனனும் அறிந்துயாக்க நட்பு.
One's nature, lineage, flaws and relations
Know them and make friends.
One's character, clan, defects and relatives must be
studied before befriending one.

794 குடிப்பிறந்து தன்கண் பழிநாணு வானைக்
கொடுத்தும் கொள்வேண்டும் நட்பு.
Secure men of noble birth who scorn vice
As good friends at any price.
One should pay any price to gain the friendship of
men of noble birth who despise disgrace.

795 அழச்சொல்லி அல்லது இடித்து வழக்குஅறிய
வல்லார்நட்பு ஆய்ந்து கொளல்.
Seek men who make you feel, reprove errors
And teach you the right ways.
One should seek worthy friends who point out one's
faults, indict and show the right path.

796 கேட்டினும் உண்டுஓர் உறுதி கிளைஞரை
நீட்டி அளப்பதோர் கோல்.
Even in ruin there is something good
It's a rod to measure a friend.
Even in misfortune there is something good, for it is
a yardstick to measure friends.

797 ஊதியம் என்பது ஒருவற்குப் பேதையார்
கேண்மை ஒரீஇ விடல்.
It's a gain for anyone to renounce
The friendship of idiots.
Getting rid of the friendship of fools is a gain to anyone
in the world.

798 உள்ளற்க உள்ளம் சிறுகுவ கொள்ளற்க
அல்லல்கண் ஆற்றறுப்பார் நட்பு.
Think not of deeds lessening your zeal
And amity of one quitting in peril.
One should not think of deeds curbing enthusiasm
and of one's friendship deserting in danger.

799 கெடுங்காலைக் கைவிடுவார் கேண்மை அடும்காலை
உள்ளினும் உள்ளம் சுடும்.
Even in death the thought of friends
Who deserted in peril rankles.
Friendship of those who deserted in distress pains
one's heart even at the time of one's death.

800 மருவுக மாசற்றார் கேண்மைஒன்று ஈத்தும்
ஒருவுக ஒப்பிலார் நட்பு.
Seek only the friendship of the blameless
Give something and give up the base.
One should seek the friendship of good people and
shake off the worthless at any cost.

81. பழைமை
LONG-STANDING INTIMACY

801 பழைமை எனப்படுவது யாதுஎனின் யாதும்
கிழமையைக் கீழ்ந்திடா நட்பு.
What is known as true intimacy
Is curbing not friend's liberty.
Intimacy is that which willingly submits to liberties
taken by old friends.

802 நட்பிற்கு உறுப்புக் கெழுதகைமை மற்றுஅதற்கு
உப்புஆதல் சான்றோர் கடன்.
Soul of old friendship is freedom of action
Accepting it is wise men's action.
The essence of old friendship is the freedom of action
which the great always cherish.

803 பழகிய நட்புஎவன் செய்யும் கெழுதகைமை
செய்தாங்கு அமையாக் கடை.
What is that intimacy if chums accept not acts
Done through liberty as their own acts?
Long-standing friendship is of no use if the friend's
freedom of action is not approved.

804 விழைதகையான் வேண்டி இருப்பர் கெழுதகையால்
கேளாது நட்டார் செயின்.
Even if friends do deeds unasked out of liberty
The wise would approve it lovingly.
The wise are not displeased even when their friends
do deeds without asking out of intimacy.

805 பேதைமை ஒன்றோ பெருங்கிழமை என்றுஉணர்க
நோதக்க நட்டார் செயின்.
Take the painful offence of friends easy
Either as folly or deep liberty.
A friend's painful offence should be ignored as it may
be due to either ignorance or deep liberty.

806 எல்லைக்கண் நின்றார் துறவார் தொலைவிடத்தும்
தொல்லைக்கண் நின்றார் தொடர்பு.
Who stand within bounds of true intimacy
Desert not even in adversity.
True friends will never abandon long-standing friends
even in adversity.

807 அழிவந்த செய்யினும் அன்புஅறார் அன்பின்
வழிவந்த கேண்மை யவர்.
True and old friends in steadfast love
Tho' harmed, won't cease to love.
True friends will not break their friendship even when
their friends do ruinous deeds.

808 கேள்இழுக்கம் கேளாக் கெழுதகைமை வல்லார்க்கு
நாள்இழுக்கம் நட்டார் செயின்.
A close friend won't listen to rumours vile
Even when hurt, he hails the day well.
An old friend won't mind the faults of his friends and
even when he gets hurt, he considers it a good day

809 கெடாஅ வழிவந்த கேண்மையார் கேண்மை
விடாஅர் விழையும் உலகு.
The whole world loves him who cherishes
The amity of old and loyal friends.
The world loves true friends who stick to long-standing
friendship.

810 விழையார் விழையப் படுப பழையார்கண்
பண்பின் தலைப்பிரியா தார்.
Even the foes will love noble friends
Who desert not old friends.
Even the enemies love those who do not desert their
old friends.

82. தீ நட்பு
BAD FRIENDSHIP

811 பருகுவார் போலினும் பண்புஇலார் கேண்மை
பெருகலின் குன்றல் இனிது.

Amity of the virtueless with feigned kindness
Had better wane than wax.

It is better for the friendship of people without genuine
love to shrink rather than shine.

812 உறின்நட்டு அறின்ஒருஉம் ஒப்பிலார் கேண்மை
பெறினும் இழப்பினும் என்.

To win or lose the amity of the unfit who dote
In gain and desert in want matters not.

It is quite useless to have friendship with the unworthy
who stay in gain and leave in loss.

813 உறுவது சீர்தூக்கும் நட்பும் பெறுவது
கொள்வாரும் கள்வரும் நேர்.

Selfish friends, whores who devour gains
And thieves are alike in their qualities.

Selfish friends, prostitutes who expect gains and thieves
are alike in their character.

814 அமரகத்து ஆற்றுஅறுக்கும் கல்லாமா அன்னார்
தமரின் தனிமை தலை.

Better be alone than be friendly with those
Who desert like an untrained war-horse.

It is better to have no friends than to have friends who,
in times of need, desert like an untrained war-horse.

815 செய்துஏமம் சாராச் சிறியவர் புன்கேண்மை
எய்தலின் எய்தாமை நன்று.

Better gain not than gain amity of the debased
Who got help but help not in times of need.

It is better to avoid bad friends who, though benefitted,
are of no help when needed.

816 பேதை பெருங்கெழீஇ நட்பின் அறிவுடையார்
ஏதின்மை கோடி உறும்.

Countless times wise men's enmity
Is better than fools' intimacy.

Enmity of the wise is far better than the intimate
friendship of fools.

817 நகைவகையர் ஆகிய நட்பின் பகைவரால்
பத்துஅடுத்த கோடி உறும்.

Hundred million times better is enmity of foes
Than the smile of feigning friends.

It is far better to have the enmity of foes than to have
the friendship of pretenders.

818 ஒல்லும் கருமம் உடற்று பவர்கேண்மை
சொல்ஆடார் சோர விடல்.

Quietly break the amity of those who spoil
And make the possible impossible.

One must silently discard the friendship of those who
make a possible task impossible.

819 கனவினும் இன்னாது மன்னோ வினைவேறு
சொல்வேறு பட்டார் தொடர்பு.

Amity of those whose words and deeds differ
Is even in dreams bitter.

The friendship of those whose words and deeds differ
gives pain even in dreams.

820 எனைத்தும் குறுகுதல் ஓம்பல் மனைக்கெழீஇ
மன்றில் பழிப்பார் தொடர்பு.

Avoid even the least amity of those who extol
In private but in public revile.

Friendship of those who act as friends in private but
curse in public must be totally avoided.

83. கூடா நட்பு
UNDESIRABLE FRIENDSHIP

821 சீர்இடம் காணின் எறிதற்குப் பட்டடை
நேரா நிரந்தவர் நட்பு.

Undesirable friendship is like an anvil
To strike at a place suitable.

Feigned friendship is like an anvil to destroy one at a
suitable place.

822 இனம்போன்று இனம்அல்லார் கேண்மை மகளிர்
மனம்போல வேறு படும்.

Friendship of those who pretend to be one's kin
Is fickle like the mind of a wanton woman.

False friendship is as unsteady as the mind of a
prostitute.

823 பலநல்ல கற்றக் கடைத்தும் மனம்நல்லர்
ஆகுதல் மாணார்க்கு அரிது.

In spite of reading numerous good books
It's rare for the foes to be good mates.

In spite of reading many good books the enemies
never become good friends.

824 முகத்தின் இனிய நகாஅ அகத்துழின்னா
வஞ்சரை அஞ்சப் படும்.

Fear cheats who smile sweeter in front
But are full of guile in their heart.

Friendship with cheats who smile outwardly but
conspire inwardly should be feared.

825 மனத்தின் அமையா தவரை எனைத்துஒன்றும்
சொல்லினால் தேறற்பாற்று அன்று.

Trust not in any matter words of those
Whose minds differ from yours.

One should not trust the words of those whose minds
are not identical.

826 நட்டார்போல் நல்லவை சொல்லினும் ஒட்டார்சொல்
ஒல்லை உணரப் படும்.
Though foes may utter good words like mates
Their evil mind will be realized at once.
Though the enemies utter friendly words, their evil
intention can soon be understood.

827 சொல்வணக்கம் ஒன்னார்கண் கொள்ளற்க வில்வணக்கம்
தீங்கு குறித்தமை யான்.
As bows bend to dart fatal arrows
Trust not humble words of foes.
One should not trust the humble words of the enemies
as they hurt like the arrows from bending bows.

828 தொழுதகை உள்ளும் படைஒடுங்கும் ஒன்னார்
அழுதகண் ணீரும் அனைத்து.
Folded hands of foes may conceal arms
Even their tears may hide evils.
Even the folded hands of the foes may conceal arms.
Likewise, their tears may have hidden dangers.

829 மிகச்செய்து தம்எள்ளு வாரை நகச்செய்து
நட்பினுள் சாப்புல்லல் பாற்று.
Feign laugh and love but break amity
Of those who extol but has enmity.
Friends who pretend to love but dislike must be
cajoled and crushed in friendly guise.

830 பகைநட்பாம் காலம் வருங்கால் முகம்நட்டு
அகம்நட்பு ஒரீஇ விடல்.
When time comes and foes seek intimacy
Feign love on face and snap amity.
When foes want to become friends, one may keep
a friendly face and give up their friendship.

84. பேதைமை
FOLLY

831 பேதைமை என்பதுஒன்று யாதெனின் ஏதம்கொண்டு
ஊதியம் போக விடல்.
Folly is clinging to what is harmful
And leaving what is fruitful.
Stupidity lies in opting for the evil and giving up what is
really good.

832 பேதைமையுள் எல்லாம் பேதைமை காதன்மை
கையல்ல தன்கண் செயல்.
Folly of follies is to love acts
Not fitting to one's status.
Folly of follies is to have the desire to do the deeds
unsuitable to one's position.

833 நாணாமை நாடாமை நார்இன்மை யாதொன்றும்
பேணாமை பேதை தொழில்.
Lack of shame, desire, love and regard
Are the marks of the stupid.
Shamelessness, desirelessness, lovelessness and
regardlessness are the qualities of a fool.

834 ஓதி உணர்ந்தும் பிறர்க்குஉரைத்தும் தான்அடங்காப்
பேதையின் பேதையார் இல்.
Fool of fools is the one who always learns
Realizes, teaches but never practises.
There is no greater fool than a man who learns, realizes
and preaches but never practises.

835 ஒருமைச் செயல்ஆற்றும் பேதை எழுமையும்
தான்புக்கு அழுந்தும் அளறு.
A fool in one birth can indulge in untold evil acts
That plunge him into hell thro' seven births.
In one birth a fool is capable of doing misdeeds which
will earn him hell through seven births.

836 பொய்படும் ஒன்றோ புனைபூணும் கையறியாப்
பேதை வினைமேல் கொளின்.

**A tactless fool who ventures into acts
Fails and finds himself in hand-cuffs.**

A fool undertaking a task without knowing how to act
not only fails but also ruins himself.

837 ஏதிலார் ஆரத் தமர்பசிப்பர் பேதை
பெருஞ்செல்வம் உற்றக் கடை.

**When fools accumulate wealth massive
Strangers prosper; relatives starve.**

When fools acquire wealth, strangers thrive but the fools'
relatives starve.

838 மையல் ஒருவன் களித்தற்றால் பேதைதன்
கையொன்று உடைமை பெறின்.

**When a fool happens to become wealthy
He will be like a lunatic drunk fully.**

A fool who becomes rich behaves like a mad man who is
fully drunk.

839 பெரிதுஇனிது பேதையார் கேண்மை பிரிவின்கண்
பீழை தருவதுஒன்று இல்.

**Very sweet is the fools' company
When parted there's no agony.**

The friendship of fools is very pleasant, since it brings
no regret on separation.

840 கழாஅக்கால் பள்ளியுள் வைத்தற்றால் சான்றோர்
குழாஅத்துப் பேதை புகல்.

**A fool arriving at the assembly of the perfect
Is like staining a clean bed with dirty feet.**

A fool's entry into a learned assembly is like putting
the unwashed feet on a clean bed.

85. புல்லறிவாண்மை
SILLY-MINDEDNESS

841   அறிவின்மை இன்மையுள் இன்மை பிறிதுஇன்மை
இன்மையா வையாது உலகு.

Lack of knowledge is the want of wants
Lack of the rest world never counts.

The worst of needs is lack of wisdom; the world does
not consider lack of others as wants.

842   அறிவிலான் நெஞ்சுஉவந்து ஈதல் பிறிதுயாதும்
இல்லை பெறுவான் தவம்.

If a fool makes a gift with a willing heart
It's by the penance of the recipient.

If a fool presents a gift willingly, it is only the result
of the receiver's penance.

843   அறிவிலார் தாம்தம்மைப் பீழிக்கும் பீழை
செறுவார்க்கும் செய்தல் அரிது.

Even enemies cannot inflict more miseries
Than what the fools inflict on themselves.

Even enemies cannot cause more troubles than what
the fools bring on themselves.

844   வெண்மை எனப்படுவது யாதுஎனின் ஒண்மை
உடையம்யாம் என்னும் செருக்கு.

What is utter folly is sin of pride
That boasts 'I am learned'.

Stupidity is nothing but arrogance which boasts of
one's own wisdom.

845   கல்லாத மேற்கொண்டு ஒழுகல் கசடுஅற
வல்லதூஉம் ஐயம் தரும்.

Pretence of learning what one hasn't learnt
Puts to doubt what one has really learnt.

A fool's pretence of knowledge makes one doubt
even what he has actually learnt.

846 அற்றம் மறைத்தலோ புல்லறிவு தம்வயின்
குற்றம் மறையா வழி.

It's foolish for one to cover one's nakedness
When one is not free from faults.

It is foolish for a person to cover his nakedness when
he is not able to guard himself against grave faults.

847 அருமறை சோரும் அறிவுஇலான் செய்யும்
பெருமிறை தானே தனக்கு.

A fool who cherishes not precious values
Brings on himself untold miseries.

A fool who neglects precious secrets brings all
miseries upon himself.

848 ஏவவும் செய்கலான் தான்தேறான் அவ்வுயிர்
போஓம் அளவும்ஓர் நோய்.

A fool who knows not and heeds not the wise
Is a plague until he dies.

A fool who neither knows nor listens to the words of the
wise suffers forever.

849 காணாதான் காட்டுவான் தான்காணான் காணாதான்
கண்டான்ஆம் தான்கண்ட வாறு.

As a fool sees only the ways of his mind
Whoever tries to guide him is stupid.

One who tries to educate a fool is a fool, for a fool
continues to see things in his own way.

850 உலகத்தார் உண்டுஎன்பது இல்என்பான் வையத்து
அலகையா வைக்கப் படும்.

Who deny what the world believes
Are, on earth, deemed as devils.

Those who reject what the whole world affirms are
considered demons on earth.

86. இகல்
DISCORDANCE

851 இகல்என்ப எல்லா உயிர்க்கும் பகல்என்னும்
பண்பின்மை பாரிக்கும் நோய்.
Hatred is a disease that breeds
Discord among all beings.
Hatred is a disease that spreads the evil of discord
among all beings.

852 பகல்கருதிப் பற்றா செயினும் இகல்கருதி
இன்னாசெய் யாமை தலை.
Tho' one does unkind deeds out of enmity
Doing evil is no good really.
Even though one does unpleasant things out of
hatred, it is good not to retaliate.

853 இகல்என்னும் எவ்வநோய் நீக்கின் தவல்இல்லாத்
தாவில் விளக்கம் தரும்.
Avoid the painful disease of discordance
And gain glory eternal and blameless.
He who discards the painful disease of hatred will
gain blameless and everlasting fame.

854 இன்பத்துள் இன்பம் பயக்கும் இகல்என்னும்
துன்பத்துள் துன்பம் கெடின்.
When malice, the misery of miseries, dies
Joy of all joys springs.
When the evil of hatred is destroyed, the greatest
delight will flourish.

855 இகல்எதிர் சாய்ந்துஒழுக வல்லாரை யாரே
மிகல்ஊக்கும் தன்மை யவர்.
Who would think of conquering him
Who possesses no hatred in him?
No one will think to overcome a person who is free
from all discordance.

856   இகலின் மிகல்இனிது என்பவன் வாழ்க்கை
             தவலும் கெடலும் நணித்து.

Life of one who thinks it's easy to succeed
By discord will fail and swiftly get ruined.

The life of one who considers it easy to win by hatred
will fail and quickly perish.

857   மிகல்மேவல் மெய்ப்பொருள் காணார் இகல்மேவல்
             இன்னா அறிவி னவர்.

A perverted genius longing for hostility
Will not see the truth causing victory.

A man with perverse knowledge and hatred for others
can never find truth leading to victory.

858   இகலிற்கு எதிர்சாய்தல் ஆக்கம் அதனை
             மிகல்ஊக்கின் ஊக்குமாம் கேடு.

Resisting hatred brings sure gain
Yielding to it brings ruin.

One who resists hatred will always gain; one who
yield to it will bring ruin on himself.

859   இகல்காணான் ஆக்கம் வருங்கால் அதனை
             மிகல்காணும் கேடு தரற்கு.

When fortune smiles, one gives up dissension
But fosters hostility to bring destruction.

When prosperity comes, one shuns hatred, but tries
to cherish discordance to bring about ruin.

860   இகலான்ஆம் இன்னாத எல்லாம் நகலான்ஆம்
             நல்நயம் என்னும் செருக்கு.

All sufferings spring only from animosity
Wealth of virtues flows from amity.

It is hatred that brings all evils and friendship brings
wealth of virtues.

87. பகைமாட்சி
MERITS OF ENMITY

861 வலியார்க்கு மாறுஎற்றல் ஓம்புக ஓம்பா
மெலியார்மேல் மேக பகை.
Avoid conflict with enemies more powerful
Cherish enmity with the less powerful.
One should not fight with a strong enemy but choose
the weaker one to fight.

862 அன்புஇலன் ஆன்ற துணைஇலன் தான்துவ்வான்
என்பரியும் ஏதிலான் துப்பு.
Can a loveless and powerless king sans allies
Crush stronger enemies?
An unkind, friendless and weak king can never over-
come his stronger enemies.

863 அஞ்சும் அறியான் அமைவுஇலன் ஈகலான்
தஞ்சம் எளியன் பகைக்கு.
Who is timid, ignorant, unsociable and miserly
Falls a prey to foes easily.
One who is shy, ignorant, unsociable and miserly
is easily defeated by one's enemies.

864 நீங்கான் வெகுளி நிறைஇலன் எஞ்ஞான்றும்
யாங்கணும் யார்க்கும் எளிது.
An angry and unrestrained man becomes a victim
To anyone, at any place and at any time.
One who is ill-tempered and uncontrolled can be
conquered by anybody, at any place and at any time.

865 வழிநோக்கான் வாய்ப்பன செய்யான் பழிநோக்கான்
பண்புஇலன் பற்றார்க்கு இனிது.
Who is erring, careless, shameless and virtueless
Is pleasant to his opponents.
One who is immoral, careless, shameless and
unrefined is an easy prey to his enemies.

866   காணாச் சினத்தான் கழிபெருங் காமத்தான்
பேணாமை பேணப் படும்.

**One with blind fury and inordinate lust
Becomes foes' easy target.**

A man blind with anger and excessive lust will be
easily overcome by his enemies.

867   கொடுத்தும் கொளல்வேண்டும் மன்ற அடுத்திருந்து
மாணாத செய்வான் பகை.

**Gain at any cost the enmity of one
Who acts friendly with treason.**

One should gain at any cost the enmity of a person
who pretends to be friendly but is disloyal.

868   குணன்இலனாய்க் குற்றம் பலஆயின் மாற்றார்க்கு
இனன்இலன்ஆம் ஏமாப்பு உடைத்து.

**Who has no virtues but a great many vices
Loses his allies and strengthens his foes.**

One who is without virtues but full of vices loses his
friends and strengthens the hands of his enemies.

869   செறுவார்க்குச் சேண்இகவா இன்பம் அறிவுஇலா
அஞ்சும் பகைவர்ப் பெறின்.

**The joy of the warriors is immense
When foes are only timid idiots.**

The joy of the warriors knows no bounds when their
enemies are fools and cowards.

870   கல்லான் வெகுளும் சிறுபொருள் எஞ்ஞான்றும்
ஒல்லானை ஒல்லாது ஒளி.

**Fame escapes the one who fails to fight
The foes who are ignorant.**

He who fails to fight the enemies who are unlearned will
never gain fame.

88. பகைத்திறம் தெரிதல்
ASSESSING THE POWER OF ENMITY

871   பகையென்னும் பண்பு இலதனை ஒருவன்
நகையேயும் வேண்டற்பாற்று அன்று.

It's not at all desirable to court
Ignoble enmity even in jest.

Enmity is an evil which should not be sought by anyone
even for fun.

872   வில்லேர் உழவர் பகைகொளினும் கொள்ளற்க
சொல்லேர் உழவர் பகை.

Even if you incur enmity of archers
Never earn enmity of orators.

A person may incur the enmity of warriors but never the
enmity of scholars.

873   ஏமுற் றவரினும் ஏழை தமியனாய்ப்
பல்லார் பகைகொள் பவன்.

Who incurs enmity of many when alone
Is worse than the insane.

One who incurs the enmity of many when alone is
more foolish than the mad.

874   பகைநட்பாக் கொண்டொழுகும் பண்புடை யாளன்
தகைமைக்கண் தங்கிற்று உலகு.

The world abides by the greatness of rulers
Who turn their foes into allies.

The world is secure under one whose love can turn even
one's enemies into friends.

875   தன்துணை இன்றால் பகைஇரண்டால் தான்ஒருவன்
இன்துணையாக் கொளகவற்றின் ஒன்று.

Helpless and alone when faced with two foes
Make one a close ally with ease.

If helpless and alone while facing two enemies, a person
should secure one of them to his side.

876 தேறினும் தேறா விடினும் அழிவின்கண்
தேறான் பகாஅன் விடல்.
Whether tested or untested is an enemy
Keep him not far nor near in adversity.
An enemy, whether tested or not, should be kept
neither close nor far in times of distress.

877 நோவற்க நொந்தது அறியார்க்கு மேவற்க
மென்மை பகைவர் அகத்து.
Reveal not to friends who know not your woes
Nor your weaknesses to foes.
One should not reveal one's woes to the unconcerned
friends nor weaknesses to the enemies.

878 வகையறிந்து தற்செய்து தற்காப்ப மாயும்
பகைவர்கண் பட்ட செருக்கு.
If one knows ways, fortifies and himself protects,
Vanity of foes will surely collapse.
The pride of enemies will fall if one strengthens and
defends himself with proper know-how.

879 இளைதுஆக முள்மரம் கொல்க களையுநர்
கைகொல்லும் காழ்த்த இடத்து.
While young and tender, destroy thorny trees
Grown hard, they hurt the cutter's hands.
A thorny tree is easy to cut when it is tender but it
injures the cutter's hands when it is well-grown.

880 உயிர்ப்ப உளர்அல்லர் மன்ற செயிர்ப்பவர்
செம்மல் சிதைக்கலா தார்.
Who fail to crush the pride of their foes
Will die at the breath of foes.
Those who fail to destroy the pride of their enemies
will surely face death from them.

89. உட்பகை
HIDDEN ENMITY

881 நிழல்நீரும் இன்னாத இன்னா தமர்நீரும்
இன்னாஆம் இன்னா செயின்.

Shade and water are bad if they breed diseases
Likewise, bad are relatives doing evils.

Shade and water are not good if they cause diseases.
Likewise, relatives doing harm are bad.

882 வாள்போல் பகைவரை அஞ்சற்க அஞ்சுக
கேள்போல் பகைவர் தொடர்பு.

Fear not the open foes like swords drawn
But fear amity of foes acting like kin.

One need not fear open enemies but one has to fear
enemies who pretend to be friends.

883 உட்பகை அஞ்சித்தற் காக்க உலைவுஇடத்து
மண்பகையின் மாணத் தெறும்.

Fear secret enmity and protect yourself, if not
When weak, like potter's knife it'll cut.

A person should guard himself against the hidden
enmity. Otherwise, it will cut him like a potter's knife.

884 மனம்மாணா உட்பகை தோன்றின் இனம்மாணா
ஏதம் பலவும் தரும்.

Unrepenting hidden enmity breeds evils
And keeps away one's relatives.

Hidden enmity will breed evils and even separate the
relatives.

885 உறல்முறையான் உட்பகை தோன்றின் இறல்முறையான்
ஏதம் பலவும் தரும்.

If there is hidden enmity among kin
Fatal faults will lead to ruin.

Hidden enmity among kinsmen will cause many
fatal faults resulting in destruction.

886 ஒன்றாமை ஒன்றியார் கண்படின் எஞ்ஞான்றும்
பொன்றாமை ஒன்றல் அரிது.
When enmity arises within kin
It is hard to escape ruin.
When serious differences arise within relatives, there
is no way to avoid destruction.

887 செப்பின் புணர்ச்சிபோல் கூடினும் கூடாதே
உட்பகை உற்ற குடி.
A family with hidden enmity seems united
But its union is like a jar and its lid.
Where there is an inner discord in the family, the
apparent unity will be like the lid on a jar.

888 அரம்பொருத பொன்போலத் தேயும் உரம்பொருது
உட்பகை உற்ற குடி.
A house with internal enmity fades
As iron, when filed, crumbles.
The strength of a family with internal hostility will wear
away like iron crumbling when it is filed.

889 எட்பக வன்ன சிறுமைத்தே ஆயினும்
உட்பகை உள்ளதாங் கேடு.
Utter destruction lies in internal enmity
Though small like a split sesame.
Though hidden enmity is small like a split sesame,
it will lead the house to total ruin.

890 உடம்பாடு இலாதவர் வாழ்க்கை குடங்கருள்
பாம்போடு உடன்உறைந் தற்று.
Living with a partner who has inward hate
Is like living with a snake in a hut.
Domestic life of persons in disagreement is like a life
of one living with a snake in a hut.

90. பெரியாரைப் பிழையாமை
NOT OFFENDING THE GREAT

891 ஆற்றுவார் ஆற்றல் இகழாமை போற்றுவார்
போற்றலுள் எல்லாம் தலை.
Not offending the might of the mighty is
The chief defence of all defences.
Not offending the might of the mighty is the chief
defence against all evils.

892 பெரியாரைப் பேணாது ஒழுகின் பெரியாரால்
பேரா இடும்பை தரும்.
Lack of reverence for the noble ones
Brings one endless sufferings.
Disrespect to the great will surely lead one to
lifelong miseries.

893 கெடல்வேண்டின் கேளாது செய்க அடல்வேண்டின்
ஆற்று பவர்கண் இழுக்கு.
Not consulting the great is to court ruin
Insulting the mighty is to get slain.
He who never consults the wise and ever insults the
mighty always courts ruin.

894 கூற்றத்தைக் கையால் விளித்தற்றால் ஆற்றுவார்க்கு
ஆற்றாதார் இன்னா செயல்.
Evil by the feeble done to the mighty men
Is like beckoning Death on their own.
The weak challenging the mighty is like inviting the
god of death and ruin.

895 யாண்டுச்சென்று யாண்டும் உளராகார் வெம்துப்பின்
வேந்து செறப்பட் டவர்.
They cannot flee and survive anywhere
If they incur the ruler's ire.
A person who incurs the wrath of a mighty ruler will
not survive wherever he goes.

896   எரியால் சுடப்படினும் உய்வுஉண்டாம் உய்யார்
       பெரியார்ப் பிழைத்துஒழுகு வார்.
One may even survive the burns of fire
But surely not the great men's ire.
One may escape even from fire-burns but certainly
not from the anger of the great.

897   வகைமாண்ட வாழ்க்கையும் வான்பொருளும் என்னாம்
       தகைமாண்ட தக்கார் செறின்.
What's the use of good life and vast riches
If one incurs the ire of the saintly ones?
If a person incurs the wrath of great men, he cannot
protect his glorious life and splendid wealth.

898   குன்றுஅன்னார் குன்ற மதிப்பின் குடியொடு
       நின்றன்னார் மாய்வர் நிலத்து.
Even the proven wealthy will perish with family
If cursed by the mountain-like mighty.
Even the wealthy will be totally ruined if they incur the
curse of powerful ascetics.

899   ஏந்திய கொள்கையார் சீறின் இடைமுறிந்து
       வேந்தனும் வேந்து கெடும்.
If men of lofty ideals become angry
The king perishes with his country.
If men of noble ideals become angry, the king loses
his state and gets ruined.

900   இறந்துஅமைந்த சார்புடையர் ஆயினும் உய்யார்
       சிறந்துஅமைந்த சீரார் செறின்.
Even great kings endowed with mighty aides
Won't survive the ire of sages.
Even mighty kings with vast army and sufficient aides
will perish if they incur the wrath of the sages.

91. பெண்வழிச் சேறல்
BEING HENPECKED

901 மனைவிழைவார் மாண்பயன் எய்தார் வினைவிழைவார்
வேண்டாப் பொருளும் அது.
Craving for wife brings no greater gain
Such a craze dutiful men disdain.
As surrendering to wife can never bring greatness,
dutiful men avoid it.

902 பேணாது பெண்விழைவான் ஆக்கம் பெரியோர்
நாணாக நாணுத் தரும்.
Wealth of one doting on wife neglecting duty
Is an utter shame and brings ignominy.
The wealth of a man infatuated with his wife unmind-
ful of his duties will bring shame and disgrace.

903 இல்லாள்கண் தாழ்ந்த இயல்புஇன்மை எஞ்ஞான்றும்
நல்லாருள் நாணுத் தரும்.
A man who is servile and henpecked
Is among the good ever disgraced.
A person who submits to his wife will always be put
to shame in the midst of the virtuous.

904 மனையாளை அஞ்சும் மறுமையி லாளன்
வினையாண்மை வீறெய்தல் இன்று.
A henpecked man who gains no heavenly bliss
Never gains glory even through manly acts.
A henpecked husband who gains no heavenly bliss
will not achieve glory even through his manly deeds.

905 இல்லாளை அஞ்சுவான் அஞ்சும்மற்று எஞ்ஞான்றும்
நல்லார்க்கு நல்ல செயல்.
Who fears his wife will always dread
To do good to the good.
He who fears his wife will always be afraid of doing
good deeds to the virtuous.

906 இமையாரின் வாழினும் பாடிலரே இல்லாள்
அமைஆர்தோள் அஞ்சு பவர்.
Who fear the bamboo-like arms of their wives
Are mean though they live like the gods.
No one will respect those who fear the tender shoulders
of their wives, though they live like gods.

907 பெண்ஏவல் செய்துஒழுகும் ஆண்மையின் நாணுடைப்
பெண்ணே பெருமை உடைத்து.
The modest womanhood is much more dignified
Than manliness of a henpecked husband.
The modest womanhood is more honoured than the
manliness of a henpecked husband.

908 நட்டார் குறைமுடியார் நன்றுஆற்றார் நன்னுதலாள்
பெட்டாங்கு ஒழுகு பவர்.
Who blindly obey the wishes of their wives
Won't help friends and do good deeds.
Men who submit to their wives cannot help their friends
and do anything good.

909 அறவினையும் ஆன்ற பொருளும் பிறவினையும்
பெண்ஏவல் செய்வார்கண் இல்.
Virtuous acts, wealth and other deeds
Are not seen in henpecked husbands.
Men who submit to their wives' instigation will gain no
virtue, wealth and joyful deeds.

910 எண்சேர்ந்த நெஞ்சத் திடனுடையார்க்கு எஞ்ஞான்றும்
பெண்சேர்ந்துஆம் பேதைமை இல்.
Those of thoughtful and strong minds
Are never foolish to dote on wives.
Men with a thoughtful and strong mind will be free from
the folly of submitting to their wives.

92. வரைவின் மகளிர்
WANTON WOMEN

911 அன்பின் விழையார் பொருள்விழையும் ஆய்தொடியார்
இன்சொல் இழுக்குத் தரும்.
Disgrace follows sweet words of bangled belles
Who talk not for love but for riches.
The sweet words of whores with their eyes only on
wealth and not on love will ruin men.

912 பயன்தூக்கிப் பண்புடைரைக்கும் பண்பின் மகளிர்
நயன்தூக்கி நள்ளா விடல்.
Analyse and shun a wanton woman who weighs
Only gains and speaks sweet words.
One should avoid an ill-natured woman who feigns love
only for her selfish gain.

913 பொருட்பெண்டிர் பொய்ம்மை முயக்கம் இருட்டுஅறையில்
ஏதில் பிணம்தழீஇ யற்று.
The false embrace of the greedy harlot's frame
Is like hugging a corpse in a dark room.
Embracing a greedy whore is like hugging a corpse in a
dark room.

914 பொருட்பொருளார் புன்நலம் தோயார் அருட்பொருள்
ஆயும் அறிவி னவர்.
The wise who seek the wealth of grace
Seek not mean joy of greedy harlots.
Men of wisdom who seek the wealth of grace will never
seek the mean joy of the prostitutes.

915 பொதுநலத்தார் புன்நலம் தோயார் மதிநலத்தின்
மாண்ட அறிவி னவர்.
Men of wits and wisdom never embrace
The mean greedy harlots.
Men of wits with true wisdom will never crave for the
mean charms of whores.

916   தம்நலம் பாரிப்பார் தோயார் தகைசெருக்கிப்
   புன்நலம் பாரிப்பார் தோள்.

Who protect their honour touch not the arms
Of whores who sell their mean charms.

Men who safeguard their honour shun the charms of
worthless whores.

917   நிறைநெஞ்சம் இல்லவர் தோய்வர் பிறநெஞ்சின்
   பேணிப் புணர்பவர் தோள்.

Men without perfect mind alone embrace
Women with minds on something else.

Men without virtue alone will seek the embrace of
whores who think of something else.

918   ஆயும் அறிவினர் அல்லார்க்கு அணங்குஎன்ப
   மாய மகளிர் முயக்கு.

A whore's embrace of men without subtle mind
Is a fatal touch of a ruinous maid.

To the fools the embrace of a whore is a fatal touch
of a ruinous maid.

919   வரைவுஇலா மாணிழையார் மென்தோள் புரையிலாப்
   பூரியர்கள் ஆழும் அளறு.

The well-decked soft shoulders of the whores
Are a deep hell for the degraded minds.

The elegant and tender shoulders of the prostitutes are
a hell for mean-minded people.

920   இருமனப் பெண்டிரும் கள்ளும் கவறும்
   திருநீக்கப் பட்டார் தொடர்பு.

The double-minded damsels, liquor and dice
Are chums of men whom wealth deserts.

Wanton women, wine and gambling are the friends of
those abandoned by fortune.

93. கள்ளுண்ணாமை
ABSTAINING FROM LIQUOR

921   உட்கப் படாஅர் ஒளியிழப்பர் எஞ்ஞான்றும்
கள்காதல் கொண்டொழுகு வார்.

Liquor addicts are not feared by foes
And light of glory they ever lose.

Men addicted to drink will never be feared by their
enemies and they never gain fame.

922   உண்ணற்க கள்ளை உணில்உண்க சான்றோரான்
எண்ணப் படவேண்டா தார்.

Drink not liquor at all ; let them drink
Who care not what the wise think.

One should not drink liquor; only those who never care
for the regards of great men may drink liquor.

923   ஈன்றாள் முகத்தேயும் இன்னாதால் என்மற்றுச்
சான்றோர் முகத்துக் களி.

A drunken son's joy pains even his mother
How will it be on men of honour?

Even the mother is hurt to see her drunken son; it is
all the more painful to the wise.

924   நாண்என்னும் நல்லாள் புறங்கொடுக்கும் கள்என்னும்
பேணாப் பெருங்குற்றத் தார்க்கு.

Modesty, the fair maiden, turns away her face
From those guilty of great sin of drunkenness.

The virtuous maid of modesty turns her face away from
those addicted to the sin of drunkenness.

925   கையறி யாமை உடைத்தே பொருள்கொடுத்து
மெய்அறி யாமை கொளல்.

Rank ignorance alone pays money
To seek drunken insensibility.

Utter ignorance alone urges one to pay money for
liquor and get insensibility in return.

926 துஞ்சினார் செத்தாரின் வேறுஅல்லர் எஞ்ஞான்றும்
நஞ்சுஉண்பார் கள்உண பவர்.

The sleeping are no different from the dead ones
The drunkards are like poison eaters.

Those who sleep do not differ from the dead. The
drunkards are always like poison takers.

927 உள்ஒற்றி உள்ளூர் நகப்படுவர் எஞ்ஞான்றும்
கள்ஒற்றிக் கண்சாய் பவர்.

When the secret drunkards lose their senses
Truth is known and laughed at by locals.

Those who drink secretly have no secrets and become
the butt of ridicule.

928 களித்துஅறியேன் என்பது கைவிடுக நெஞ்சத்து
ஒளித்ததூஉம் ஆங்கே மிகும்.

Never say, 'Liquor I have ever tasted not.'
When drunk, comes out the secret.

A drunkard should not pretend that he does not get
drunk. The secret will be out when he is drunk.

929 களித்தானைக் காரணம் காட்டுதல் கீழ்நீர்க்
குளித்தானைத் தீத்துரீஇ யற்று.

Coaxing a drunkard to become sane is similar
To seeking with a lamp one sunk in water.

Convincing a drunkard of the evils of drinking is like
searching with a lamp for a man drowned in water.

930 கள்உண்ணாப் போழ்தில் களித்தானைக் காணும்கால்
உள்ளான்கொல் உண்டதன் சோர்வு.

In sobriety, if a drinker sees a drinker's fate
Won't he see ills of his drunken state?

When not drunk, if a drunkard sees another in a drunken
state, he learns the evil effects of his own drinking.

94. சூது
GAMBLING

931   வேண்டற்க வென்றிடினும் சூதினை வென்றதூஉம்
தூண்டில்பொன் மீன்விழுங்கி யற்று.

Gambling should be avoided though one can win
Its gains are like a baited hook a fish gulped in.

One should avoid gambling for gains. Its gains are
like a baited hook swallowed by a fish.

932   ஒன்றுஎய்தி நூறுஇழக்கும் சூதர்க்கும் உண்டாம்கொல்
நன்றுஎய்தி வாழ்வதோர் ஆறு.

Can gamblers have a life rich and good
By gaining one and losing a hundred?

Gamblers who gain one and lose a hundred can never
dream of a prosperous life.

933   உருள்ஆயம் ஓவாது கூறின் பொருளாயம்
போஒய்ப் புறமே படும்.

If one bets on the rolling dice always
Wealth and gains will go to foes.

The wealth and income of one who endlessly indulges in
gambling will go into the hands of one's enemies.

934   சிறுமை பலசெய்து சீர்அழிக்கும் சூதின்
வறுமை தருவதுஒன்று இல்.

Nothing else brings poverty like the dice game
Which causes misery and ruins fame.

Nothing brings poverty like gambling that causes
misery and spoils one's fame.

935   கவறும் கழகமும் கையும் தருக்கி
இவறியார் இல்லாகி யார்.

Men clinging to dice, dicing hall and skill
Will become poor though placed well.

Men who take pleasure in gambling will soon be
reduced to poverty though they may be rich.

936 அகடுஆரர் அல்லல் உழப்பர்ஃகுது என்னும்
முகடியால் மூடப்பட் டார்.
One ensnared by Misfortune called gambling
Faces hunger and suffering.
One, seized by the goddess of misfortune called
gambling, suffers the torments of hunger and misery.

937 பழகிய செல்வமும் பண்பும் கெடுக்கும்
கழகத்துக் காலை புகின்.
If one wastes precious time at a gambling den
Inherited riches and virtue come to ruin.
Inherited wealth and goodness will be wiped out if
one wastes time in a gambling house.

938 பொருள்கெடுத்துப் பொய்மேல் கொளீஇ அருள்கெடுத்து
அல்லல் உழப்பிக்கும் சூது.
Gambling ruins one's fortune, breeds lies,
Spoils grace and causes miseries.
Gambling ruins one's wealth, leads to falsehood,
spoils grace and brings in utter miseries.

939 உடைசெல்வம் ஊண்ஒளி கல்விஎன்று ஐந்தும்
அடையாவாம் ஆயம் கொளின்.
Clothing, fortune, food, fame and learning —
These five desert the one gambling.
Clothing, wealth, food, glory and education depart
from a man who indulges in gambling.

940 இழத்தொறூஉம் காதலிக்கும் சூதேபோல் துன்பம்
உழத்தொறூஉம் காதற்று உயிர்.
As love for gambling grows with each defeat
Love for life grows with every torment.
At every loss, craving for gambling increases. Likewise,
the love for life grows as sufferings grow.

95. மருந்து
MEDICINE

941 மிகினும் குறையினும் நோய்செய்யும் நூலோர்
வளிமுதலா எண்ணிய மூன்று.

**Gas, bile and phlegm less or excess
Lead to diseases, say experts.**

Experts say that excess or deficiency of the three
humours, i.e. gas, bile and phlegm, causes diseases.

942 மருந்துஎன வேண்டாவாம் யாக்கைக்கு அருந்தியது
அற்றது போற்றி உணின்.

**If man eats after digesting what he has taken
The body surely needs no medicine.**

No medicine is needed if man eats only after digesting
what he has already taken.

943 அற்றால் அளவுஅறிந்து உண்க அஃதுடம்பு
பெற்றான் நெடிதுஉயிக்கும் ஆறு.

**Eating with moderation after digestion
Is a way to live for long duration.**

Eating moderately after digestion is a sure way of
attaining longevity.

944 அற்றது அறிந்து கடைப்பிடித்து மாறுஅல்ல
துய்க்க துவரப் பசித்து.

**Choose always agreeable food and eat it
After digestion with keen appetite.**

One should eat what is agreeable to the system with
proper appetite after digestion.

945 மாறுபாடு இல்லாத உண்டி மறுத்துஉண்ணின்
ஊறுபாடு இல்லை உயிர்க்கு.

**No disease will ever afflict the life of those
Who moderately eat agreeable meals.**

Agreeable food in moderation ensures the absence
of diseases in our life.

946 இழிவுஅறிந்து உண்பான்கண் இன்பம்போல் நிற்கும்
கழிபே ரிரையான்கண் நோய்.

As joy stays with the moderate eater
Sickness stays with the overeater.

Moderate eating ensures good health; likewise,
overeating breeds diseases.

947 தீயளவு அன்றித் தெரியான் பெரிதுஉண்ணின்
நோயளவு இன்றிப் படும்.

Eating beyond one's hunger limits
Results in countless ailments.

Eating food beyond the limit of one's digestion leads
to all kinds of ailments.

948 நோய்நாடி நோய்முதல் நாடி அதுதணிக்கும்
வாய்நாடி வாய்ப்பச் செயல்.

Examine disease, cause and means of cure
And then resort to remedial measure.

Physicians should diagnose the disease, find out
the cause and its remedy before treatment.

949 உற்றான் அளவும் பிணிஅளவும் காலமும்
கற்றான் கருதிச் செயல்.

A doctor must note the sick man's state,
Sickness and time, and then treat.

A doctor should study the patient's condition, nature of
sickness and time before treatment.

950 உற்றவன் தீர்ப்பான் மருந்துஉழைச் செல்வான்என்று
அப்பால்நாற் கூற்றே மருந்து.

The patient, healer, remedy and nurse
Are four parts of medical science.

The patient, physician, medicine and nurse are the
four aspects of medical science.

96. குடிமை
NOBLE BIRTH

951

இற்பிறந்தார் கண்அல்லது இல்லை இயல்பாகச்
செப்பமும் நாணும் ஒருங்கு.

Impartiality combined with fear of sin
Is natural only to the noble-born.

The principles of honesty in word and deed and a sense
of shame are natural only to the noble-born.

952

ஒழுக்கமும் வாய்மையும் நாணும்இம் மூன்றும்
இழுக்கார் குடிப்பிறந் தார்.

Right conduct, truthfulness and modesty —
The noble won't part with these three.

The noble-born never deviate from the path of good
conduct, truthfulness and a sense of shame.

953

நகைஈகை இன்சொல் இகழாமை நான்கும்
வகையென்ப வாய்மைக் குடிக்கு.

Smile, charity, pleasant words and civility —
These four are marks of true nobility.

Cheerful face, generous heart, sweet words and
courtesy are the four signs of true nobility.

954

அடுக்கிய கோடி பெறினும் குடிப்பிறந்தார்
குன்றுவ செய்தல் இலர்.

Men of noble birth shun evil deeds
Even if they gain many millions.

Men of noble birth will never stoop to mean acts even
if they are given immense wealth.

955

வழங்குவது உள்வீழ்ந்தக் கண்ணும் பழங்குடி
பண்பில் தலைப்பிரிதல் இன்று.

Though by charity their wealth becomes less
Noble families forsake not their traits.

Though their sources of charity diminish, noble
families will continue to be charitable.

956 சலம்பற்றிச் சால்புஇல செய்யார்மாசு அற்ற
குலம்பற்றி வாழ்தும்என் பார்.
Who live in conformity with spotless tradition
Never do unfitting deeds of deception.
Those who live up to the traditions of their family will
never stoop to ignoble deeds of deceit.

957 குடிப்பிறந்தார் கண்விளங்கும் குற்றம் விசும்பின்
மதிக்கண் மறுப்போல் உயர்ந்து.
Faults of the noble-born are prominently seen
Just like the spots on the moon.
The faults of the noble are exposed as clearly as the
dark spots on the moon.

958 நலத்தின்கண் நார்இன்மை தோன்றின் அவனைக்
குலத்தின்கண் ஐயப் படும்.
Ancestry of one's breed is suspected
If lack of love is seen by the world.
If one is found lacking in love for others, one's very
noble birth will be doubted.

959 நிலத்தில் கிடந்தமை கால்காட்டும் காட்டும்
குலத்தில் பிறந்தார்வாய்ச் சொல்.
As the nature of the soil is seen from sprouts
Nature of birth is seen from one's talks.
As sprouts indicate the nature of the soil, speech
reveals the nature of one's birth.

960 நலம்வேண்டின் நாண்உடைமை வேண்டும் குலம்வேண்டின்
வேண்டுக யார்க்கும் பணிவு.
Who desire goodness must have modesty
Who desire nobility must have humility.
One's goodness springs from the sense of shame and
one's family's honour comes out of humility.

97. மானம்
HONOUR

961 இன்றி அமையாச் சிறப்பின ஆயினும்
   குன்ற வருப விடல்.

Avoid deeds degrading family honour, how far
Indispensably vital they are.

One should avoid mean acts that degrade the family
honour, even if they are inevitable.

962 சீரினும் சீர்அல்ல செய்யாரே சீரொடு
   பேராண்மை வேண்டு பவர்.

Who yearn for great honour and manliness
Won't do, even for fame, mean acts.

Those who desire honour and majesty will not do
mean deeds even for the sake of fame.

963 பெருக்கத்து வேண்டும் பணிதல் சிறிய
   சுருக்கத்து வேண்டும் உயர்வு.

Practise utmost humility in prosperity
Uphold due dignity in adversity.

One should be humble in prosperity and maintain
honour in poverty.

964 தலையின் இழிந்த மயிர்அனையர் மாந்தர்
   நிலையின் இழிந்தக் கடை.

Men are like the hair fallen from the crown
When from eminence they fall down.

Men of noble family, if fallen from their high position,
are like the hair fallen from the head.

965 குன்றின் ·அனையாரும் குன்றுவர் குன்றுவ
   குன்றி அனைய செயின்.

Great men of hill-like status will surely be debased
Tho' their flaws are as small as a _kunri_ seed.

The great will sink to nothing if they commit even the
smallest fault.

966 புகழ்இன்றால் புத்தேள்நாட்டு உய்யாதால் என்மற்று
இகழ்வார்பின் சென்று நிலை.

Why follow those who always scorn
As it leads not to glory or heaven.

Men of high birth need not go after those who despise
them, for it brings them no fame or heaven.

967 ஒட்டார்பின் சென்றுஒருவன் வாழ்தலின் அந்நிலையே
கெட்டான் எனப்படுதல் நன்று.

It is far better to die in starvation
Than serve those who scorn.

It is much better for a man to die than to serve those
who scorn him.

968 மருந்தோமற்று ஊன்ஓம்பும் வாழ்க்கை பெருந்தகைமை
பீடழிய வந்த இடத்து.

Is nourishing one's body an antidote·to death
After losing glory of one's noble birth?

Life which is saved at the cost of honour is not a cure
to immortality.

969 மயிர்நீப்பின் வாழாக் கவரிமா அன்னார்
உயிர்நீப்பர் மானம் வரின்.

Men, like a deer that lives not at the loss of hair
Give up life to retain their honour.

As a deer kills itself at the loss of its hair, the noble
will die to uphold their honour.

970 இளிவரின் வாழாத மானம் உடையார்
ஒளிதொழுது ஏத்தும் உலகு.

The world will bow and admire the glory
Of men who prefer death to infamy.

The world will admire the glory of men who would prefer
to die when they face dishonour.

98. பெருமை
GREATNESS

971 ஒளிஒருவற்கு உள்ள வெறுக்கை இளிஒருவற்கு
அஃதுஇறந்து வாழ்தும் எனல்.
Glory is doing with mental fervour
Disgrace is a life sans ardour.
Greatness lies in doing things with zeal. To live without
ardent desire for good is ignoble.

972 பிறப்புஒக்கும் எல்லா உயிர்க்கும் சிறப்புஒவ்வா
செய்தொழில் வேற்றுமை யான்.
Tho' human beings in their birth are the same
By diverse trade their worth isn't the same.
All are equal by birth. But the worth of each person
depends on his trade.

973 மேல்இருந்தும் மேல்அல்லார் மேல்அல்லர் கீழ்இருந்தும்
கீழ்அல்லார் கீழ்அல் லவர்.
Tho' highly placed, the low never become great
Tho' placed low, the great won't fall in state.
Even when lifted high, the low will never be great; the
great, though placed low, will never become mean.

974 ஒருமை மகளிரே போலப் பெருமையும்
தன்னைத்தான் கொண்டொழுகின் உண்டு.
Greatness, like single-minded women's purity
Abides in one guarded by integrity.
Like chastity in women, greatness is found in one
who is true to oneself.

975 பெருமை உடையவர் ஆற்றுவார் ஆற்றின்
அருமை உடைய செயல்.
Men of greatness do rare deeds
In proper and perfect ways.
Great men are capable of performing rare deeds in a
proper and perfect manner.

976 சிறியார் உணர்ச்சியுள் இல்லை பெரியாரைப்
பேணிக்கொள் வேம்என்னும் நோக்கு.
In the minds of the mean enters not the thought
To seek and revere the great.
The petty-minded have no respect for the great and
avoid seeking their company.

977 இறப்பே புரிந்த தொழிற்றாம் சிறப்பும்தான்
சீரல் லவர்கண் படின்.
If the mean-minded attain greatness
Deeds of vanity breed in excess.
If unworthy men gain power and wealth, they will
soon resort to insolent deeds.

978 பணியுமாம் என்றும் பெருமை சிறுமை
அணியுமாம் தன்னை வியந்து.
Greatness always bows with humility
Meanness prides itself in vanity.
Great minds are always humble but the petty-minded
take pride in their deeds.

979 பெருமை பெருமிதம் இன்மை சிறுமை
பெருமிதம் ஊர்ந்து விடல்.
Greatness is free from vanity
Pettiness rides on vanity.
Greatness is free from pride. Meanness is marked
with pride.

980 அற்றம் மறைக்கும் பெருமை சிறுமைதான்
குற்றமே கூறி விடும்.
Greatness ignores others' shortcomings
Pettiness exposes only their flaws.
Greatness never minds the faults of others but
pettiness exposes them clearly.

99. சான்றாண்மை
PERFECTNESS

981 கடன்என்ப நல்லவை எல்லாம் கடன்அறிந்து
சான்றாண்மை மேற்கொள் பவர்க்கு.
All good deeds are indeed natural to the great
Who are duty-conscious and perfect.
All good deeds stay in those who are duty-conscious
and perfect.

982 குணநலம் சான்றோர் நலனே பிறநலம்
எந்நலத்து உள்ளதூஉம் அன்று.
Goodness of heart is the virtue of the great
All else are not at all great.
Good character is the virtue of the great. All other
qualities are not so great.

983 அன்புநாண் ஒப்புரவு கண்ணோட்டம் வாய்மையொடு
ஐந்துசால்பு ஊன்றிய தூண்.
Love, modesty, charity, mercy and truthfulness
Are five supporting pillars of perfectness.
Love, modesty, benevolence, mercy and truthfulness
are the five pillars of perfectness.

984 கொல்லா நலத்தது நோன்மை பிறர்தீமை
சொல்லா நலத்தது சால்பு.
Penance is indeed a virtue of not slaughtering
Perfectness is a virtue of not backbiting.
Penance is a virtue arising from non-killing and
perfectness lies in not speaking ill of others.

985 ஆற்றுவார் ஆற்றல் பணிதல் அதுசான்றோர்
மாற்றாரை மாற்றும் படை.
Humility alone is the might of the mighty
It's a weapon to transform enmity.
Humility is the strength of the mighty and it is the
weapon to demolish one's enmity.

986

சால்பிற்குக் கட்டளை யாதெனில் தோல்வி
துலையல்லார் கண்ணும் கொளல்.

The touchstone to test one's excellence
Is to accept defeat from his inferiors.

The touchstone of one's perfection is to acknowledge
defeat even at the hands of his inferiors.

987

இன்னாசெய் தார்க்கும் இனியவே செய்யாக்கால்
என்ன பயத்ததோ சால்பு.

Of what avail is the perfection of character
If it fails to do good even to an evil-doer?

Nobility is of no value if it does not do pleasing deeds
even to those who have caused pain.

988

இன்மை ஒருவற்கு இளிவுஅன்று சால்புஎன்னும்
திண்மைஉண் டாகப் பெறின்.

Penury is not at all a disgrace
If one is firm in perfectness.

Poverty is not at all a disgrace to one who possesses
perfection of character.

989

ஊழி பெயரினும் தாம்பெயரார் சான்றாண்மைக்கு
ஆழி எனப்படு வார்.

Though seas may overflow shores around
Men of goodness cross not the bound.

Men who are called the ocean of perfect goodness
will never change, even at the time of deluge.

990

சான்றவர் சான்றாண்மை குன்றின் இருநிலம்தான்
தாங்காது மன்னோ பொறை.

The vast world will not sustain its own burden
If the perfect shrink in perfection.

If the great fall from their noble nature, even this huge
earth cannot bear its burden.

100. பண்புடைமை
COURTESY

991   எண்பதத்தால் எய்தல் எளிதுஎன்ப யார்மாட்டும்
பண்புடைமை என்னும் வழக்கு.
One can gain virtue called courtesy
If one is accessible easily.
Accessibility to all is the easy way to gain the virtue
called courtesy.

992   அன்புடைமை ஆன்ற குடிப்பிறத்தல் இவ்விரண்டும்
பண்புடைமை என்னும் வழக்கு.
Love and high-born dignity
Are two ways of courtesy.
Love for all and noble tradition are the two ways of
courtesy in one's life.

993   உறுப்புஒத்தல் மக்கள்ஒப்பு அன்றால் வெறுத்தக்க
பண்புஒத்தல் ஒப்பதாம் ஒப்பு.
To be a human is not mere bodily resemblance
Likeness in courtesy is real semblance.
To be a human is not merely a matter of physical
resemblance. It is found only in courtesy.

994   நயனொடு நன்றி புரிந்த பயன்உடையார்
பண்புபா ராட்டும் உலகு.
All the world will commend the excellence
Of men who serve all with justice and grace.
The world will praise the excellence of men whose
service results in justice and charity.

995   நகையுள்ளும் இன்னாது இகழ்ச்சி பகையுள்ளும்
பண்புஉள பாடுஅறிவார் மாட்டு.
Even in jest, words of contempt hurt
Even to foes, the kind are polite.
Even in jest, mockery is painful; hence the courteous
will not hurt even their enemies.

996 பண்புடையார்ப் பட்டுஉண்டு உலகம் அதுஇன்றேல்
மண்புக்கு மாய்வது மன்.

The world goes on because of courteous men
Else, it'll bury itself in dust and ruin.

The world subsists only because of courteous men.
Otherwise, it will perish.

997 அரம்போலும் கூர்மைய ரேனும் மரம்போல்வர்
மக்கட்பண்பு இல்லா தவர்.

The discourteous tho' sharp as files
Are similar to the trees.

Those without manners, though sharp like files, are
just like trees.

998 நண்புஆற்றா ராகி நயம்இல செய்வார்க்கும்
பண்புஆற்றார் ஆதல் கடை.

Discourtesy even to the hostile and the wicked
Is utterly bad indeed.

It is a disgrace to be discourteous even to those who
are unfriendly and harmful.

999 நகல்வல்லர் அல்லார்க்கு மாயிரு ஞாலம்
பகலும்பாற் பட்டன்று இருள்.

To those who are unfriendly and cannot rejoice
Even in daylight earth is buried in darkness.

The wide world is in darkness even by daytime to
those who do not lovingly mix with others.

1000 பண்புஇலான் பெற்ற பெருஞ்செல்வம் நன்பால்
கலம்தீமை யால்திரிந் தற்று.

The immense wealth of the discourteous is futile
Like the milk gone sour in an unclean vessel.

The great wealth of discourteous men is useless like
the pure milk spoilt in an unclean vessel.

101. நன்றியில் செல்வம்
FUTILE WEALTH

1001 வைத்தான்வாய் சான்ற பெரும்பொருள் அஃதுஉண்ணான்
செத்தான் செயக்கிடந்தது இல்.
Who hoards vast wealth and keeps it unused
Is deemed dead as his wealth is wasted.
One who hoards wealth but never uses it, is as good as
a dead man.

1002 பொருளான்ஆம் எல்லாம்என்று ஈயாது இவறும்
மருளான்ஆம் மாணாப் பிறப்பு.
An ignorant miser who thinks he gains all by wealth
And shares it not has only ignoble birth.
The miser who thinks that wealth is all and hoards
it without giving it to anyone is of mean birth only.

1003 ஈட்டம் இவறி இசைவேண்டா ஆடவர்
தோற்றம் நிலக்குப் பொறை.
Birth of one who craves not for fame but wealth
Is indeed a burden to the earth.
A man bent on earning wealth but not a worthy name
is a burden to the earth.

1004 எச்சம்என்று என்எண்ணும் கொல்லோ ஒருவரால்
நச்சப் படாஉ தவன்.
What can one ever think of leaving behind
If one is not loved by mankind?
One who is not loved by anyone cannot think of leaving
any legacy behind.

1005 கொடுப்பதூஉம் துய்ப்பதூஉம் இல்லார்க்கு அடுக்கிய
கோடிஉண் டாயினும் இல்.
What is the use of countless millions earned
If it is not shared and enjoyed?
It is of no use to store immense wealth, if one neither
gives nor enjoys it.

1006   ஏதம் பெருஞ்செல்வம் தான்துவ்வான் தக்கார்க்குஒன்று
         ஈதல் இயல்பிலா தான்.
         If one denies the needy nor enjoys,
         To his wealth, he is a disease.
         He who neither gives his wealth to those in want nor
         himself enjoys it is a curse to it.

1007   அற்றார்க்குஒன்று ஆற்றாதான் செல்வம் மிகநலம்
         பெற்றாள் தமியள்மூத் தற்று.
         One's vast wealth not used for the poverty-stricken
         Is like a fair spinster growing old and shrunken.
         The wealth of a man who gives nothing to the needy is
         like an unmarried pretty woman growing old.

1008   நச்சப் படாதவன் செல்வம் நடுஊருள்
         நச்சு மரம்பழுத் தற்று.
         The wealth of a stingy man not loved by anyone
         Is like a poison tree bearing fruit in mid-town.
         The wealth of a man who is not liked by others is like
         a poison-tree bearing fruit in the middle of a town.

1009   அன்புஒறீஇத் தன்செற்று அறம்நோக்காது ஈட்டிய
         ஒண்பொருள் கொள்வார் பிறர்.
         Others will easily take away the shining riches
         Gained without love, comfort and morals.
         The wealth accumulated without love, comfort and
         scruples will be taken away by others.

1010   சீருடைச் செல்வர் சிறுதுனி மாரி
         வறம்கூர்ந் தனையது உடைத்து.
         The short-lived poverty of the glorious rich
         Is like brief dryness of clouds very much.
         The short-lived poverty of the honourable rich is like the
         benevolent clouds becoming dry.

102. நாணுடைமை
SENSE OF SHAME

1011 கருமத்தால் நாணுதல் நாணுத் திருநுதல்
நல்லவர் நாணுப் பிற.

Sense of shame is the fear of evil action
The rest belong only to women.

Sense of shame is the fear of unworthy deeds. Other
forms of shame are found only in women.

1012 ஊணுடை எச்சம் உயிர்க்குஎல்லாம் வேறுஅல்ல
நாண்உடைமை மாந்தர் சிறப்பு.

Food, dress and the rest are common to all men
Sense of shame is peculiar to good men.

Food, clothing and other needs are common to all men
but modesty is the pride of good men.

1013 ஊனைக் குறித்த உயிரெல்லாம் நாண்என்னும்
நன்மை குறித்தது சால்பு.

All beings abide in their own physical body
Perfection is in goodness of modesty.

All lives dwell in the body. Likewise, perfection dwells
in modesty.

1014 அணிஅன்றோ நாண்உடைமை சான்றோர்க்கு அஃதுஇன்றேல்
பிணிஅன்றோ பீடு நடை.

Isn't modesty an ornament to the perfect?
Without it stately gait is an ailment.

Modesty is the jewel of the noble. Without it, their
majestic gait is only a disease.

1015 பிறர்பழியும் தம்பழியும் நாணுவார் நாணுக்கு
உறைபதி என்னும் உலகு.

Who dreads others' faults as his own faults
Is an abode where modesty rests.

He who feels ashamed of others' faults as his own
is an embodiment of modesty.

1016 நாண்வேலி கொள்ளாது மன்னோ வியன்ஞாலம்
பேணலர் மேலா யவர்.

The noble without choosing modesty as a shield
Never long to live in the wide world.

The great will never long for the worldly life without having
modesty as a shield.

1017 நாணால் உயிரைத் துறப்பர் உயிர்ப்பொருட்டால்
நாண்துறவார் நாண்ஆள் பவர்.

The modest give up their life for shame
To save life they won't lose shame.

The great would give up their life for the sense of
shame but not modesty for the sake of life.

1018 பிறர்நாணத் தக்கது தான்நாணான் ஆயின்
அறம்நாணத் தக்கது உடைத்து.

Virtue forsakes one who feels no shame
For what others feel as shame.

Virtue abandons the man who shamelessly does what
others are ashamed of doing.

1019 குலம்சுடும் கொள்கை பிழைப்பின் நலம்சுடும்
நாணின்மை நின்றக் கடை.

Lack of good principles burns one's race
Lack of shame burns all goodness.

Misconduct injures one's clan; shamelessness
destroys all good deeds.

1020 நாண்அகத்து இல்லார் இயக்கம் மரப்பாவை
நாணால் உயிர்மருட்டி யற்று.

Movements of those without modesty in the heart
Are like the life-like acts of a stringed puppet.

Movements of those without a sense of shame are like
the movements of the puppets controlled by strings.

103. குடிசெயல் வகை
PROMOTING FAMILY WELFARE

1021 கருமம் செயஒருவன் கைதூரவேன் என்னும்
பெருமையின் பீடுஉடையது இல்.
Nothing is indeed more dignified than saying
'I'll dutifully raise my family's well-being.'
Nothing is greater than one's tireless efforts to uplift
one's own family.

1022 ஆள்வினையும் ஆன்ற அறிவும் எனஇரண்டின்
நீள்வினையால் நீளும் குடி.
One's lineage grows by one's ceaseless acts
Based on effort and profound genius.
Untiring effort and ripe wisdom are the two basic needs
to promote one's family.

1023 குடிசெய்வல் என்னும் ஒருவற்குத் தெய்வம்
மடிதற்றுத் தான்முந் துறும்.
God fastens His robes and rushes to help him
Who strives to exalt his home.
Even God would rush to help a man who works hard to
elevate his family.

1024 சூழாமல் தானே முடிவுஎய்தும் தம்குடியைத்
தாழாது உஞற்று பவர்க்கு.
Who strains ceaselessly to elevate his family
Gains success spontaneously.
One who labours for the betterment of the family will
succeed in one's efforts naturally.

1025 குற்றம் இலனாய்க் குடிசெய்து வாழ்வானைச்
சுற்றமாச் சுற்றும் உலகு.
The world revolves around him who leads really
A blameless life and elevates his family.
People seek the relationship of a man who raises the
glory of his family righteously.

1026 நல்ஆண்மை என்பது ஒருவற்குத் தான்பிறந்த
இல்ஆண்மை ஆக்கிக் கொளல்.
**True manliness is to elevate one's family
And make oneself a leader worthy.**
True manliness is the ability to raise the honour of
the family in which one was born.

1027 அமர்அகத்து வன்கண்ணர் போலத் தமர்அகத்தும்
ஆற்றுவார் மேற்றே பொறை.
**Just as the brunt of the battle falls on the valiant
Family's burden rests on the competent.**
The burden of the battle falls on the brave. Likewise,
the burden of the family falls on the able member.

1028 குடிசெய்வார்க்கு இல்லை பருவம் மடிசெய்து
மானம் கருதக் கெடும்.
**There is no season to elevate one's family
As sloth and pride bring disgrace surely.**
There is no time or season to promote one's family as
laziness and false prestige will bring disgrace.

1029 இடும்பைக்கே கொள்கலம் கொல்லோ குடும்பத்தைக்
குற்றம் மறைப்பான் உடம்பு.
**If a man protects his family from flaws
Will his body be a cup of miseries?**
The body of one who protects the family from troubles
will never feel the burden.

1030 இடுக்கண்கால் கொன்றிட வீழும் அடுத்தூன்றும்
நல்ஆள் இலாத குடி.
**A tree of family without great men as props
Falls when the axe of misery cuts.**
A family will face misfortune and also disintegrate
without good men to support it.

209

104. உழவு
FARMING

1031   சுழன்றும்ஏர்ப் பின்னது உலகம் அதனால்
உழந்தும் உழவே தலை.
Though laborious, farming is the best
All trades in the world rely on it.
Though laborious, farming is an excellent industry, for
all the people in the world depend on it for food.

1032   உழுவார் உலகத்தார்க்கு ஆணிஅஃது ஆற்றாது
எழுவாரை எல்லாம் பொறுத்து.
Farmers are the linchpin of the whole world
As they feed even those not in the field.
The farmers are the linchpin of the society, as they
support all those who practise other professions.

1033   உழுதுஉண்டு வாழ்வாரே வாழ்வார்மற்று எல்லாம்
தொழுதுஉண்டு பின்செல் பவர்.
Who live by ploughing and eating alone live
The rest bow and follow others to live.
Only the farmers who plough the field and eat live; the
rest depend on others for their sustenance.

1034   பலகுடை நீழலும் தம்குடைக்கீழ்க் காண்பர்
அலகுஉடை நீழ லவர்.
Benign farmers of bounteous crops bring
All states under their king.
Prosperous and kind-hearted farmers will bring all
other states under the control of their own king.

1035   இரவார் இரப்பார்க்குஒன்று ஈவர் கரவாது
கைசெய்துஊண் மாலை யவர்.
Tillers who work with their hands
Beg not but give the seekers.
Tillers who eat by manual labour never beg but only
give alms to those who seek.

1036   உழவினார் கைம்மடங்கின் இல்லை விழைவதூஉம்
விட்டேம்என் பார்க்கும் நிலை.
**If tillers plough not and slacken their hands
There's no life even for the ascetic ones.**
If farmers remain without doing any cultivation,
even the ascetics will suffer.

1037   தொடிப்புழுதி கஃசா உணக்கின் பிடித்துஎருவும்
வேண்டாது சாலப் படும்.
**If the ploughed soil is fully dried up to a quarter
Good crops follow, sans handful of manure.**
Ploughing and drying the fields sufficiently will yield
plentifully even without manuring.

1038   ஏரினும் நன்றால் எருஇடுதல் கட்டபின்
நீரினும் நன்றுஅதன் காப்பு.
**Manuring is more rewarding than mere ploughing
After weeding, guarding is better than watering.**
Manuring is more gainful than ploughing. After weeding,
guarding is more vital than watering.

1039   செல்லான் கிழவன் இருப்பின் நிலம்புலந்து
இல்லாளின் ஊடி விடும்.
**If the landowner stays away from his fields
They'll sulk like a neglected spouse.**
If the landowner fails to visit his fields, they will sulk
like a neglected wife and yield nothing.

1040   இலம்என்று அசைஇ இருப்பாரைக் காணின்
நிலம்என்னும் நல்லாள் நகும்.
**The earth, the good maiden, will laugh surely
If idlers are idle on the plea of penury.**
The maiden earth will laugh to herself when she finds
the lazy sitting idle pleading poverty.

105. நல்குரவு
POVERTY

1041 இன்மையின் இன்னாதது யாதுஎனின் இன்மையின்
இன்மையே இன்னா தது.
What else is more painful than poverty?
Poverty alone is as painful as poverty.
Poverty alone is the most painful and no other suffering
is so miserable as poverty.

1042 இன்மை எனஒரு பாவி மறுமையும்
இம்மையும் இன்றி வரும்.
Poverty, the matchless sinner, brings no delight
In this life and in the life next.
Poverty is the sinner who destroys the joys of this
life and those of the next world.

1043 தொல்வரவும் தோலும் கெடுக்கும் தொகையாக
நல்குரவு என்னும் நசை.
Craving called poverty ruins totally
Ancestral pride along with glory.
The state of poverty will totally destroy the honour and
glory of an ancestry.

1044 இற்பிறந்தார் கண்ணேயும் இன்மை இளிவந்த
சொற்பிறக்கும் சோர்வு தரும்.
Penury drives even the high-born to laziness
That leads to speak words of meanness.
Poverty will force even men of high-birth to the moral
weakness of speaking mean words.

1045 நல்குரவு என்னும் இடும்பையுள் பல்குரைத்
துன்பங்கள் சென்று படும்.
The pain of woes called poverty brings
A trail of endless miseries.
The pain of poverty brings in its course many kinds of
sufferings.

1046   நற்பொருள் நன்குஉணர்ந்து சொல்லினும் நல்கூர்ந்தார்
சொற்பொருள் சோர்வு படும்.

The words of the poor are often ignored
Even tho' deep truth is clearly uttered.

Although sound in thought, the words of the poor will
go unheeded.

1047   அறம்சாரா நல்குரவு ஈன்றதா யானும்
பிறன்போல நோக்கப் படும்.

Even a mother despises her son as a stranger
If his poverty is devoid of good behaviour.

Even a mother treats her son as a stranger if his
poverty is not related with virtue.

1048   இன்றும் வருவது கொல்லோ நெருநலும்
கொன்றது போலும் நிரப்பு.

Will the fatal penury of yesterday
Torment me even today?

People in utter penury always fear whether there will be
no end to their poverty.

1049   நெருப்பினுள் துஞ்சலும் ஆகும் நிரப்பினுள்
யாதுஒன்றும் கண்பாடு அரிது.

One may even sleep on a fiery bed
But not in penury indeed.

One may sleep even in the midst of fire but not in the
midst of poverty.

1050   துப்புரவு இல்லார் துவரத் துறவாமை
உப்பிற்கும் காடிக்கும் கூற்று.

The destitute · who renounce not completely
Are death to others' salt and soup really.

The poor who do not renounce the world completely
depend on their neighbours for food.

106. இரவு
BEGGING

1051 இரக்க இரத்தக்கார்க் காணின் கரப்பின்
அவர்பழி தம்பழி அன்று.
Beg from the worthy; if they refuse
Fault is theirs and not yours.
One may beg from the worthy. If they refuse, they alone
are to be blamed.

1052 இன்பம் ஒருவற்கு இரத்தல் இரந்தவை
துன்பம் உறாஅ வரின்.
Even begging is a joy if what is sought
Is got without discomfort.
If one gets alms without suffering, even begging will
become a delight.

1053 கரப்புஇலா நெஞ்சின் கடன்அறிவார் முன்நின்று
இரப்பும்ஓர் ஏஎர் உடைத்து.
There is grace in begging from the generous
Who always remain duty-conscious.
There is beauty in begging, if one begs from those who
are liberal and duty-conscious.

1054 இரத்தலும் ஈதலே போலும் கரத்தல்
கனவிலும் தேற்றாதார் மாட்டு.
Begging from men who deny not even in dreams
Is as good as giving alms.
Begging is as good as giving alms when one begs
from those who never deny alms even in dreams.

1055 கரப்பிலார் வையகத்து உண்மையால் கண்ணின்று
இரப்பவர் மேற்கொள் வது.
The world has liberal men who never deny charity
So the needy stand before them for mercy.
As there are men who never refuse alms, the poor resort
to begging.

1056   கரப்புஇடும்பை இல்லாரைக் காணின் நிரப்புஇடும்பை
எல்லாம் ஒருங்கு கெடும்.

All the pangs of penury will soon wither away
Before the generous who never deny.

At the sight of the generous who never deny charity,
all the evils of poverty will vanish.

1057   இகழ்ந்துஉள்ளாது ஈவாரைக் காணின் மகிழ்ந்துஉள்ளம்
உள்ளுள் உவப்ப துடைத்து.

When the generous donate with no contempt
The beggar's heart is filled with delight.

The heart of a beggar rejoices, when he meets men
who give alms without contempt.

1058   இரப்பாரை இல்லாயின் ஈர்ங்கண்மா ஞாலம்
மரப்பாவை சென்றுவந் தற்று.

Happenings of grand cool world sans beggars
Are like movements in puppet-shows.

Without beggars the vast world will only resemble a
puppet show.

1059   ஈவார்கண் என்உண்டாம் தோற்றம் இரந்துகோள்
மேவார் இலாஅக் கடை.

What would be the glory of givers
If at all there were no beggars?

If there are no beggars, there will be no glory at all to
the givers.

1060   இரப்பான் வெகுளாமை வேண்டும் நிரப்புஇடும்பை
தானேயும் சாலும் கரி.

A beggar should not frown when not given
His own want is a proof of misfortune.

A beggar should not get angry when not given, for his
own poverty serves as an evidence.

107. இரவச்சம்
FEAR OF BEGGING

1061   கரவாது உவந்துஈயும் கண்ணன்னார் கண்ணும்
        இரவாமை கோடி யுறும்.

Not begging even from the most generous ones
Who gladly give is worth ten million times.

Not begging even from the most generous ones who
give lovingly without refusing is worth ten million times.

1062   இரந்தும் உயிர்வாழ்தல் வேண்டின் பரந்து
        கெடுக உலகுஇயற்றி யான்.

Let the Creator of the world roam and rot
If living by begging is someone's lot.

If the Creator of the world intends begging as human
fate, He Himself should wander and perish.

1063   இன்மை இடும்பை இரந்துதீர் வாம்என்னும்
        வன்மையின் வன்பாட்டது இல்.

Nothing is harder than giving up effort saying
'We seek to abolish penury by begging'.

Nothing is harder to understand than remaining
effortless saying that they can end poverty by begging.

1064   இடம்எல்லாம் கொள்ளாத் தகைத்தே இடம்இல்லாக்
        காலும் இரவுஒல்லாச் சால்பு.

Even the world is too small before the perfect
Who beg not even in their want.

Even the whole world is too small before the great
who never beg even in poverty.

1065   தெள்நீர் அடுபுற்கை ஆயினும் தாள்தந்தது
        உண்ணலின் ஊங்குஇனியது இல்.

Nothing is sweeter than watery gruel
If obtained by one's own toil.

Even watery gruel obtained by one's own sustained
effort is sweeter than anything else.

1066   ஆவிற்கு நீர்என்று இரப்பினும் நாவிற்கு
       இரவின் இளிவந்தது இல்.
       Nothing is so shameful to the tongue as begging
       For water even for a cow dying.
       It will be very disgraceful to the tongue even to beg
       water for feeding a cow.

1067   இரப்பன் இரப்பாரை எல்லாம் இரப்பின்
       கரப்பார் இரவன்மின் என்று.
       If at all they have to beg, I beseech those begging
       'Not to beg from those who hide everything.'
       If at all one has to beg, one should not beg from the
       unwilling misers.

1068   இரவுஎன்னும் ஏமாப்புஇல் தோணி கரவுஎன்னும்
       பார்தாக்கப் பக்கு விடும்.
       The unsafe raft called begging smashes
       When on the rock of refusal it dashes.
       The unsafe raft of begging will break if it strikes the
       rock of denial.

1069   இரவுஉள்ள உள்ளம் உருகும் கரவுஉள்ள
       உள்ளதூஉம் இன்றிக் கெடும்.
       The thought of begging melts the heart,
       The thought of denial breaks it apart.
       Mere thought of begging melts one's heart but the
       thought of refusal breaks the heart itself.

1070   கரப்பவர்க்கு யாங்குஒளிக்கும் கொல்லோ இரப்பவர்
       சொல்லாடப் போஓம் உயிர்.
       The life of a beggar ends just on hearing 'No'.
       Where goes life of a miser who says 'No'?
       Saying 'no' to a beggar would take away his life; the
       same word would also kill one who says 'no'.

108. கயமை
MEANNESS

1071 மக்களே போல்வர் கயவர் அவரன்ன
ஒப்பாரி யாம்கண்டது இல்.

The base resemble humans only outwardly
Nowhere such likeness I've seen truly.

The base resemble others in outward form and there
is no such similarity found anywhere.

1072 நன்றுஅறி வாரின் கயவர் திருஉடையர்
நெஞ்சத்து அவலம் இலர்.

The mean-minded are luckier than the good
As there's no pang in their heart's abode.

The baser ones are luckier than those who know what
is good, as the former never care for any wrongs.

1073 தேவர் அனையர் கயவர் அவரும்தாம்
மேவன செய்தொழுக லான்.

The base are like gods, for they do
Whatever they desire to do.

The base resemble gods, for they too act according to
their own will and pleasure.

1074 அகப்பட்டி ஆவாரைக் காணின் அவரின்
மிகப்பட்டுச் செம்மாக்கும் கீழ்.

When the mean-minded find others meaner
They boast of their own behaviour.

When the mean-minded find others meaner than them,
they feel very proud of themselves.

1075 அச்சமே கீழ்களது ஆசாரம் எச்சம்
அவாஉண்டேல் உண்டாம் சிறிது.

For the base, fear is the code of good conduct
Desire also results in such conduct.

Fear is the code of conduct for the base. Desire is
another motive for good conduct.

1076   அறைபறை அன்னர் கயவர்தாம் கேட்ட
        மறைபிறர்க்கு உய்த்துஉரைக்க லான்.
The mean-minded are like the beaten drum
As others' secrets they tom-tom.
The mean-minded are like a drum that is beaten, as
they make others' secrets public.

1077   ஈர்ங்கை விதிரார் கயவர் கொடிறுஉடைக்கும்
        கூன்கையர் அல்லா தவர்க்கு.
The mean-minded shake not even their wet hands
Except to clenched fists that break their jaws.
The ignoble never give charity except to those who would
break their jaws.

1078   சொல்லப் பயன்படுவர் சான்றோர் கரும்புபோல்
        கொல்லப் பயன்படும் கீழ்.
The perfect ones lend support when merely asked
The mean yield like sugarcane when crushed.
Perfect men help immediately on a request but the
mean render help only when they are forced.

1079   உடுப்பதூஉம் உண்பதூஉம் காணின் பிறர்மேல்
        வடுக்காண வற்றாகும் கீழ்.
On seeing the fine dress and food of others
The mean envy and wantonly find flaws.
Seeing others having good food and fine clothing, the mean
would envy them and point out only their faults.

1080   எற்றிற்கு உரியர் கயவர்ஒன்று உற்றக்கால்
        விற்றற்கு உரியர் விரைந்து.
What are the mean fit for? If misfortune falls
They rush to sell themselves.
During calamity the mean who are fit for nothing would
hasten to sell even themselves.

III

இன்பத்துப்பால்
LOVE

109. தகையணங்குறுத்தல்
BEAUTY'S DART

Hero speaks to himself:

1081 அணங்குகொல் ஆய்மயில் கொல்லோ கனங்குழை
மாதர்கொல் மாலும்என் நெஞ்சு.

**Is she an angel, a peahen or a jewelled maid?
She is only a puzzle to my mind.**

She is so beautiful that he wonders whether she is
an angel or a peahen or a bejewelled lady.

1082 நோக்கினாள் நோக்கெதிர் நோக்குதல் தாக்குஅணங்கு
தானைக்கொண் டன்னது உடைத்து.

The counter-glance of my *love appears to be
A nymph coming to attack with an army.**

The responding glance of the beautiful lady is like a
nymph coming with a band of army.

1083 பண்டுஅறியேன் கூற்றுஎன் பதனை இனிஅறிந்தேன்
பெண்தகையால் பேரமர்க் கட்டு.

**Never have I seen Death, but now I see his form
In warring eyes and feminine charm.**

He never knew the god of death. Now he sees the god
of death in the maiden's guise and warring eyes.

1084 கண்டார் உயிருண்ணும் தோற்றத்தால் பெண்தகைப்
பேதைக்கு அமர்த்தன கண்.

**Eyes that seem to drink the life of gazers
Are contrary to her graceful gaze.**

This innocent maiden has devouring eyes which take
away the life of those gazing at her.

1085 கூற்றமோ கண்ணோ பிணையோ மடவரல்
நோக்கம்இம் மூன்றும் உடைத்து.

**Is it Death, eye or doe? All these
Three are in this lady's gaze.**

In the young maiden's glance, there are Death, bliss
and timidity of a deer.

---

* Love indicates his beloved.

1086   கொடும்புருவம் கோடா மறைப்பின் நடுங்குஅஞர்
செய்யல மன்இவள் கண்.

If the cruel eyebrows bow and conceal her eyes
They cause no trembling sorrows.

The maiden's eyes do not harm her lover, if her
eyebrows are bent.

1087   கடாஅக் களிற்றின்மேல் கண்படாம் மாதர்
படாஅ முலைமேல் துகில்.

The soft mantle lying on the maiden's firm breast
Resembles the eye-cover of a mad elephant.

The cloth on the firm breast of the maiden looks like a
veil covering the forehead of a mad elephant.

1088   ஒள்நுதற்கு ஒஒ உடைந்ததே ஞாட்பினுள்
நண்ணாரும் உட்கும்என் பீடு.

What a shining forehead that ruins my might
Feared even by dauntless foes in fight !

The forehead of this maiden shatters her lover's
strength feared even by his mighty enemies.

1089   பிணையேர் மடநோக்கும் நாணும் உடையாட்கு
அணிஎவனோ ஏதில தந்து.

What jewels can adorn this maiden's prettiness
As she has doe-like looks and shyness?

No jewels can add to the beauty of this maiden who
has meek looks and modesty.

1090   உண்டார்கண் அல்லது அடுநறாக் காமம்போல்
கண்டார் மகிழ்செய்தல் இன்று.

Wine gives delight only when tasted
Love delights even when sighted.

Wine gives joy only when it is tasted but love gives joy
even at sight.

110. குறிப்பறிதல்
DIVINING THE HEART
Hero speaks to himself:

1091

இருநோக்கு இவள்உண்கண் உள்ளது ஒருநோக்கு
நோய்நோக்கொன்று அந்நோய் மருந்து.

**Her painted eyes possess twofold looks
One harms while the other treats.**

Her painted eyes have two different looks; one injures,
the other heals.

1092

கண்களவு கொள்ளும் சிறுநோக்கம் காமத்தில்
செம்பாகம் அன்று பெரிது.

**Her swift stealthy glance gives more pleasure
Than half of sexual pleasure.**

Her secret momentary look gives more joy than half of
the sexual pleasure.

1093

நோக்கினாள் நோக்கி இறைஞ்சினாள் அஃதவள்
யாப்பினுள் அட்டிய நீர்.

**She looked; as I looked, her head drooped
It resembled watering our love-plant.**

She looked and when he looked she lowered her
head. Her action was like watering their love-plant.

1094

யான்நோக்கும் காலை நிலன்நோக்கும் நோக்காக்கால்
தான்நோக்கி மெல்ல நகும்.

**When I look at the maiden, down she gazes
When I don't, she looks and gently smiles.**

When he looks at her, her head droops to the earth.
When he turns, she looks at him with a gentle smile.

1095

குறிக்கொண்டு நோக்காமை அல்லால் ஒருகண்
சிறக்கணித்தாள் போல நகும்.

**She casts a side glance and smiles softly
Without looking straight at me.**

She casts a stealthy glance at her lover and smiles
gently at him.

1096 உறாஅ தவர்போல் சொலினும் செறாஅர்சொல்
ஒல்லை உணரப் படும்.

Though, like a stranger, she speaks harshly
Her words are soon found to be friendly.

She appears to speak harshly like a stranger but her
words are really friendly.

1097 செறாஅச் சிறுசொல்லும் செற்றார்போல் நோக்கும்
உறாஅர்போன்று உற்றார் குறிப்பு.

Seemingly bitter words and angry stares
Are but feigned signs of lovers.

Seemingly harsh words and angry looks are only inner
expressions of true lovers.

Hero speaks to the heroine:

1098 அசைஇயற்கு உண்டுஆண்டுஒர் ஏள்யான் நோக்கப்
பசையினள் பைய நகும்.

Great is the charm the slender maiden owns
When I gaze, in love, she gently smiles.

The slender maiden has a gracious look. She smiles
at her lover when he looks at her.

Confidante speaks to herself:

1099 ஏதிலார் போலப் பொதுநோக்கு நோக்குதல்
காதலார் கண்ணே யுள.

Looking at each other as strangers
Belongs only to lovers.

They look at each other as strangers, but really they are
lovers. Such practice is found only among lovers.

1100 கண்ணொடு கண்ணிணை நோக்குஒக்கின் வாய்ச்சொற்கள்
என்ன பயனும் இல.

When eye to eye lovers lock their looks
Spoken words are of no use.

Words are of no use when lovers convey the message
of love through their eyes.

111. புணர்ச்சி மகிழ்தல்
JOY OF SEX

Hero speaks to himself:

1101 கண்டுகேட்டு உண்டுஉயிர்த்து உற்றறியும் ஐம்புலனும்
ஒண்தொடி கண்ணே உள.

All joys of sight, hearing, taste, smell and touch
Has this bangled maiden very much.

The joy of five sensuous pleasures is present in the fair
maiden with pretty bangles.

1102 பிணிக்கு மருந்து பிறமன் அணியிழை
தன்நோய்க்குத் தானே மருந்து.

Remedy for all other illnesses is found elsewhere
For my illness caused by her, herself is the cure.

Normally the cure for all ills is elsewhere. But, for his
illness caused by her, she herself is the cure.

Hero speaks to his friend:

1103 தாம்வீழ்வார் மென்தோள் துயிலின் இனிதுகொல்
தாமரைக் கண்ணான் உலகு.

Joy of repose on soft shoulders of the beloved
Is more than that of lotus-eyed god's abode.

The joy of resting on the soft shoulders of the beloved
is sweeter than the joy of heaven itself.

Hero speaks to himself:

1104 நீங்கின் தெறூஉம் குறுகும்கால் தண்என்னும்
தீயாண்டுப் பெற்றாள் இவள்.

When I leave, it burns; it's cool when I come near
Wherefrom has she got this fire?

Away from her, he burns with love. When she is closer, he
feels cool. She has got such a strange fire in her.

1105 வேட்ட பொழுதின் அவைஅவை போலுமே
தோட்டார் கதுப்பினாள் தோள்.

Shoulder of the flower-decked maiden brings
Varied joys at once as he desires.

The flower-decked maiden instantly gives her lover
various joys as he desires.

1106   உறுதோறு உயிர்தளிர்ப்பத் தீண்டலால் பேதைக்கு
        அமிழ்தின் இயன்றன தோள்.

This simple damsel has arms of divine nectar
For, embracing her revives my vigour.

The maiden's shoulders are made of divine nectar;
embracing her revives his drooping spirit.

Hero speaks to the confidante:

1107   தம்மில் இருந்து தமதுபாத்து உண்டற்றால்
        அம்மா அரிவை முயக்கு.

The joy of embracing the fair, golden dame
Is like sharing self-earned food at home.

Embracing the fair maiden is as delightful as sharing
one's food with guests at home.

1108   வீழும் இருவர்க்கு இனிதே வளியிடை
        போழப் படாஅ முயக்கு.

The tight clasping that admits no air between
Is sweet to lovers whose love is genuine.

Embracing so tightly that not even air passes between
them gives great joy to true lovers.

1109   ஊடல் உணர்தல் புணர்தல் இவைகாமம்
        கூடியார் பெற்ற பயன்.

Sulking, relenting and love-making
Are the gains of lovers' meeting.

Feigned dislike, reconciliation and love-making are the
fruits enjoyed by the lovers.

Hero speaks to himself:

1110   அறிதோறு அறியாமை கண்டற்றால் காமம்
        செறிதோறும் சேயிழை மாட்டு.

As repeated learning reveals past ignorance
Repeated union shows passion intense.

As repeated learning reveals one's earlier ignorance,
sex with the fair maiden gives new pleasure every time.

112. நலம் புனைந்துரைத்தல்
PRAISING HER BEAUTY

Hero speaks to himself:

1111
நல்நீரை வாழி அனிச்சமே நின்னினும்
மெல்நீரள் யாம்வீழ் பவள்.

**Hail, O, anicham flower! You are tender
But my sweetheart is more tender.**

The beloved maiden is more tender than the sensitive
anicham flower.

1112
மலர்காணின் மையாத்தி நெஞ்சே இவள்கண்
பலர்காணும் பூவொக்கும் என்று.

**O, my heart ! How deluded you are and unwise
To match her eyes with common flowers!**

The lover is confused at the sight of flowers as they
resemble the eyes of his beautiful maiden.

Hero speaks to his friend:

1113
முறிமேனி முத்தம் முறுவல் வெறிநாற்றம்
வேல்உண்கண் வேய்த்தோ எவட்கு.

**The dame has bamboo-like shoulders, golden hue,
Pearly teeth, aroma and spear-like eyes too.**

She has tender shoulders, shining appearance, pearly
teeth, natural fragrance and piercing eyes.

Hero speaks to himself:

1114
காணின் குவளை கவிழ்ந்து நிலன்நோக்கும்
மாணிழை கண்ஒவ்வேம் என்று.

**If lilies see the jewelled maiden, they will bow
And say, 'We can't rival your eyes now.'**

Even lilies will bend their heads thinking that they cannot match the eyes of his beautiful maiden.

1115
அனிச்சப்பூக் கால்களையாள் பெய்தாள் நுசுப்பிற்கு
நல்ல படாஅ பறை.

**When she wears anicham without removing stalks
Her thin waist breaks and sad drum beats.**

On wearing *anicham* flowers with the stalks, her thin
waist may break and she may die.

1116   மதியும் மடந்தை முகனும் அறியா
பதியிற் கலங்கிய மீன்.

The stars are confused to see no difference
Between the moon and my maiden's face.

The stars are puzzled unable to differentiate between
the moon and the maiden's face.

1117   அறுவாய் நிறைந்த அவிர்மதிக்குப் போல
மறுஉண்டோ மாதர் முகத்து.

Are there any spots on the face of the maiden
Like those on the altering phase of the moon?

There are no dark spots on the fair maiden's face like
those on the waxing and waning moon.

1118   மாதர் முகம்போல் ஒளிவிட வல்லையேல்
காதலை வாழி மதி.

If you could shine like the face of my maiden
You'd merit my love, O moon!

He will love the moon if it shines as brightly as his
maiden's sweet face.

1119   மலர்அன்ன கண்ணாள் முகம்ஒத்தி யாயின்
பலர்காணத் தோன்றல் மதி.

If you like to be my flower-eyed maiden's face
O moon, shine not for all with grace.

If the moon wants to be like his maiden's face, it
should not be seen by others except her lover.

Hero speaks to the confidante:

1120   அனிச்சமும் அன்னத்தின் தூவியும் மாதர்
அடிக்கு நெருஞ்சிப் பழம்.

Anicham flower and swan's soft feathers
Are like nettle to the feet of damsels.

Even the delicate *anicham* flower and the swan's soft
feathers are like thorns to the maidens' soft feet.

113. காதற்சிறப்புரைத்தல்
GLORIFICATION OF LOVE

Hero speaks to himself:

1121 பாலொடு தேன்கலந் தற்றே பணிமொழி
வால்எயிறு ஊறிய நீர்.

The dew at the teeth of the soft-spoken lady
Is like a mixture of milk and honey.

The saliva at his soft maiden's teeth is like the sweet
mixture of milk and honey to the lover.

1122 உடம்பொடு உயிரிடை என்னமற்று அன்ன
மடந்தையொடு எம்மிடை நட்பு.

The intimacy between this dame and me
Is like the union of soul and body.

The intimacy between the lovers is similar to the union
of the body and the soul.

1123 கருமணியிற் பாவாய்நீ போதாயாம் வீழும்
திருநுதற்கு இல்லை இடம்.

O pupil of my eye! Leave and make room
In my eye for my fair-browed dame.

The image in the pupil of the lover's eye should go
away giving place to his love.

1124 வாழ்தல் உயிர்க்குஅன்னள் ஆயிழை சாதல்
அதற்குஅன்னள் நீங்கும் இடத்து.

Union with my jewelled maiden is like living
Parting with her is like dying.

Union with his lady is like living and parting with her
is like death to him.

Hero speaks to the confidante:

1125 உள்ளுவன் மன்யான் மறப்பின் மறப்பறியேன்
ஒள்ளமர்க் கண்ணாள் குணம்.

If I forget I can recall but I forget not the qualities
Of my maiden with bright warring eyes.

If the lover forgets her rare qualities, he can recall them.
But he never forgets them.

Heroine speaks to herself:

1126 கண்உள்ளின் போகார் இமைப்பின் பருவரார்
நுண்ணியர்எங் காத லவர்.
**My subtle lover never leaves my eyes
Even if I wink, pain he never feels.**
The lover always remains in his love's eyes. Even when
she winks, he is not hurt.

1127 கண்உள்ளார் காத லவராகக் கண்ணும்
எழுதேம் கரப்பாக்கு அறிந்து.
**As my lover resides in my eyes forever
I paint them not, for he may disappear.**
As the lover is within her eyes, she does not paint
them fearing he would disappear.

1128 நெஞ்சத்தார் காத லவராக வெய்துஉண்டல்
அஞ்சுதும் வேபாக்கு அறிந்து.
**My lover dwells forever within my heart
I shun hot food lest he should be hurt.**
The lover lives in her heart; so she avoids hot food for
fear of harming him.

1129 இமைப்பின் கரப்பாக்கு அறிவல் அனைத்திற்கே
ஏதிலர் என்னும்இவ் வூர்.
**I never wink my eyes lest he should disappear
Not knowing it villagers blame him forever.**
She never winks her eyes fearing her lover will dis-
appear but the villagers call him heartless.

1130 உவந்துஉறைவர் உள்ளத்துள் என்றும் இகந்துஉறைவர்
ஏதிலர் என்னும்இவ் வூர்.
**My lover always dwells happily in my heart
Yet villagers decry he lives unkindly apart.**
The lover always resides in her heart. Even then, the
villagers blame him as a heartless deserter.

114. நாணுத்துறவுரைத்தல்
DECORUM DEFIED

Hero speaks to himself:

1131 காமம் உழந்து வருந்தினார்க்கு ஏமம்
மடல்அல்லது இல்லை வலி.

Lovers with pangs of love find no safety
But in riding the *palm-horse* only.

There is no solution for those suffering from lovesickness except riding the *palm-horse*.

Hero speaks to the confidante:

1132 நோனா உடம்பும் உயிரும் மடல்ஏறும்
நாணினை நீக்கி நிறுத்து.

Unable to bear pangs of love, my body and soul
Will shamelessly resort to riding the *madal*.

Unable to bear the grief of separation, the lover's body
and mind are prepared to mount the *madal*.

1133 நாணொடு நல்லாண்மை பண்டுடையேன் இன்றுடையேன்
காமுற்றார் ஏறும் மடல்.

Once I had fine manliness and modesty
Now I have the lovers' *madal* only.

Once the lover was full of manliness and modesty.
Now he has only the lovers' *palm-horse*.

1134 காமக் கடும்புனல் உய்க்குமே நாணொடு
நல்லாண்மை என்னும் புணை.

Fierce torrent of passion at once sweeps
Off the raft of modesty and manliness.

Fierce floods of love will sweep away the raft of both
modesty and manliness at once.

1135 தொடலைக் குறுந்தொடி தந்தாள் மடலொடு
மாலை உழக்கும் துயர்.

The *palmyra ride* and the anguish of eventide
Are gifts of garland-like bangled maid.

The *palm-horse* and the pangs of evening are the
gifts of the bangled maiden.

---

* madal - an ancient practice of carrying a lover on a palmyra
horse to get consent for marriage

1136   மடல்ஊர்தல் யாமத்தும் உள்ளுவேன் மன்ற
         படல்ஒல்லா பேதைக்குஎன் கண்.
I think of *palm-horse* riding even at midnight
Pining for the maiden my eyes sleep not.
Even at midnight, the lover thinks of riding the *palm-horse*. He is sleepless thinking of the maiden.

1137   கடல்அன்ன காமம் உழந்தும் மடல்ஏறாப்
         பெண்ணின் பெருந்தக்கது இல்.
Nothing is nobler than woman who goes not
For *madal* tho' tormented by a sea of lust.
Nothing is so noble as the womanly nature that does not resort to *madal* when suffering from love.

Heroine speaks to herself:

1138   நிறைஅரியர் மன்அளியர் என்னாது காமம்
         மறைஇறந்து மன்று படும்.
Passionate love reveals itself at once
Despite purity and tenderness.
Despite modesty and gentleness, intense love breaks its secrecy and comes out in public.

1139   அறிகிலார் எல்லாரும் என்றேஎன் காமம்
         மறுகின் மறுகும் மருண்டு.
Thinking that nobody knows the secret
My lust reels confused in the street.
Thinking that no one knows her secret love, her passion tends to exhibit itself.

1140   யாங்கண்ணின் காண நகுப அறிவுஇல்லார்
         யாம்பட்ட தாம்படா வாறு.
The fools laugh at me before my eyes
For they've suffered not my pains.
The ignorant make fun of her in her presence, for they have never suffered the pangs of love like her.

115. அலர் அறிவுறுத்தல்
ANNOUNCEMENT OF RUMOUR

Hero speaks to the confidante:

1141

அலர்எழ ஆருயிர் நிற்கும் அதனைப்
பலர்அறியார் பாக்கியத் தால்.

Rumour saves my life that is precious
Luckily, others are not aware of this.

Rumour preserves his precious life. It is his good
fortune that many do not realize this.

1142

மலர்அன்ன கண்ணாள் அருமை அறியாது
அலர்எமக்கு ஈந்ததுஇவ் வூர்.

Talk of town has given me this flower-eyed lass
Not knowing her excellence.

Not knowing the value of the fair maiden, the rumour of
the townsfolk has gifted her to the lover.

1143

உறாஅதோ ஊரறிந்த கௌவை அதனைப்
பெறாஅது பெற்றன்ன நீர்த்து.

I surely benefit by this village rumour
Tho' I have not, I feel, I have her.

The lover profits by the public rumour. As a result of it,
he feels as if he possessed her.

1144

கவ்வையால் கவ்விது காமம் அதுஇன்றேல்
தவ்வென்னும் தன்மை இழந்து.

My passion increases by means of rumour
If not, it will languish losing power.

His love grows because of this rumour. Or else, it will
become pale and weak.

1145

களித்தொறும் கள்ளுண்டல் வேட்டற்றால் காமம்
வெளிப்படுந் தோறும் இனிது.

The more a drunkard drinks the more he desires
The more the rumour is the sweeter love grows.

Each cup of liquor adds to the joy of the drunkard.
Likewise, every rumour adds to the delight of lovers.

Heroine speaks to her confidante:

1146 கண்டது மன்னும் ஒருநாள் அலர்மன்னும்
திங்களைப் பாம்புகொண் டற்று.

Meeting of my lover was on only one occasion
Rumour spread like snake swallowing moon.

She met her lover only once. But the rumour spread
like the news of a lunar eclipse.

1147 ஊரவர் கௌவை எருவாக அன்னைசொல்
நீராக நீளும்இந் நோய்.

Lovesickness grows manured by village talk
And watered by mother's rebuke.

The plant of lovesickness grows, manured by rumours
and watered by mother's scolding.

1148 நெய்யால் எரிநுதுப்பேம் என்றற்றால் கௌவையால்
காமம் நுதுப்பேம் எனல்.

Quenching the burning lust by rumour wild
Is like dousing fire with ghee poured.

The flame of love cannot be put out by rumour, just as
fire cannot be put out by pouring ghee on it.

1149 அலர்நாண ஒல்வதோ அஞ்சல்ஓம்பு என்றார்
பலர்நாண நீத்தக் கடை.

Why should this rumour make me ashamed
When he who said, 'Fear not' has parted?

As the lover has assured her not to fear and has left,
she need not be ashamed of the rumour.

Confidante speaks to the heroine:

1150 தாம்வேண்டின் நல்குவர் காதலர் யாம்வேண்டும்
கௌவை எடுக்கும்இவ் வூர்.

The village spreads the rumour I require
If I want, he will grant my desire.

She wanted the rumour to be spread by the village
so that he would agree to take her with him.

116. பிரிவாற்றாமை
PANGS OF SEPARATION

Confidante speaks to the hero:

1151 செல்லாமை உண்டேல் எனக்குஉரை மற்றுநின்
வல்வரவு வாழ்வார்க்கு உரை.

Tell me only when you do not ever leave
About your fast return tell those alive.

The *lover** must tell her only if he does not part; if it is
about his speedy return, he must inform the survivors.

Heroine speaks to her confidante:

1152 இன்கண் உடைத்தவர் பார்வல் பிரிவுஅஞ்சும்
புன்கண் உடைத்தால் புணர்வு.

The very sight of the lover was once delightful
Fear of departure now makes union fearful.

Once the mere look of her lover was a joy. But now the
thought of separation makes even the union fearful.

1153 அரிதரோ தேற்றம் அறிவுடையார் கண்ணும்
பிரிவுஓர் இடத்துஉண்மை யான்.

Knowing the pain of separation, he leaves
How can I trust his consoling words?

Though he knows the pain of separation, he leaves
and so his words cannot be trusted.

1154 அளித்துஅஞ்சல் என்றுஅவர் நீப்பின் தெளித்தசொல்
தேறியார்க்கு உண்டோ தவறு.

If he who openly said to me, 'Fear not' now leaves
Can I be blamed for trusting his words?

As the lover, who consoled her not to fear, has left,
none can blame her faith in him.

1155 ஓம்பின் அமைந்தார் பிரிவுஓம்பல் மற்றவர்
நீங்கின் அரிதால் புணர்வு.

To save my life, stop my lover from leaving
If he leaves, impossible is rejoining.

If the lover wants to save her life, he must not leave.
If it happens, she will not be alive for reunion.

---

* Lover indicates husband.

1156 பிரிவுரைக்கும் வன்கண்ணர் ஆயின் அரிதுஅவர்
நல்குவர் என்னும் நசை.

If he is so heartless to announce his departure
Hope of regaining his love is lost forever.

If he is so hard-hearted to talk of his departure, it is
vain to hope for his return and revival of love.

1157 துறைவன் துறந்தமை தூற்றாகொல் முன்கை
இறைஇறவா நின்ற வளை.

Won't the gliding bangles on my forearm utter
My seashore chieftain's departure?

The departure of her lover is proclaimed by the
loosening of her bangles.

1158 இன்னாது இனன்இல்லூர் வாழ்தல் அதனினும்
இன்னாது இனியார்ப் பிரிவு.

Bitter is life without friends in a place
Worse it is in lover's absence.

It is bitter to live with no friends in a place and it is
more bitter to be without one's lover.

1159 தொடிற்சுடின் அல்லது காமநோய் போல
விடிற்சுடல் ஆற்றுமோ தீ.

Fire burns certainly when touched
But love burns when left.

Fire injures only when touched. But lovesickness
burns the lovers when separated.

1160 அரிதுஆற்றி அல்லல்நோய் நீக்கிப் பிரிவுஆற்றிப்
பின்இருந்து வாழ்வார் பலர்.

Agreeing to separation and enduring the pain
Many women accept it and live on.

Many women survive tolerating separation and
bearing its pain.

117. படர்மெலிந்திரங்கல்
PINING

Heroine speaks to her confidante:

1161 மறைப்பேன்மன் யான்இஃதோ நோயை இறைப்பவர்க்கு
ஊற்றுநீர் போல மிகும்.

I try to conceal my intense love-suffering
But it swells like a spring.

She is trying to hide her lovesickness but it swells
like a spring.

1162 கரத்தலும் ஆற்றேன்இந் நோயைநோய் செய்தார்க்கு
உரைத்தலும் நாணுத் தரும்.

I can neither conceal my lovesickness
Nor tell my lover due to shyness.

She can neither conceal her lovesickness nor tell her
lover about it because of her shyness.

1163 காமமும் நாணும் உயிர்காவாத் தூங்கும்என்
நோனா உடம்பின் அகத்து.

My soul as the shoulder-pole with love and shame
At both ends, burdens within my weary frame.

Her frail body is unable to bear torments of her soul
torn between love and shame.

1164 காமக் கடல்மன்னும் உண்டே அதுநீந்தும்
ஏமப் புணைமன்னும் இல்.

There is indeed a great sea of lust
But no raft of safety to cross it.

The vast sea of love exists in her. But she has no
safe raft to cross it.

1165 துப்பின் எவன்ஆவர் மன்கொல் துயர்வரவு
நட்பினுள் ஆற்று பவர்.

What harm will he not do in animosity
If he gives pain even in amity?

He who causes pain even in friendship will do greater
harm in enmity.

1166 இன்பம் கடல்மற்றுக் காமம் அஃதுஅடும்கால்
துன்பம் அதனின் பெரிது.

With union the pleasure of love is oceanful
Without it love pangs are more painful.

The joy of love is as great as the ocean. But the
pain of separation is far greater than the ocean.

1167 காமக் கடும்புனல் நீந்திக் கரைகாணேன்
யாமத்தும் யானே உளேன்.

I swim but cannot find the shore of love
Alone at midnight I'm pining for love.

While swimming in the flood of love, she is unable to
see the shore. At midnight she pines all alone.

1168 மன்னுயி ரெல்லாம் துயிற்றி அளித்துஇரா
என்அல்லது இல்லை துணை.

Night gracefully lulls all beings to rest
But I alone give company to night.

Night makes all beings sleep. But she is awake to
give company to the night.

1169 கொடியார் கொடுமையின் தாம்கொடிய இந்நாள்
நெடிய கழியும் இரா.

Crueller than the heartless
Are the unending nights.

The long and slow moving nights are crueller than
the heartless lover, who has deserted her.

1170 உள்ளம்போன்று உள்வழிச் செல்கிற்பின் வெள்ளநீர்
நீந்தல மன்னோஎன் கண்.

If my eyes, like my mind, could go where he is
They needn't swim in flood of tears.

If her eyes could travel like her thought to her lover's
abode, she need not shed tears.

239

118. கண் விதுப்பழிதல்
GRIEVING EYES

Heroine speaks to her confidante:

1171
கண்தாம் கலுழ்வது எவன்கொலோ தண்டாநோய்
தாம்காட்ட யாம்கண் டது.

**As eyes showed him, I got sickness of love
Why should they cry for him now?**

Her eyes saw him and brought her incurable lovesickness. So they should not weep now.

1172
தெரிந்துஉணரா நோக்கிய உண்கண் பரிந்துஉணராப்
பைதல் உழப்பது எவன்.

**My eyes loved him without foresight
But why do they now regret?**

After thoughtlessly falling in love, her eyes should not
regret for their folly.

1173
கதுமெனத் தாம்நோக்கித் தாமே கலுழும்
இதுநகத் தக்கது உடைத்து.

**The eyes eagerly loved him that day
Is it not a mockery to weep today?**

It is ridiculous to see that the eyes which eagerly loved
him, now weep for him.

1174
பெயல்ஆற்றா நீர்உலந்த உண்கண் உயல்ஆற்றா
உய்வுஇல்நோய் என்கண் நிறுத்து.

**The eyes that brought me fatal lovesickness
Are dried up now with no tear-drops.**

The eyes that brought her the incurable pain are now
completely dry because of constant weeping.

1175
படல்ஆற்றா பைதல் உழக்கும் கடல்ஆற்றாக்
காமநோய் செய்தளன் கண்.

**The eyes that caused oceanic lovesickness
Now suffer the pain of sleeplessness.**

The eyes that plunged her into the vast sea of love
suffer without sleep now.

1176 ஓஒ இனிதே எமக்குஇந்நோய் செய்தகண்
தாஅம் இதற்பட் டது.

Oh, the eyes that caused lovesickness once
Fall victims to the pain of sleeplessness.

It is sweet that the eyes which are responsible for her
pain should themselves grieve in sorrow.

1177 உழந்துஉழந்து உள்நீர் அறுக விழைந்துஇழைந்து
வேண்டி யவர்க்கண்ட கண்.

The eyes that feasted on him lovingly
May dry up pining deeply.

The eyes which once feasted on her lover lovingly
now suffer pain and dry up.

1178 பேணாது பெட்டார் உளர்மன்னோ மற்றுஅவர்க்
காணாது அமைவில கண்.

Only his lips but not his heart loved me
Yet my eyes long to see him near me.

He did not love her sincerely, yet her eyes are
restless to see him.

1179 வாராக்கால் துஞ்சா வரின்துஞ்சா ஆயிடை
ஆரஞர் உற்றன கண்.

Whether he comes or not, I sleep not
Either way my eyes are in torment.

Her eyes do not sleep whether he comes or not. They
suffer all the time.

1180 மறைபெறல் ஊரார்க்கு அரிதுஅன்றால் எம்போல்
அறைபறை கண்ணா ரகத்து.

As all my miseries my tell-tale eyes trumpet
People here easily know my secret.

She cannot conceal her secret from the townsfolk, as
her eyes reveal her sufferings.

119. பசப்புறு பருவரல்
SUFFERING FROM PALLOR

Heroine speaks to herself:

1181
நயந்தவர்க்கு நல்காமை நேர்ந்தேன் பசந்தஎன்
பண்பியார்க்கு உரைக்கோ பிற.

I myself agreed to the parting with my lover
To whom can I now complain of my pallor?

She willingly consented to part with her lover and
now she cannot complain of her lovesickness.

Heroine speaks to her confidante:

1182
அவர்தந்தார் என்னும் தகையால் இவர்தந்துளன்
மேனிமேல் ஊரும் பசப்பு.

As sickly pallor is the gift of my dear lover
It proudly spreads all over my figure.

This pallor is the gift of her lover and so it spreads
all over her body.

1183
சாயலும் நாணும் அவர்கொண்டார் கைம்மாறா
நோயும் பசலையும் தந்து.

He robbed me of my beauty and modesty
Giving in return pain and pallor to me.

He took away her beauty and modesty giving her
pain and lovesickness in return.

1184
உள்ளுவன் மன்யான் உரைப்பது அவர்திறமால்
கள்ளம் பிறவோ பசப்பு.

I think of his words and talk of his worth only
How then pallor betrays me stealthily?

Though she always thinks and speaks of her lover,
pallor quietly seizes her.

1185
உவக்காண்எம் காதலர் செல்வார் இவக்காண்என்
மேனி பசப்புஊர் வது.

Look there! My beloved lover parts with me
Look here! Pallor spreads on my body.

As soon as her lover leaves her, pallor spreads all
over her body.

1186   விளக்குஅற்றம் பார்க்கும் இருளேபோல் கொண்கன்
முயக்குஅற்றம் பார்க்கும் பசப்பு.

Just as darkness waits for the light to fade
Pallor waits for lover's embrace to end.

Just as darkness waits for the failing light, pallor
waits for an interval in the lover's embrace.

1187   புல்லிக் கிடந்தேன் புடைபெயர்ந்தேன் அவ்வளவில்
அள்ளிக்கொள் வற்றே பசப்பு.

I turned a little away from my lover's embrace
And found pallor seize me at once.

The moment she moved away from her lover's embrace,
pallor seized her immediately.

1188   பசந்தாள் இவள்என்பது அல்லால் இவளைத்
துறந்தார் அவர்என்பார் இல்.

People cast aspersions, 'She has got pallor.'
None blames, 'He has deserted her.'

Everyone blames her for her lovesickness. But no
one blames the lover for leaving her.

1189   பசக்கமன் பட்டாங்குஎன் மேனி நயப்பித்தார்
நல்நிலையர் ஆவர் எனின்.

Let my body suffer even from pallor
If my parted lover is to prosper.

She is willing to suffer from pallor, so as to let her
lover prosper in a distant land.

1190   பசப்புஎனப் பேர்பெறுதல் நன்றே நயப்பித்தார்
நல்காமை தூற்றார் எனின்.

Better I bear with myself being ridiculed as pallid
If they hate not my parted lover as unkind.

She may bear with people ridiculing her pallor, if
people do not blame her parted lover as unkind.

120. தனிப்படர் மிகுதி
PINING ALONE

Heroine speaks to her confidante:

1191
தாம்வீழ்வார் தம்வீழப் பெற்றவர் பெற்றாரே
காமத்துக் காழில் கனி.

Who love and are loved with loving care
Gain the seedless fruit of love so rare.

They who love and are loved alone are blessed. They
gain the seedless fruit of love.

1192
வாழ்வார்க்கு வானம் பயந்தற்றால் வீழ்வார்க்கு
வீழ்வார் அளிக்கும் அளி.

Like the seasonal rains to the world
Is the lover's love to the beloved.

The lover's kindness to his beloved is similar to the
timely rain to the world.

1193
வீழுநர் வீழப் படுவார்க்கு அமையுமே
வாழுநம் என்னும் செருக்கு.

The pride of saying 'We shall live' belongs
Only to those loved by their beloveds.

Women who are loved by their husbands alone may
boast that they possess life's very best.

1194
வீழப் படுவார் கெழீஇயிலர் தாம்வீழ்வார்
வீழப் படாஅர் எனின்.

Even those loved by the purest are wretched ones
Unless loved by their husbands.

Even the women loved by the purest are considered
as evil ones if not loved by their husbands.

1195
நாம்காதல் கொண்டார் நமக்குஎவன் செய்பவோ
தாம்காதல் கொள்ளாக் கடை.

What good will my beloved do to me
If he returns not his love to me?

Her love is of no use at all if she is not loved by her
beloved husband.

1196 ஒருதலையான் இன்னாது காமம்காப் போல
இருதலை யானும் இனிது.
Mutual love poised like shoulder-poles is sweeter
One-sided love is indeed very bitter.
One-sided love causes sufferings. Mutual love is plea-
sant like the balanced weight on shoulder-poles.

1197 பருவரலும் பைதலும் காணான்கொல் காமன்
ஒருவர்கண் நின்றுஒழுகு வான்.
Cupid staying on one side assails me alone
Does he not know my pallor and pain?
The god of love tortures only the maiden without knowing
her pallor and grief.

1198 வீழ்வாரின் இன்சொல் பெறாஅது உலகத்து
வாழ்வாரின் வன்கணார் இல்.
None is harder than the one who can live
Without her lover's words of love.
There is no one bolder than a woman who endures
life without her lover's sweet words.

1199 நசைஇயார் நல்கார் எனினும் அவர்மாட்டு
இசையும் இனிய செவிக்கு.
Though my lover gives not my heart's desire
A word from him is sweeter to my ear.
Though her lover does nothing to delight her, even a
word from him is a sweet melody to hear.

Heroine speaks to her heart:
1200 உறாஅர்க்கு உறுநோய் உரைப்பாய் கடலைச்
செறாஅஅய் வாழிய நெஞ்சு.
O heart, why tell the heartless your pains?
Rather fill the sea of sorrow with tears.
Instead of telling her grief to her loveless lover, it is
better to fill the sea of sorrow with tears.

245

121. நினைந்தவர் புலம்பல்
SAD MEMORIES OF LOVE

Hero speaks to his friend:

1201 உள்ளினும் தீராப் பெருமகிழ் செய்தலால்
கள்ளினும் காமம் இனிது.

Endless joy comes from thought of love fine
Love is, therefore, sweeter than wine.

Even the very thought of love brings joy but wine delights
only when drunk. So love is sweeter than wine.

1202 எனைத்துஒன்று இனிதேகாண் காமம்தாம் வீழ்வார்
நினைப்ப வருவதுஒன்று இல்.

No pain of separation, when I think of my *love*
By any measure sweeter is love.

His pain disappears at the thought of the beloved.
Such a love is sweeter in all aspects.

Heroine speaks to her confidante:

1203 நினைப்பவர் போன்று நினையார்கொல் தும்மல்
சினைப்பது போன்று கெடும்.

My lover seemed to think of me but forgot
For I felt like sneezing but could not.

She felt like sneezing but could not. Probably her
lover wanted to think of her but forgot.

1204 யாமும் உளேம்கொல் அவர்நெஞ்சத்து எம்நெஞ்சத்து
ஓஒ உளரே அவர்.

My lover ever resides in my heart
Do I too reside in his heart?

He always dwells in her heart but she doubts if she
has a place in his heart.

1205 தம்நெஞ்சத்து எம்மைக் கடிகொண்டார் நாணார்கொல்
எம்நெஞ்சத்து ஓவா வரல்.

He often enters my heart; is he ashamed not
When he keeps me out of his heart?

He is not ashamed of coming into her heart even though
he keeps her out of his heart.

---

* Love indicates wife.

1206   மற்றுயான் என்உளேன் மன்னோ அவரொடுயான்
உற்றநாள் உள்ள உளேன்.
I live only on memories of union with him
How could I have lived without them?
She lives only by remembering the happier days of
her union with her lover.

1207   மறப்பின் எவன்ஆவன் மற்கொல் மறப்புஅறியேன்
உள்ளினும் உள்ளம் சுடும்.
Thoughts of his separation burn my bosom
What would happen if I forgot him?
Her heart burns at the thought of his separation. She
will not survive if she forgets him.

1208   எனைத்து நினைப்பினும் காயார் அனைத்துஅன்றோ
காதலர் செய்யும் சிறப்பு.
However much I think of him, he never frets
It's the only privilege to me he grants.
Her lover never resents however much she thinks of him.
It is a great honour her lover confers on her.

1209   விளியும்என் இன்னுயிர் வேறல்லம் என்பார்
அளிஇன்மை ஆற்ற நினைந்து.
My life ends thinking of the lovelessness
Of my lover who avowed our oneness.
Her precious life passes on thinking too much of him
who once promised they would be one forever.

Heroine speaks to herself:
1210   விடாஅது சென்றாரைக் கண்ணினால் காணப்
படாஅதி வாழி மதி.
O moon, set not until my eyes find my lover
Who lived with me but has left me forever.
The moon should not set till her eyes find her parted
lover who lived with her.

122. கனவுநிலை உரைத்தல்
RELATING HER DREAMS
Heroine speaks to her confidante:

1211
காதலர் தூதொடு வந்த கனவினுக்கு
யாதுசெய் வேன்கொல் விருந்து.

What feast shall I give this dream now
That brings my lover's word of love?

She would like to honour the dream that comforts her
with a message from her beloved.

1212
கயல்உண்கண் யான்இரப்பத் துஞ்சின் கலந்தார்க்கு
உயல்உண்மை சாற்றுவேன் மன்.

If my painted fish-like eyes, as I wish, sleep
I'll tell my lover in dream my pangs deep.

She tries to sleep so that she can tell her painful
sufferings to her lover in her dream.

1213
நனவினால் நல்கா தவரைக் கனவினால்
காண்டலின் உண்டுஎன் உயிர்.

No kindness is shown in waking hours
Yet I survive meeting him in dreams.

Her lover does not show his love when she is awake.
Yet she lives because she meets him in her dreams.

1214
கனவினான் உண்டாகும் காமம் நனவினான்
நல்காரை நாடித் தரற்கு.

Dreams fetch my lover missing in waking hours
To enjoy bliss in my dreams.

She loves dreams for she meets her lover, who is missing
in waking hours.

1215
நனவினால் கண்டதூஉம் ஆங்கே கனவும்தான்
கண்ட பொழுதே இனிது.

Seeing him in waking hours is so sweet
Seeing him in dreams is also sweet.

It is a joy to see her lover during waking hours. It is
also delightful to see him in her dreams.

1216 நனவுள ஒன்றில்லை ஆயின் கனவினால்
காதலர் நீங்கலர் மன்.

If there was no such time as waking hours
My lover would not part in my dreams.

If there was no such time as waking hours, her lover,
who appeared in her dreams, would never part.

Heroine speaks to herself:

1217 நனவினால் நல்காக் கொடியார் கனவினால்
என்எம்மைப் பீழிப் பது.

When awake, my cruel lover showed no passions
How could he torment me in my dreams?

Her unkind lover gave her no pleasure in waking hours.
So he has no right to trouble her in her dreams.

Heroine speaks to her confidante:

1218 துஞ்சும்கால் தோள்மேலர் ஆகி விழிக்கும்கால்
நெஞ்சத்தர் ஆவர் விரைந்து.

While asleep, he leans on my shoulders
While awake, into my heart he hastens.

When she is asleep, he rests on her shoulders. When
she is awake, he hides in her heart.

1219 நனவினால் நல்காரை நோவர் கனவினால்
காதலர்க் காணா தவர்.

Who have never seen their lovers in dreams
Blame my lover's absence in waking hours.

Women who have never met their lovers in dreams
complain of her lovers' absence while awake.

1220 நனவினால் நம்நீத்தார் என்பர் கனவினால்
காணார்கொல் இவ்ஊ ரவர்.

People blame my parted lover in waking hours
As they see not his visit in my dreams.

Villagers blame her parted lover for parting her while
awake as they do not see him coming in her dreams.

123. பொழுது கண்டிரங்கல்
EVENING WOES

1221
Heroine speaks to herself:

மாலையோ அல்லை மணந்தார் உயிர்உண்ணும்
வேலைநீ வாழி பொழுது.

O evening, you are in fact no eventide at all
To parted wives you are a death knell.

Evening is the worst time which tortures the wives who
are separated from their husbands.

1222
புன்கண்ணை வாழி மருள்மாலை எம்கேள்போல்
வன்கண்ண தோநின் துணை.

Long live, you muddled pallid eventide
Is your lover as mine so unkind?

Evening time is sad and pale and so its lover must
also be unkind like her lover.

1223
Heroine speaks to her confidante:

பனிஅரும்பிப் பைதல்கொள் மாலை துனிஅரும்பித்
துன்பம் வளர வரும்.

Evening that came trembling with dimness before
Now brings hardships more.

The evening that came trembling with dimness before
boldly adds to her bitterness and miseries now.

1224
காதலர் இல்வழி மாலை கொலைக்களத்து
எதிலர் போல வரும்.

Eventide arrives when my lover is away
Like the enemy coming only to slay.

In the absence of her lover, evening arrives like an
enemy in the field of slaughter.

1225
காலைக்குச் செய்தநன்று என்கொல் எவன்கொல்யான்
மாலைக்குச் செய்த பகை.

What good have I done to the morning?
What evil have I done to the evening?

She fails to understand why morning should bring her
relief and evening misery.

1226 மாலைநோய் செய்தல் மணந்தார் அகலாத
காலை அறிந்தது இலேன்.
I never knew the woes of eventide
Till parting with my beloved.
She never experienced the pain of evenings till her
lover parted with her.

1227 காலை அரும்பிப் பகல்எல்லாம் போதுஆகி
மாலை மலரும்இந் நோய்.
Buds at dawn, grows through daytime
Lovesickness blooms in eve-time.
Her lovesickness buds in the morning, grows all day
and blossoms in the evening.

1228 அழல்போலும் மாலைக்குத் தூதுஆகி ஆயன்
குழல்போலும் கொல்லும் படை.
Shepherd's flute once sweet now burns me
Heralding eve as a deadly army.
The shepherd's flute, once sweet, has now become
a weapon to slay her in the evening.

1229 பதிமருண்டு பைதல் உழக்கும் மதிமருண்டு
மாலை படர்தரும் போழ்து.
When the deceiving eventide spreads
Village grieves for my lovesickness.
When the deluding evening sets in, the whole village
grieves for her lovesickness.

1230 பொருள்மாலை யாளரை உள்ளி மருள்மாலை
மாயும்என் மாயா உயிர்.
Remembering the lover gone to amass riches
My life in this deluding eve slowly perishes.
Thinking of her parted lover bent on making wealth,
she is slowly dying in this bewildering evening.

124. உறுப்புநலன் அழிதல்
LOSING PHYSICAL BEAUTY

Confidante speaks to the heroine:

1231
சிறுமை நமக்குஒழியச் சேண்சென்றார் உள்ளி
நறுமலர் நாணின கண்.

Brooding over him who left us in great pains
Your dim eyes feel shy at sweet flowers.

Thinking of her lover, who had gone away, her eyes
have lost their grace and feel shy to see flowers.

1232
நயந்தவர் நல்காமை சொல்லுவ போலும்
பசந்து பனிவாரும் கண்.

Your pallid eyes with streaming tears look like
Proclaiming your lover's dislike.

Her pale and moist eyes seem to declare the unkind -
ness of her beloved lover.

1233
தணந்தமை சால அறிவிப்ப போலும்
மணந்தநாள் வீங்கிய தோள்.

Your shoulders that swelled on the day of union
Have shrunk now declaring his separation.

Her shoulders that swelled on her marriage day have
now shrunk as if to proclaim his separation.

1234
பணைநீங்கிப் பைந்தொடி சோரும் துணைநீங்கித்
தொல்கவின் வாடிய தோள்.

Lover away, your arms lose grace and shrink
Your gold bangles slip and sink.

Her lover's separation takes away the beauty of her
arms and her golden bracelets slip down.

1235
கொடியார் கொடுமை உரைக்கும் தொடியொடு
தொல்கவின் வாடிய தோள்.

Your arms with loose bangles and faded beauty
Proclaim loudly your lover's cruelty.

Her loosened bracelets and faded beauty proclaim
the cruelty of the heartless lover.

1236 தொடியொடு தோள்நெகிழ நோவல் அவரைக்
கொடியர் எனக்கூறல் நொந்து.

With shrunken arms and loose bangles I wail
As others call my lover cruel.

She can bear her arms becoming thin and bangles
slipping down but not her lover being rebuked

Heroine speaks to her heart:

1237 பாடு பெறுதியோ நெஞ்சே கொடியார்க்கென்
வாடுதோள் பூசல் உரைத்து.

O heart, carry the news of my withering arms
To my cruel lover and earn his praise.

Her heart should carry her miserable message to the
unkind parted lover and thus earn glory.

Hero speaks to himself:

1238 முயங்கிய கைகளை ஊக்கப் பசந்தது
பைந்தொடிப் பேதை நுதல்.

The forehead of this timid maiden turned pallid
As my embracing arms relaxed their hold.

Even when he loosened his embracing arms slightly,
her forehead turned pale at once .

1239 முயக்குஇடைத் தண்வளி போழப் பசப்புஉற்ற
பேதை பெருமழைக் கண்.

When cool air pierced through our embrace
Her large cool eyes paled at once.

Even when cool air entered through them in tight
embrace, her tearful eyes became pale at once.

1240 கண்ணின் பசப்போ பருவரல் எய்தின்றே
ஒண்ணுதல் செய்தது கண்டு.

The sign of pallor on the shining forehead
Pained the dim eyes of the fair maid.

Seeing the bright forehead turning pale, her eyes
became pale showing her anguish.

125. நெஞ்சொடு கிளத்தல்
SPEAKING TO THE HEART

Heroine speaks to her heart:

1241 நினைத்துஒன்று சொல்லாயோ நெஞ்சே எனைத்துஒன்றும்
எவ்வநோய் தீர்க்கும் மருந்து.

O heart, can't you suggest any remedy
To cure the incurable malady?

She seeks prescription of some medicine to cure her
incurable lovesickness.

1242 காதல் அவர்இலர் ஆகநீ நோவது
பேதைமை வாழியென் நெஞ்சு.

O heart, longing for him is folly
When he has no love for me.

It is the folly of her heart to long for her unkind lover and
grieve at the separation.

1243 இருந்துஉள்ளி என்பரிதல் நெஞ்சே பரிந்துள்ளல்
பைதல்நோய் செய்தார்கண் இல்.

Why suffer and pine for him, O heart !
Who caused pallor but loves me not.

Her sufferings and longing for her lover are in vain as
he has caused lovesickness but has no love for her.

1244 கண்ணும் கொளச்சேறி நெஞ்சே இவைஎன்னைத்
தின்னும் அவர்க்காணல் உற்று.

O heart, take my eyes to my lover
Or else they will kill me for sure.

She is pleading to her heart to take her eyes to the
lover. Or else her eyes will kill her.

1245 செற்றார் எனக்கை விடல்உண்டோ நெஞ்சேயாம்
உற்றால் உறாஅது தவர்.

O heart, he forsook my love and yet
Can I desert him who has no heart?

She cannot abandon her heartless lover though he
shows no love for her.

1246 கலந்துஉணர்த்தும் காதலர்க் கண்டால் புலந்துஉணராய்
பொய்க்காய்வு காய்திஎன் நெஞ்சு.
O my heart, your anger becomes false
Face to face you rush to embrace.
She cannot maintain her anger when she meets her
lover and yields to him.

1247 காமம் விடுஒன்றோ நாண்விடு நல்நெஞ்சே
யானோ பொறேன்இவ் இரண்டு.
O noble heart, give up lust or shyness
I can't tolerate both these traits.
She should forsake either her lust or her shame as
she cannot endure both the feelings.

1248 பரிந்துஅவர் நல்கார்என்று ஏங்கிப் பிரிந்தவர்
பின்செல்வாய் பேதைஎன் நெஞ்சு.
O heart, you're a fool to chase
Him crying, 'He is pitiless.'
Without pity the lover deserted his beloved. Yet she
longs for him.

1249 உள்ளத்தார் காத லவர்ஆக உள்ளிநீ
யாருழைச் சேறிஎன் நெஞ்சு.
O heart, why are you seeking him elsewhere
While your dear one is within you ever?
As her lover is residing within her heart, her heart
need not search for him elsewhere.

1250 துன்னாத் துறந்தாரை நெஞ்சத்து உடையேமா
இன்னும் இழத்தும் கவின்.
By retaining my deserted lover in my heart
My inner beauty is lost.
By remembering her lover, who deserted her, she is
losing all her inner beauty.

126. நிறை அழிதல்
LOSING SELF-RESTRAINT
Heroine speaks to her confidante:

1251 காமக் கணிச்சி உடைக்கும் நிறையென்னும்
நாணுத்தாழ் வீழ்த்த கதவு.
Axe of passion smashes the bolt of modesty
Which protects the door of purity.
The axe of love will break open the door of chastity
bolted with modesty.

1252 காமம் எனஒன்றோ கண்ணின்றுஎன் நெஞ்சத்தை
யாமத்தும் ஆளும் தொழில்.
The merciless thing that is called lust
Sways my heart even at midnight.
Her mind is tossed by the heartless thing called lust
even at midnight.

1253 மறைப்பேன்மன் காமத்தை யானோ குறிப்புஇன்றித்
தும்மல்போல் தோன்றி விடும்.
How can I conceal my passion that exposes
Itself like a sneeze coming unawares?
It is hard to conceal passionate love which breaks
out like a sudden sneeze.

1254 நிறைஉடையேன் என்பேன்மன் யானோஎன் காமம்
மறைஇறந்து மன்று படும்.
I claimed pride in my being highly modest
But now my lust in public breaks out.
She claimed pride in her modesty. But her lust
reveals itself in public.

1255 செற்றார்பின் செல்லாப் பெருந்தகைமை காமநோய்
உற்றார் அறிவதுஒன்று அன்று.
Dignity is in desisting from seeking the deserters
It is unknown to those with lovesickness.
Dignity is not known to the lovelorn as they can't
resist going after their lovers, who have parted.

1256   செற்றவர் பின்சேரல் வேண்டி அளித்தரோ
எற்றுள்ளை உற்ற துயர்.

How cruel is my passion that sends me
After my lover who parted with me?

Lovesickness is such a horrible thing that makes her
go after her unkind lover, who parted with her.

1257   நாண்எள ஒன்றோ அறியலம் காமத்தால்
பேணியார் பெட்ப செயின்.

I know not anything like shameful reserve
When my lover gives desired love.

She has no sense of shame when her lover gives the
love she desires.

1258   பன்மாயக் கள்வன் பணிமொழி அன்றோநம்
பெண்மை உடைக்கும் படை.

Luring words of artful lover with great love
Are weapons to break feminine reserve.

The tempting words of the deluding lover are the
weapons that break the feminine firmness.

1259   புலப்பல் எனச்சென்றேன் புல்லினேன் நெஞ்சம்
கலத்தல் உறுவது கண்டு.

I went to sulk, but seeing my heart join him,
I tightly embraced him.

She went there to pretend to dislike him. But she
embraced him on seeing him.

1260   நிணம்தீயில் இட்டன்ன நெஞ்சினார்க்கு உண்டோ
புணர்ந்துஊடி நிற்பேம் எனல்.

Maidens with hearts melting like fat in fire
Can't feign sulk seeking sexual pleasure.

It is impossible to feign sulking for maidens who
melt like fat in fire while making love.

127. அவர்வயின் விதும்பல்
LONGING FOR THE LOVER

Heroine speaks to herself:

1261
வாள்அற்றுப் புற்கென்ற கண்ணும் அவர்சென்ற
நாள்ஒற்றித் தேய்ந்த விரல்.

My bright eyes dimmed and lost shining
Fingers thinned listing days of parting.

Her shining eyes have dimmed and her fingers worn
out marking the days of separation on the wall.

Heroine speaks to her confidante:

1262
இலங்கிழாய் இன்று மறப்பின்என் தோள்மேல்
கலம்கழியும் காரிகை நீத்து.

If I forget my lover now, O bejewelled maiden
Beauty wanes, bracelets slip down.

When she forgets her lover, she becomes thin, her
bangles slide and she loses her beauty and grace.

1263
உரன்நசைஇ உள்ளம் துணையாகச் சென்றார்
வரல்நசைஇ இன்னும் உளேன்.

He has gone with zeal as an aide to win
I am alive only to see him return.

Her lover has gone to the battlefield with enthusiasm
to win. She sustains her life hoping to meet him again.

1264
கூடிய காமம் பிரிந்தார் வரவுஉள்ளிக்
கோடுகொடு ஏறும்என் நெஞ்சு.

My heart swells in great rapture to note
The parted lover returning to dote.

She swells in great delight to see the return of her
separated lover with renewed love.

1265
காண்கமன் கொண்கனைக் கண்ணாரக் கண்டபின்
நீங்கும்என் மென்தோள் பசப்பு.

Pallor on·my tender arms flees instantly
As I gaze at him quite intently.

Her paleness will disappear the moment she looks
passionately at her lover.

1266 வருகமன் கொண்கன் ஒருநாள் பருகுவன்
பைதல்நோய் எல்லாம் கெட.
My parted lover will surely come back some day
Sex with him will keep lovesickness away.
The return of her lover and their union will drive away
all her lovesickness.

1267 புலப்பேன்கொல் புல்லுவேன் கொல்லோ கலப்பேன்கொல்
கண்அன்ன கேளிர் வரின்.
While my eye-like darling comes back home
Shall I sulk, hug or do both with him?
When her parted lover returns, she does not know
whether to sulk, embrace or do both.

Hero speaks to himself:
1268 வினைகலந்து வென்றீக வேந்தன் மனைகலந்து
மாலை அயர்கம் விருந்து.
Let our king shine in battle with conquest
I'll embrace my love to feast the night.
When the king wins the battle, the husband can rejoin
his wife and enjoy bliss at night.

1269 ஒருநாள் எழுநாள்போல் செல்லும்சேண் சென்றார்
வருநாள்வைத்து ஏங்கு பவர்க்கு.
A day seems like seven long days to those
Yearning for the return of their lovers.
One day is as long as seven days for those who long
for the return of their husbands from afar.

1270 பெறின்என்னாம் பெற்றக்கால் என்னாம் உறின்என்னாம்
உள்ளம் உடைந்துஉக்கக் கால்.
If my beloved's heart is broken and dead
My return, meeting and sex are no good.
There is no use in returning, meeting and embracing his
dame after her heart is broken due to separation.

128. குறிப்பு அறிவுறுத்தல்
REVEALING THE MIND

Hero speaks to the heroine:

1271 கரப்பினும் கையிகந்து ஒல்லாநின் உண்கண்
உரைக்கல் உறுவதுஒன்று உண்டு.

Though you hide something, there is a secret
Your eyes expose breaking restraint.

Though she hides her feelings, her eyes expose
them overcoming restraint.

Hero speaks to the confidante:

1272 கண்நிறைந்த காரிகைக் காம்புஎர்தோள் பேதைக்குப்
பெண்நிறைந்த நீர்மை பெரிது.

With eyeful beauty and bamboo-like arms
My maiden has great feminine charms.

This simple beautiful lady with tender shoulders is full
of lovable feminine charms.

1273 மணியில் திகழ்தரு நூல்போல் மடந்தை
அணியில் திகழ்வதுஒன்று உண்டு.

Something is implied in her feminine charms
Like a string seen through crystal beads.

Like the thread passing through crystal beads, there
is some significance in her feminine beauty.

1274 முகைமொக்குள் உள்ளது நாற்றம்போல் பேதை
நகைமொக்குள் உள்ளதுஒன்று உண்டு.

Certain secret lies in the smile of the artless maid
Like the latent fragrance in a bud.

Like the hidden fragrance in the bud there is some
hidden significance in the smile of this simple lady.

1275 செறிதொடி செய்திறந்த கள்ளம் உறுதுயர்
தீர்க்கும் மருந்துஒன்று உடைத்து.

The closely-bangled wife's secret sign
Has cure for love pain.

The secret sign of his bangled wife has a remedy to
cure his lovesickness.

Heroine speaks to her confidante:

1276 பெரிதுஆற்றிப் பெட்பக் கலத்தல் அரிதுஆற்றி
அன்புஇன்மை சூழ்வது உடைத்து.

**His ardent love-making comforts my pain
But signals his parting soon.**

His passionate love comforts her but signifies the impending painful separation.

1277 தண்அம் துறைவன் தணந்தமை நம்மினும்
முன்னம் உணர்ந்த வளை.

**Before I could foresee, my bracelets foresaw
The separation of my lord of cool seashore.**

Her bangles foretold the departure of her lover, who is the chief of the cool seashore.

1278 நெருநற்றுச் சென்றார்எம் காதலர் யாமும்
எழுநாளேம் மேனி பசந்து.

**My loved one left me only the day earlier
But I feel as if I had a week's pallor.**

Her lover left her only the previous day. But her pallor spreads faster as if he had left her a week ago.

Confidante speaks to the hero:

1279 தொடிநோக்கி மென்தோளும் நோக்கி அடிநோக்கி
அஃதுஆண்டு அவள்செய் தது.

**She looks at her bangles, tender arms
And feet; these are her indications.**

She looks at her bangles, thin shoulders and feet; they are the signs of her desire to accompany him.

1280 பெண்ணினால் பெண்மை உடைத்துஎன்ப கண்ணினால்
காமநோய் சொல்லி இரவு.

**Eyes that reveal love-pain and beg for remedy
Add feminine charm to femininity.**

The way in which her eyes reveal her lovesickness and long for remedy adds charm to her femininity.

129. புணர்ச்சி விதும்பல்
LONGING FOR SEX
Heroine speaks to her confidante:

1281 உள்ளக் களித்தலும் காண மகிழ்தலும்
கள்ளுக்குஇல் காமத்திற்கு உண்டு.
Delight at thought and cheer at sight
Are peculiar not to liquor but to lust.
Joy at the mere thought and cheer at the very sight
of the lover belong not to liquor but to lust.

1282 தினைத்துணையும் ஊடாமை வேண்டும் பனைத்துணையும்
காமம் நிறைய வரின்.
When intense love grows palmyra tall
Sulking is wrong tho' millet small.
When passionate love is very intense, there should
be no sulking even as small as a millet.

1283 பேணாது பெட்பவே செய்யினும் கொண்கனைக்
காணாது அமையல கண்.
He cares not for me but does what pleases him
Still my eyes are restless to see him.
Though he does as he pleases without caring for her,
her eyes will find no rest unless they see him.

1284 ஊடற்கண் சென்றேன்மன் தோழி அதுமறந்து
கூடற்கண் சென்றதுஎன் நெஞ்சு.
O my friend, I intended to feign sulks
Forgetting it, my heart longs for sex.
She wanted to feign dislike but, at his very sight, her
heart forgot it and longed for union with him.

1285 எழுதுங்கால் கோல்காணாக் கண்ணேபோல் கொண்கன்
பழிகாணேன் கண்ட இடத்து.
Like the eyes that see not the pencil that paints
On meeting, I'm blind to my lover's faults.
Like the eyes that cannot see the brush painting them
she cannot see her lover's faults while meeting him.

1286   காணும்கால் காணேன் தவறாய காணாக்கால்
காணேன் தவறல் லவை.

**When I am close to my lover, I see no error
But only errors when he isn't near.**

When he is with her, she finds no fault. When he is away, she finds nothing but faults.

1287   உய்த்தல் அறிந்து புனல்பாய் பவரேபோல்
பொய்த்தல் அறிந்துஎன் புலந்து.

**As a diver dives into flood knowing its peril
I sulk, knowing it can't last but fail.**

Sulking with her lover is as useless as a diver battling against a strong current.

Confidante speaks to the hero:

1288   இளித்தக்க இன்னா செயினும் களித்தார்க்குக்
கள்ளற்றே கள்வநின் மார்பு.

**Wine brings shame, yet drunkards love it ever
So is your bosom to her, O traitor!**

Liquor is loved by drunkards, though it brings disgrace to them. So is the lover's bosom to his love.

Hero speaks to himself:

1289   மலரினும் மெல்லிது காமம் சிலர்அதன்
செவ்வி தலைப்படு வார்.

**Love is more delicate than a tender flower
Only a few enjoy it knowing its nature.**

Love is softer than a tender flower. Only a few enjoy it realizing its fineness.

1290   கண்ணின் துனித்தே கலங்கினாள் புல்லுதல்
என்னினும் தான்விதுப் புற்று.

**She feigned sulk in her eyes and pined
Rushing to embrace faster than I did.**

She showed dislike only in her eyes and pined rushing faster than her lover to embrace him.

130. நெஞ்சொடு புலத்தல்
REBUKING THE HEART

Heroine speaks to her heart:

1291
அவர்நெஞ்சு அவர்க்குஆதல் கண்டும் எவன்நெஞ்சே
நீஎமக்கு ஆகா தது.

O my heart, his heart is with him alone
Why not you be mine?

His heart remains with him without thinking of her. So
she would also like to keep her heart to herself alone.

1292
உறாஅது தவர்க்கண்ட கண்ணும் அவரைச்
செறாஅரெனச் சேறிஎன் நெஞ்சு.

O my heart, you know he has no love for me
Yet you go after him as if he were not angry.

She knows that he has no love for her but still she
seeks him trusting that he has no dislike for her.

1293
கெட்டார்க்கு நட்டார்இல் என்பதோ நெஞ்சேநீ
பெட்டாங்கு அவர்பின் செலல்.

O my heart, you go after the separated lover
Knowing the ruined have no friends ever.

Her heart goes after her lover hoping that the ruined
have no friends.

1294
இனிஅன்ன நின்னொடு சூழ்வார்யார் நெஞ்சே
துனிசெய்து துவ்வாய்காண் மற்று.

O heart, who'll consult you about the joy of sulk
If you unite with him without sulk?

When she yields to him without even a sulk, none will
discuss the joy of sulk with her.

Heroine speaks to her confidante:

1295
பெறாஅமை அஞ்சும் பெறின்பிரிவு அஞ்சும்
அறாஅது இடும்பைத்துஎன் நெஞ்சு.

Without him it fears and with him too it fears
Fearing separation my heart forever grieves.

Her heart grieves without his company and even in
his company it grieves fearing separation.

1296   தனியே இருந்து நினைத்தக்கால் என்னைத்
       தினிய இருந்ததுஎன் நெஞ்சு.
       When I ponder over him and stay alone
       My heart eats my flesh and bone.
       When she is alone pondering over her lover's separation,
       her grief affects her body and soul.

1297   நாணும் மறந்தேன் அவர்மறக் கல்லாஎன்
       மாணா மடநெஞ்சில் பட்டு.
       Swayed by foolish heart that forgets him not
       My unforgettable blush I forget.
       She has forgotten her inseparable blush because of
       her mad love for her lover whom she cannot forget.

1298   எள்ளின் இளிவாம்என்று எண்ணி அவர்திறம்
       உள்ளும் உயிர்க்காதல் நெஞ்சு.
       My loving heart thinks of nothing but his fame
       I feel that it is mean to deride him.
       Her loving heart always thinks of her lover and his
       greatness, as despising him is a disgrace.

Hero speaks to himself:

1299   துன்பத்திற்கு யாரே துணையாவார் தாழுடைய
       நெஞ்சம் துணையல் வழி.
       Who else would come to help in grief
       If one's own heart refuses relief?
       None will comfort a man in sorrow if his own heart
       does not support him.

1300   தஞ்சம் தமர்அல்லர் ஏதிலார் தாம்உடைய
       நெஞ்சம் தமர்அல் வழி.
       When your own heart owns you not
       No wonder others also own you not.
       When a person's own heart is not friendly with him, it
       will not be strange if others desert him.

131. புலவி
SULKING

Confidante speaks to the heroine:

1301

புல்லாது இராஅப் புலத்தை அவர்உறும்
அல்லல்நோய் காண்கம் சிறிது.

**Feign dislike and embrace him not
Let us witness his misery a bit.**

She should pretend to sulk and not embrace him so
that they could, for a while, watch him suffer.

1302

உப்புஅமைந்த தற்றால் புலவி அதுசிறிது
மிக்கற்றால் நீள விடல்.

**Feigning sulk in limit is like adding salt to food
Too much of it is like excess of salt in food.**

Just as salt is to food, sulk is to sex. Prolonged sulk
is like excess of salt in food.

Heroine speaks to the hero:

1303

அலந்தாரை அல்லல்நோய் செய்தற்றால் தம்மைப்
புலந்தாரைப் புல்லா விடல்.

**To leave the sulking woman unembraced
Is like torturing one already distressed.**

To leave the sulking woman without fond embrace is
like grieving one already in agony.

1304

ஊடி யவரை உணராமை வாடிய
வள்ளி முதல்அரிந் தற்று.

**Not to appease the pretty maiden who is sulking
Is like cutting the root of a creeper withering.**

Not to comfort a sulking maiden is like cutting the root
of a withering creeper.

Hero speaks to himself:

1305

நலத்தகை நல்லவர்க்கு ஏஎர் புலத்தகை
பூஅன்ன கண்ணார் அகத்து.

**The lovely grace of a good and virtuous man
Is the sulk of the flower-eyed woman.**

The lovely charm of a worthy lover is the feigning dislike
of his beloved.

1306　துனியும் புலவியும் இல்லாயின் காமம்
கனியும் கருக்காயும் அற்று.

Love sans long sulks is like an over-ripe fruit
Love sans brief sulks is like an unripe fruit.

Love without prolonged sulking is like an over-ripe fruit
and love without brief sulking is like an unripe fruit.

1307　ஊடலின் உண்டுஆங்குஒர் துன்பம் புணர்வது
நீடுவது அன்றுகொல் என்று.

In feigned sulk there is a painful doubt
Whether the union will last or not.

The lovers' sulking in excess puts to doubt whether
the union will last long or not.

Hero speaks to the heroine:
1308　நோதல் எவன்மற்று நொந்தார்என்று அஃதுஅறியும்
காதலர் இல்லா வழி.

What's the use of the painful lament
When the beloved one is absent?

There is no use in wailing when the beloved one is not
by the side to feel and comfort.

1309　நீரும் நிழலது இனிதே புலவியும்
வீழுநர் கண்ணே இனிது.

Sweet is the water in shades of groves
So is sulking between lovers.

Water in the shade of trees is sweet. Likewise, feigned
anger between lovers is sweet.

1310　ஊடல் உணங்க விடுவாரோடு என்நெஞ்சம்
கூடுவேம் என்பது அவா.

It's but my desire that makes my heart ache
For union with one who leaves me in sulk.

Though his lady love does not comfort him, he longs for
union with her due to desire.

132. புலவி நுணுக்கம்
NUANCES OF SULKING

Heroine speaks to the hero:

1311 பெண்இயலார் எல்லாரும் கண்ணின் பொதுஉண்பர்
நண்ணேன் பரத்தநின் மார்பு.

All women feast on you with their eyes
Your lewd chest I won't squeeze.

She finds all women gazing at his bosom. Therefore,
she will not embrace him.

Heroine speaks to her confidante:

1312 ஊடி இருந்தேமாத் தும்மினார் யாம்தம்மை
நீடுவாழ்க என்பாக்கு அறிந்து.

He sneezed in the course of my sulking
Thinking I would say, "Live long!"

He sneezed while she was sulking, expecting that
she would say, "Live long."

Hero speaks to the confidante:

1313 கோட்டுப்பூச் சூடினும் காயும் ஒருத்தியைக்
காட்டிய சூடினீர் என்று.

"Which woman is it for?" she frowns
When I wear fresh flowers.

Even when he wears fresh flowers, she would say that
he was doing it to please another woman.

1314 யாரினும் காதலம் என்றேனா ஊடினாள்
யாரினும் யாரினும் என்று.

"I love you more than anyone else," I expressed
"More than whom?" she sulked.

When he said that he loved her more than anyone else,
she angrily asked who the other one was.

1315 இம்மைப் பிறப்பில் பிரியலம் என்றேனாக்
கண்நிறை நீர்கொண் டனள்

I declared, "In this life we will never part."
Fearing parting in other births, she wept.

When he said he would never part with her in this life,
she cried bitterly fearing separation in other births.

1316　உள்ளினேன் என்றேன்மற்று என்மறந்தீர் என்றென்னைப்
புல்லாள் புலத்தக் கனள்.

"I thought of you," I said to her. "Why forgot?"
She said; not embracing me, she sulked.

He said he had thought of her. But she sulked angrily
and asked him why he had forgotten her.

1317　வழுத்தினாள் தும்மினே னாக அழித்துஅழுதாள்
யார்உள்ளித் தும்மினீர் என்று.

I sneezed, she blessed; but soon she cried
"Who thought of you and you sneezed?"

When he sneezed, she blessed. Soon she cried who
thought of him and he sneezed.

1318　தும்முச் செறுப்ப அழுதாள் நுமர்உள்ளல்
எம்மை மறைத்திரோ என்று.

I suppressed my sneeze; she wept saying
"Who are you now concealing?"

When he suppressed his sneezing, she cried that he
was hiding another woman who was thinking of him.

1319　தன்னை உணர்த்தினும் காயும் பிறர்க்குநீர்
இந்நீரர் ஆகுதிர் என்று.

When I cajole her, she sulks and says
"Is this the way you coax others?"

Even when he pleads with her, she is displeased and
asks whether that is how he cajoles other women.

1320　நினைத்துஇருந்து நோக்கினும் காயும் அனைத்துநீர்
யார்உள்ளி நோக்கினீர் என்று.

When I think of her and gaze at her, asks she
"Who are you thinking of looking at me?"

When he gazes at her admiring her beauty, she angrily
asks him who he was thinking of looking at her.

133. ஊடல் உவகை
JOY OF SULKING

Heroine speaks to her confidante:

1321   இல்லை தவறுஅவர்க்கு ஆயினும் ஊடுதல்
வல்லது அவர்அளிக்கு மாறு.

He is faultless; I sulk however
To make him love me ever.

He is without fault; yet she sulks to make him love her
forever.

1322   ஊடலில் தோன்றும் சிறுதுனி நல்அளி
வாடினும் பாடு பெறும்.

Feigned dislike causes a little pain
But it glorifies love again.

Sulking causes only a little pain but it always
strengthens love.

1323   புலத்தலின் புத்தேள்நாடு உண்டோ நிலத்தொடு
நீர்இயைந் தன்னார் அகத்து.

Is there a heavenly world like feigned anger
If hearts of lovers join as earth and water?

There is no heavenly joy that gives more happiness to
lovers than sulking.

1324   புல்லி விடாஅப் புலவியுள் தோன்றும்என்
உள்ளம் உடைக்கும் படை.

In a long sulk that ends in an embrace sweet
Lies a weapon to break my heart.

In a long sulking that leads to a sweet embrace lies
a weapon that can break her resolution.

Hero speaks to himself:

1325   தவறிலர் ஆயினும் தாம்வீழ்வார் மென்தோள்
அகறலின் ஆங்குஒன்று உடைத்து.

It is a great joy even for the faultless
To forego briefly love's embrace.

Though he is faultless, denial of sweet embrace of
her tender arms, for a while, has a unique charm.

1326   உணலினும் உண்டது அறல்இனிது காமம்
      புணர்தலின் ஊடல் இனிது.

Digestion is better than eating again
In love, sulk is sweeter than union.

Digestion is better than having food again. In love,
sulking is sweeter than having sex.

1327   ஊடலில் தோற்றவர் வென்றார் அதுமன்னும்
      கூடலில் காணப் படும்.

In the game of sulk the loser is the winner
And this will be seen in the union later.

In the game of sulk, the loser actually wins. This will
be known in the bliss of their union.

1328   ஊடிப் பெறுகுவம் கொல்லோ நுதல்வெயர்ப்பக்
      கூடலில் தோன்றிய உப்பு.

Can't the feigned dislike give more delight
Than the joy of sex causing sweat?

He can get more delight in feigned dislike than the
joy of sex.

1329   ஊடுக மன்னோ ஒளியிழை யாம்இரப்ப
      நீடுக மன்னோ இரா.

Sulk on! O shining jewelled charmer
Stay on! O night, till I appease her.

The bright-jewelled lady may sulk and the night may
last long enough to conciliate her.

1330   ஊடுதல் காமத்திற்கு இன்பம் அதற்குஇன்பம்
      கூடி முயங்கப் பெறின்.

Sulking is the delight of passionate loving
And union is the bliss of sulking.

Sulking is the charming delight of passionate lovers
and the joy of sulking lies in the bliss of union.